THE CHANGING
EUROPEAN COMMISSION

Published in our
centenary year
～ 2004 ～
MANCHESTER
UNIVERSITY
PRESS

EUROPE IN CHANGE SERIES EDITORS *Thomas Christiansen and Emil Kirchner*

Dionyssis G. Dimitrakopoulos
EDITOR

THE CHANGING
EUROPEAN COMMISSION

MANCHESTER UNIVERSITY PRESS
Manchester and New York

distributed exclusively in the USA by Palgrave

Copyright © Manchester University Press 2004

While copyright in the volume as a whole is vested in Manchester University Press, copyright in individual chapters belongs to their respective authors, and no chapter may be reproduced wholly or in part without the express permission in writing of both author and publisher.

Published by Manchester University Press
Oxford Road, Manchester M13 9NR, UK
and Room 400, 175 Fifth Avenue, New York, NY 10010, USA
www.manchesteruniversitypress.co.uk

Distributed exclusively in the USA by
Palgrave, 175 Fifth Avenue, New York,
NY 10010, USA

Distributed exclusively in Canada by
UBC Press, University of British Columbia, 2029 West Mall,
Vancouver, BC, Canada V6T 1Z2

British Library Cataloguing-in-Publication Data
A catalogue record for this book is available from the British Library

Library of Congress Cataloging-in-Publication Data applied for

ISBN 0 7190 6776 6 *hardback*
      0 7190 6777 4 *paperback*

First published 2004

13 12 11 10 09 08 07 06 05 04   10 9 8 7 6 5 4 3 2 1

Typeset in Minion with Lithos
by Northern Phototypesetting Co Ltd, Bolton
Printed in Great Britain
by CPI, Bath

CONTENTS

FIGURES AND TABLES

Figures

Tables

CONTRIBUTORS

Irène Bellier is Senior Research Fellow at CNRS/Centre for the Anthropology of Social Institutions and Organisations, Maison des Sciences de l'Homme, Paris.

Fraser Cameron is Director of Studies at the European Policy Centre, Brussels.

Michelle Cini is Senior Lecturer in Politics in the Department of Politics, University of Bristol.

Véronique Dimier is Professor of Politics in the Faculty of Social, Political and Economic Sciences, Université Libre de Bruxelles.

Dionyssis G. Dimitrakopoulos is Lecturer in Politics in the School of Politics and Sociology, Birkbeck College, University of London.

Hussein Kassim is Senior Lecturer in Politics in the School of Politics and Sociology, Birkbeck College, University of London.

Anand Menon is Professor of European Politics and Director, European Research Institute, University of Birmingham.

Argyris G. Passas is Associate Professor of Political Institutions, Department of Law, Panteion University of Social and Political Sciences, Athens.

John Peterson is Professor of Politics and Jean Monnet Professor of European Political Integration in the Department of Politics, University of Glasgow.

Susanne K. Schmidt is Research Fellow in the Max-Planck Institute for the Study of Societies, Cologne.

David Spence is First Counsellor at the European Commission's delegation to the United Nations in Geneva.

ACKNOWLEDGEMENTS

This book stems from a workshop that I organised in May 2001 while I was a Marie Curie Post-Doctoral Fellow in Oxford. I should like to thank the Centre for European Politics, Economics and Society and the Department of Politics and International Relations, for hosting this event. In particular, I want to thank Professor Jeremy Richardson, the Director of the Centre, for enabling me to organise the workshop.

I should also like to thank the contributors, especially Anand Menon for advice, encouragement and constructive criticism and Susanne K. Schmidt for her unparalleled patience. Thanks are also due to Argyris G. Passas for providing useful comments on parts of the book. Finally, I should like to thank Anne Deighton and David Levi-Faur for chairing sessions of the workshop, and Tony Mason and his team at Manchester University Press who know how to deal with an inexperienced editor.

Most important of all, though, was the support that I received from my colleagues in the School of Politics and Sociology at Birkbeck College, especially Hussein Kassim (who also read and commented on parts of this book) and Bill Tompson. Naturally, the usual disclaimer applies.

Dionyssis G. Dimitrakopoulos
Bloomsbury, London

Abbreviations

AAR	Annual Activity Report
ABB	Activity-Based Budgeting
ABM	Activity-Based Management
ACP	African, Caribbean and Pacific countries
AMP	Annual Management Plan
APS	Annual Policy Strategy
ASP	Annual Strategy Paper
BAT	*Bureau d'Assistance Technique*
CESDP	Common European Security and Defence Policy
CFSP	Common Foreign and Security Policy
CIE	Committee of Independent Experts
COREU	*Correspondants Européens*
DG	Directorate-General
ECA	European Court of Auditors
EDF	European Development Fund
EEA	European Environmental Agency
EMU	European Monetary Union
EP	European Parliament
EPC	European Political Co-operation
ESDP	European Security and Defence Policy
EUMC	European Union Military Committee
EUMS	European Union Military Staff
FIDES	*Fonds d'Investissement pour le Développement Economique et Social* (Investment Fund for Economic and Social Development)
HLG	High Level Group
HR	High Representative
IAS	Internal Audit Service
IGC	Intergovernmental Conference
IMF	International Monetary Fund
IRMS	Integrated Resource Management System
JHA	Justice and Home Affairs
MAP	Modernisation of Administration and Personnel Policy
MEP	Member of the European Parliament
NATO	North Atlantic Treaty Organisation
OECD	Organisation for Economic Co-operation and Development
OMC	Open Method of Co-ordination
PCG	Planning and Co-ordinating Group
PSC	Political and Security Committee
QMV	Qualified Majority Vote
SAA	Stabilisation and Association Agreement

SEM	Sound and Efficient Financial Management
SITCEN	Situation Centre
SME	small and medium-sized enterprises
SPP	Strategic Planning and Programming
TAO	technical assistance office
TFAR	Task Force on Administrative Reform
UMP	Unit Management Plan
WEU	Western European Union

Dionyssis G. Dimitrakopoulos

Introduction

The dual nature of the European Commission

The European Commission is at the heart of the process of integration and central to the debates between the two main schools of thought in the theory of European integration. Indeed, the European Commission can be described as the barometer of integration and the key organisation whose formal powers and actual operation are thought to reflect the patterns of integration in Europe. This is so because the Commission performs a wide range of roles that frequently confront it with another key protagonist, the nation-state.[1] Two main types of roles can be identified. Systemic roles concern the credibility and the maintenance of the EU as a system of government while sub-systemic roles are policy related. Both types of roles are inherently political for they are meant to regulate conflict between self-interested actors. Systemic roles include the Commission's powers of (a) guardian of the Treaties and (b) external negotiator. Sub-systemic roles include policy initiation and (partial) implementation. Both types of roles rely on the assumptions of institutional coherence and autonomy (March and Olsen, 1989: 17).

However, the Commission – like all governmental and quasi-governmental organisations (Allison, 1971) is both an *arena* for the exercise of power, since it comprises (Coombes, 1970) an explicitly political element (the College of Commissioners) and an administrative (and implicitly political) element, i.e. its administrative services, as well as an *actor* in its own right.[2] The assumptions of coherence and autonomy relate only to the second aspect of the Commission's dual nature. More importantly, they permeate the roles that the 'grand' theories of integration ascribe to the Commission.

Neglect of the dual nature of the European Commission as both an arena and an actor in its own right is a common feature of neo-functionalism and inter-governmentalism.[3] Indeed, the two theories which occupy the same conceptual space, seem unable to deal with this duality, not least because of the level of abstraction at which they operate. They conceptualise the Commission only as an actor who has the capacity to act either as the purposeful promoter of integrationas or an obedient agent of the Member States.

The role of 'supranational' purposeful actors highlighted by neo-functionalists (Haas, [1958] 1968; Lindberg, 1963) was a key departure from Mitrany's (1946) initial rather technocratic and 'automatic' functionalism (Rosamond, 2000: 55). The European Commission was construed as a cardinal component of the emerging 'European polity'. It would generate solutions to common problems and eventually come to command – along with other parts of the emerging institutional system – the loyalty of interest groups. The ensuing role of the Commission as the self-interested promoter of both the process of integration and the institutionalisation of the emerging system relied implicitly on the idea of rational, calculated and coherent action. This action would, on the one hand, highlight the need for linkages between integrated and other sectors (and would then seek to provide them) and, on the other hand, it would sponsor the emergence of regional interest associations (Rosamond, 2000: 58–9). The Commission was expected to seek 'to provide for a maximum role for the central institutions' not least because the institutional arrangement of the Communities of the 1950s actually offered clear opportunities to do so (Lindberg, 1963: 71–2).

Hoffmann's intergovernmentalism relies on the notion of the state as a unitary actor that would remain the dominant player in the emerging European political system. The authority of the organisations (including the Commission) of that system remained (in the mid-1960s) 'limited, its structure weak, its popular base restricted and distant' (Hoffmann, 1966: 885). Moravcsik's more sophisticated (liberal) version of intergovernmentalism is much more explicit about the role of the Commission. His view is premised on the functional theory of regimes (Keohane, 1984: Ch 6) where institutions reduce transaction costs between Member States, facilitate agreements, provide unbiased information and ensure compliance. Moravcsik (1993: 511–13) identifies three functions performed by the Commission after the end of intergovernmental conferences where grand bargains are struck: agenda setting, enforcement (which is meant to enhance the credibility of national commitments) and external representation. This view construes the European Commission as an agent of the Member States (acting in the Council of Ministers). It is expected to act as a gatekeeper of mutual agreements, thereby limiting the cost of monitoring – which could be high if undertaken by individual Member States – and increases the credibility of the EU system as a whole.

Equally important is a particular conception of rationality that is built into both grand theories of integration. Indeed, both roles rely heavily on what Herbert Simon has termed *substantive rationality*.[4] 'Behavior is substantively rational when it is appropriate to the achievement of given *goals* within the limits imposed by given conditions and constraints' (Simon, 1976: 130; emphasis added). This type of rationality, however, does not preclude the possibility that unintended consequences may stem from action as well as inaction. Simon underlines the limits of the model of objective rationality by stating that 'it is obviously impossible for the individual to know *all* his alternatives or *all* their consequences' (Simon, 1947 [1997]: 77, emphasis in original). Moreover, what is known is heavily mediated by a number of 'givens', that is 'premises that are accepted by the subject as basis for his choice; behavior is adaptive only within the limits set by these givens' (Simon, [1947] 1997: 92). Therefore, rationality is bounded and 'human beings . . . *satisfice* because they have not the wits to *maximize*' (Simon, [1947] 1997: 118, original emphasis). The problem of bounded rationality is compounded by the typically problematic[5] allocation of attention (March and Olsen, 1979).

Although both theories of integration rely on the assumptions of institutional coherence, autonomy[6] and substantive rationality and ascribe significant – though variable – importance to the Commission, there is no obvious *a priori* reason to think that the Commission cannot suffer from the problems of internal organisation and operation that plague other governmental actors. Indeed, omissions and deliberate actions resulting from the inherent deficiencies of the actors that produce them (Simon, [1947] 1997; Pierson, 2000) may well have a detrimental impact on the European Commission and its capacity to fulfil the roles delegated to it by the Treaty.

Internal reform – which includes both administrative reform and the re-organisation of the College is the obvious case in point. The contradictory conclusions of two internal reports commissioned towards the end of Jacques Delors' second tenure (Stevens and Stevens, 2001: 186) seem to confirm the idea that internal systematic and comprehensive thinking about the Commission as an organisation was certainly not a major priority.[7] This neglect was at least as important as Jacques Santer's apparent inability to impose himself as the undisputed leader of the College.[8]

Romano Prodi's initially successful attempt to 'presidentialise' his post (Peterson, Ch 1 this volume) was followed by the reforms agreed by the Member States at Nice whereby the role of the President was enhanced. Individual Commissioners now 'carry out their duties devolved upon them by the President under his authority' (art. 217 para. 2). This sequence of events has highlighted not only the dual nature of the Commission but, more importantly, the existence of a threshold beyond which the Member States felt the need to intervene and restore the credibility of this organisation. If the appointment in 1999 of a promising and ambitious (Norman, 1999; *The Economist*, 11 September 1999) new President seemed to match the need to reform the organisation and to re-launch it in a manner that would allow it to fulfil its systemic role in (a) economic integration and (b) the most challenging enlargement in the history of the EU, it has also reflected the existence of a rather pre-determined agenda.

Established agendas and the Prodi Commission

Agenda setting is typically contested and reflects the balance of power in a given political system (Bachrach and Baratz, 1962; 1963). However, when Romano Prodi took office there was no disagreement between the new President and the governments of the Member States on the need to revitalise the European Commission. Romano Prodi's appointment as President of the European Commission in 1999 was a response to a number of major issues that appeared on both the *systemic* agenda of the European Union (EU) and the *institutional* agenda of the European Commission.[9] Indeed, Prodi's appointment was hailed as the beginning of a new era for this troubled but pivotal organisation of the EU (Duhamel, 1999; *Frankfurter Allgemeine Zeitung*, 26 April 1999: 16; *La Stampa*, 25 March 1999: 9).

Prodi, a former Italian Prime Minister and academic who had played an important role in Italy's accession to the euro-zone (*Guardian*, 24 March 1999), seemed to combine two features of fundamental importance for any Commission President who aspires to make a significant contribution to the process of European integration: he was both a political 'heavyweight' (and one from a large Member State) and a man of not inconsiderable intellect who commanded the respect of many European leaders (Walker and Traynor, 1999; *Il Sole 24 Ore*, 25 March 1999: 5; *Le Monde*, 27 March 1999; *Neue Zürcher Zeitung*, 10 April 1999: 21). In that sense, Prodi's appointment could be construed as an attempt to revitalise the European Commission which had reached a 'nadir' (Peterson, Ch 1 this volume; Kassim and Menon, Ch 5 this volume) under Jacques Santer.[10]

This choice presented a challenge to researchers who are interested in both the European Commission and the process of integration as a whole. Indeed, 1999 (the year when Prodi was appointed) was a very important year on both the 'domestic' and the 'external' fronts. In the first case, it was marked by the official launch of the euro (January), the decision on the 2000–6 financial perspective (March), the entry in to force of the Treaty of Amsterdam (May), the European elections (June) and the decision to convene a new intergovernmental conference (December). In the second case, Javier Solana (former NATO Secretary-General) was appointed High Representative for the Common Foreign and Security Policy and Council Secretary-General (June) as part of a more pronounced effort on the part of the EU to play a more significant role in international affairs – also evidenced by the first joint strategy (on Russia), the declarations on Kosovo and, more importantly, the declaration of the European Council on strengthening the common European policy on security and defence (European Council, 1999a). In addition, the decision to open accession negotiations with Romania, Slovakia, Latvia, Lithuania, Bulgaria and Malta and to recognise Turkey as a candidate for membership (December) increased to thirteen the number of prospective members. In other words, the context in which the Commission had to operate was highly complex and increasingly fluid.

In the absence of a new inspiring idea, the new President was acutely aware of the Commission's clear need for a sense of political direction, if his ambition to turn the Commission into 'a political driving force to shape the new Europe' (Prodi, 2000) were to become reality. His initial formal statements seemed to reflect this reality in a number of ways. For example, he stressed his own status by highlighting (a) the fact that the President's powers were 'enhanced' as a result of the entry into force of the Treaty of Amsterdam[11] and (b) his need to 'have total confidence in each and every candidate' (Prodi, 1999b). Moreover, by stating that his aim was to 'ensure that the European Commission concentrates on its real job and does it efficiently and well' (Prodi, 2000: 7), Prodi rightly highlighted the idea that leadership entails the choice of priorities. In addition, aware as he was of the importance of the Commission's (and his own) public profile, he stressed the fact that the Commission's spokesman ought to command the confidence of the President, and should therefore be chosen personally by him.

Second, the way in which Jacques Santer's Commission collapsed in 1999 (Stevens, 2000) had placed the issue of administrative reform firmly on the agenda of *any* future Commission President, irrespective of status and ambitions. His own administrative reform agenda consisted of two sets of elements (Prodi, 1999b: 4–5). On the one hand, immediate reforms included the attempt to clarify the division of labour between Commissioners' *cabinets* and the administrative services, the effort to reduce the size and increase the number of nationalities present in each *cabinet*, the idea that Commissioners and their Directorates-General should be located in the same building, the enhanced role of the Secretariat General within the Commission and the rotation of senior Commission officials (Directors-General and Directors).

On the other hand, a more ambitious long-term reform agenda was 'one of the core priorities throughout [his] term of office' and was meant to take two to three years to implement (Prodi, 1999b: 5) and could lead to an even more far-reaching set of changes which would entail improving management skills of Commission staff, better use of public money and a more fundamental 'shift from a procedure-oriented organisation to a policy-oriented one'. The combination of these elements exemplifies Prodi's (at least implicit) belief in the incremental approach to reform and was also a expression of his pragmatism.

Third, Prodi chose to link internal reform with the workload of the Commission and boldly stated (2000: 7) that 'unless we are given the resources needed, we shall . . . refuse to take on any further non-core tasks'. This decision was more in line with Santer's decision to focus on doing less and doing it better (Cini, this volume, p. 66) than the Commission's determined drive under Delors to accumulate more formal powers. By opting for this approach Prodi clearly sought to place emphasis on the consolidation of the role of the Commission in the wider institutional framework of the Union but also seemed to believe that additional resources were probably not forthcoming.

Fourth, Prodi placed emphasis on the *political* element of the integration process. By stating (Prodi, 1999a: 3) that integration will '[F]rom now on be an

increasingly political process' and by explicitly linking the reform in the management of external aid to the credibility of the EU as an international actor[12] he
highlighted foreign affairs as one of the important areas of his term of office. Two
major factors allowed one to believe that this was the almost natural next 'target'
for the Commission: (a) its powerful role in the EU's external trade (a key foreign
policy instrument) and (b) the appointment of Chris Patten, another political
heavyweight, as Commissioner in charge of external relations alongside Pascal
Lamy, the new Commissioner in charge of external trade. These choices[13] can be
construed as an indication of Prodi's intention to seek ways that would allow the
Commission to play a more active role in the EU's 'foreign policy'.[14]

Progress in the area of economic integration in the quest for growth and job
creation was Prodi's final objective (1999a: 2). This is an area in which the Commission had accumulated both very significant powers and the capacity to
exploit them (Schmidt, 2000; Ch 6 this volume). There were, however, earlier
signs of a new determination on the part of, at least some, national governments
to play a more active role in EU affairs (Kassim and Menon, Ch 5 this volume).
The introduction of the 'open method of co-ordination' was an indication of this
trend. This pattern was neither uniform nor unchallenged. Although its officials
had learned to use the Commission's roles of (a) guardian of the Treaty and (b)
key actor in the area of competition policy to promote economic integration
(Schmidt, Ch 6 this volume), the immediate post-Delors era was marked by the
absence of a central idea that would mobilise Commission officials. Indeed, after
the formal completion of the Single Market project, emphasis was placed on the
important but mundane and rather uninspiring issues of (a) compliance[15] and
(b) simplification of internal market legislation.

The extant literature on the European Commission typically attempts to
examine the way in which this organisation attempts to affect political (in particular policy) outcomes. This literature can be classified in one of the following
two categories. On the one hand, the Commission is examined as a determined
actor who seeks to affect the EU legislative process (Schmidt, 2000) or post-
decisional politics (Smith, 1998; Franchino, 2000b; Dimitrakopoulos, 2001)
even in adverse conditions (Dimitrakopoulos, 2003). In addition, scholars who
build (to varying extents) on rational choice tend to highlight the problems
faced by the Member States in controlling the Commission over time (e.g. Pierson, 1996; Pollack, 1997; Kassim and Menon, 2003). On the other hand, in addition to these analyses of the Commission as a more or less coherent *actor*, a new
type of work has appeared which (a) rightly stresses the need to look *inside* the
Commission and to analyse it as an evolving organisation (see Page, 1997;
Stevens and Stevens, 2001) and (b) analyses both aspects of the Commission
(see e.g. Cini, 1996; Nugent, 2001). Important and useful though they are, their
main problem is the fact that they remain removed from the specific context in
which the Commission operates.[16] Finally, a much more interesting type of work
has appeared recently and is hopefully going to provide the incentive for further
work: Hooghe's work (2001) offers excellent analysis of the preferences of senior

Commission officials while Joana and Smith (2002) have opened the 'black box' of the College and have discussed in a thought-provoking way key Commissioners, their political advisers and their impact on political outcomes.

The objective of the present volume is to combine elements of these broad groups of work by analysing the Commission as both an arena and an actor and to do so in a manner that allows one to comprehend this dual identity in a specific period: the late 1990s (broadly) and, in particular, Romano Prodi's tenure which essentially was meant to lead the Commission out of a crisis of a *systemic* nature. Certainly, it is early to assess Prodi's long-term impact on the Commission. However, by focusing on this period and by combining a number of approaches, we can at least gain a better understanding of the nature of this key organisation at a certain point in time.

The structure and foci of the book

The balance between the notion of the Commission as an arena/organisation and actor as analytic foci changes over time, but if there was ever one period in which these two facets of the Commission were most inextricably linked, Prodi's tenure was it. If the Commission is to upgrade the common interest or act as the (more or less obedient) agent of the Member States, it must have both a degree of *autonomy* from competing interests (national, private or other) as well as a minimum of internal *coherence* which will allow it to perform the role that is expected of it.

The structure and contents of this book reflect this agenda and constitute a collective attempt to shed light on the Commission at a critical moment in its history. The choice of approach and methodology was left to the discretion of the contributors who were asked to address key elements of the Commission's two aforementioned facets during Romano Prodi's tenure. The book has two main parts that reflect the notions of the Commission as an organisation/arena for the exercise of power and as an actor in its own right. The first part examines the European Commission as an organisation. It constitutes an attempt to analyse two elements of Prodi's reforms, namely the presidency, composition and operation of the College on the one hand, and administrative reform on the other.

John Peterson (Chapter 1) examines the Presidency of the Commission and evaluates the performance of the College of Commissioners under Prodi. Two main patterns emerge from this analysis. On the one hand, Prodi's Commission was more presidential than most of its predecessors, not least because of its President's tendency to lead from the front on big issues, such as the role of the EU in the Balkans. On the other hand, Prodi's decision[17] to bring together a 'top class team' (Prodi, 1999b: 2) whose quality – and distribution of portfolios (Mény, 1999) – arguably rivalled that of Jacques Delors' first team (Kassim and Menon, Ch 5 this volume) – was reflected in the actual operation of the College which, Peterson argues, has become more ministerial under Prodi. This pattern mirrored the qualities of the individual Commissioners, especially – though not exclusively – the economics team (Peterson, this volume), and led to some important public disagreements.[18] The public 'unease' with which Commissioners Patten, Kinnock and de Palacio have approached the announcement of Romano Prodi's blueprint for the Union (Parker, 2002b; *Financial Times*, 30 November 2002; *Le Monde*, 7 December 2002) and his need to resort to a secret process (*Le Monde*, 5 December 2002) for the preparation of this document indicate that Prodi's determination *de facto* to presidentialise his post did not remain unchallenged, despite the fact that the operation of this College was usually underpinned by a 'very powerful culture of avoiding votes' (Peterson, Ch 1 this volume).

Hussein Kassim (Chapter 2) provides a very detailed and empirically rich discussion of the current process of administrative reform. More specifically, Kassim discusses in detail the origin, content and (crucially) the implementation of Kinnock's administrative reform. His argument is threefold. He argues that although the timing and the content of the reform were to a large extent externally imposed, the reform programme reflects (at least in part) a pre-existing *internal* reform agenda. Second, the reform *strategy* was formulated by Vice-President Kinnock whose work was explicitly based on the institution's past experience. Third, despite problems that typically characterise administrative reforms in any context, this reform has been 'remarkably successful' (Kassim, this volume p. 33).

Michelle Cini (Chapter 3) draws on organisation theory and, using the concept of 'organisational culture', examines a particular aspect of this administrative reform, namely Neil Kinnock's White Paper. Her analysis highlights two culture-related elements of Kinnock's approach, namely leadership and inclusiveness. In turn, these procedural elements reflect the substantive requirements of the attempted reform. Indeed, as Cini demonstrates, the analysis of the reform-related discourse reveals an emphasis on 'propriety' and 'public service' and, more importantly, an attempt to introduce a *common* management culture into the administration of the Commission which in the past was permeated by multiple cultures (Cini, 2000a). Finally, Cini's analysis reveals that Kinnock's approach combines the logic of incrementalism (since it emphasises the need for 'continuous improvement') and planned, voluntaristic change (since this is an 'one-in-a-generation programme').

In Chapter 4 Véronique Dimier examines administrative reform from the perspective of the balance of power between self-interested internal actors and focuses on Directorate-General (DG) Development (ex DG VIII). Building on Selznick's (1957) concept of 'institutionalisation' Dimier's analysis covers the first seventeen years of the life of that DG. It shows that the process of reform has a power political dimension, for it alters the balance of power between key office holders. Indeed, Dimier shows that the first enlargement led to the partial reform of the management practices used by DG VIII. Despite the sustained use of the concepts of 'efficiency' and 'effectiveness' which figure prominently in re-organisation discourse (March and Olsen, 1983: 282), reform was met with scepticism or even outright hostility. This conflict has revealed the fact that the personal, bureaucratic and national interests are frequently closely intertwined. In so doing, Dimier essentially highlights a significant barrier to the current ambitious reform process and echoes a familiar theme in the literature on administrative reform (March and Olsen, 1983: 283).

The second part of the book focuses on the role of the European Commission as an actor. The relationship between the Commission and the Member States is the key theme that permeates this part of the book. Hussein Kassim and Anand Menon (Chapter 5) argue that the Commission's decline – which was evident prior to Prodi's appointment – has continued after this event and that it concerned both the systemic and the policy-related aspects of the Commission's role. Their analysis implicitly relies on the principal–agent model (see also Kassim and Menon, 2003) and traces the decline in the Commission's autonomy in its successes under Jacques Delors. It reveals a gradual process whereby the Member States have re-shaped their (collective) relationship with the Commission 'with a view to preventing or thwarting the kinds of ambitious, entrepreneurial initiatives' that had marked Jacques Delors' first tenure. They do so by highlighting examples relating to all three pillars. As regards Prodi's tenure specifically, Kassim and Menon highlight a process of 'continuing intergovernmentalisation' which they attribute in part to the agenda and the realisation of key Treaty objectives. In doing so, they ascribe (albeit indirectly) this pattern to Prodi's inability to come up with a powerful idea that would either mobilise Commission officials, or at least counter-balance the negative effects on morale of the necessarily introspective exercise of internal reform.

Susanne K. Schmidt (Chapter 6) focuses on the Single Market. Her analysis relies on the aforementioned assumption of rationality and institutional coherence (see pp. 105–6) and examines the capacity of the Commission to shape the content of EU legislation on the basis of its powers of guardian of the Treaty and administrator of EU competition law. Schmidt argues that the Council is forced by the Commission to adopt legislative proposals 'which would have been rejected' if the Commission did not possess this specific combination of powers'. The Commission, Schmidt argues, relies on this power base to present the Member States with the following options: a particular market/sector can be liberalised through either the acceptance on their part of a relatively modest[19] legislative proposal from the Commission or the Commission's use of its horizontal powers under competition law (whereby the Commission can claim that extant national practices violate EU competition law even in the absence of a sector-specific provision in the Treaty). In the light of the fact that the latter is not unlikely to be much more far-reaching than the former, acceptance on their part of a legislative proposal represents for the Member States what Schmidt calls 'the lesser evil strategy'. Schmidt's analysis shows that this powerful combination of roles allows the Commission to shape – at least in part –

policy outcomes and to promote market liberalisation, despite (indeed, even after) the crisis of 1998-9.

Fraser Cameron and David Spence (Chapter 7) examine the operation of the Commission-Council tandem in the foreign policy arena which is one of the areas singled out by Romano Prodi in his initial speeches as President of the Commission (see p. 6). Their analysis focuses on the Patten–Solana tandem and highlights a threefold pattern. On the one hand, these experienced politicians have curved out a good personal relationship and have, at times, worked closely together. On the other, the bureaucracies they are in charge of have engaged in turf battles, without, as Cameron and Spence argue, damaging the climate of co-operation between the Council and the Commission, probably because of the complementary roles of the two senior officials. Finally, and perhaps more importantly, Cameron and Spence highlight the Commission's ambitious CFSP-related proposals to the Convention (European Commission, 2002b) which would, in practice, entail the absorption of the recently established post of High Representative for CFSP by one of the Commission's Vice Presidential posts.

The second part of the volume concludes with anthropologist Irène Bellier's discussion (Chapter 8) of the role of the European Commission in the accession negotiations. Bellier's analysis highlights the eminently political role of the Commission in the process of accession negotiation. This role of 'mediator of meaning' entails, as Bellier argues, the definition and actual use of metaphors, which, nevertheless, cannot hide the clear power asymmetries that exist between the applicant countries on the one hand and the Union on the other.

In the final chapter of this volume, Dionyssis G. Dimitrakopoulos and Argyris G. Passas first link the previous chapters to Prodi's agenda and then contrast Prodi's proposals and the recent calls for the explicit 'parliamentarisation' of the Commission with Majone's thesis (2002) on the perils inherent in this idea.

Notes

1 Coombes (1970: 234–8) offers an alternative classification entailing four types of functions: initiative, normative, administrative and meditative (see also Cini, 1996: Ch 1).
2 The recent literature has not sought to capture the interplay between the two facets of the European Commission. One important exception is Page's excellent analysis of the Commission as a bureaucracy (Page and Wouters, 1994; Page, 1997) which, however, was published before the crisis of 1999.
3 This applies both to its initial (Hoffmann, 1966; 1982) and liberal (Moravcsik, 1991; 1993; 1998) variants.
4 Simon distinguished this form of rationality from 'procedural rationality' which he defined as 'the outcome of appropriate deliberation' (Simon, 1976: 131).
5 This is so for three reasons. First, attention is limited. Individuals, organisational units and organisations as a whole cannot attend to everything all the time. Second, at any moment there is more than one issue seeking attention within an organisation. Third, structural constraints (e.g. rules) are imposed on the allocation of attention (March and Olsen, 1979: 39).

6 Clearly, the two theories differ from each other in that respect. While neo-functionalists rely on the idea of the Commission as an autonomous promoter of integration who can go beyond the mere aggregated wishes of the Member States en bloc, liberal intergovernmentalism is couched in the idea that the Commission can act, in individual cases, as a credible (i.e. autonomous) enforcer of the agreements made by national governments.

7 The efforts made between 1985 and 1994 (Stevens and Stevens, 2001: 184–6) were not insignificant but did not amount to a comprehensive reform programme.

8 For example, Jacques Santer did not manage to get Commissioner Edith Cresson's resignation.

9 Agenda setting is a significant part of the actual operation of any political system. Agendas can be systemic or institutional (Cobb and Elder, 1971: 906). While the former concerns the political system as a whole and includes the issues that according to the members of a political community warrant government action, the latter includes issues that are under the explicit consideration of government bodies.

10 If private discussions with Commission officials are anything to go by, morale had indeed reached a nadir in 1999.

11 The new provision of art. 219 (ex art. 163) stated that 'The Commission shall work under the political guidance of its President'.

12 His statement was clear: 'Here, if anywhere, the gap between rhetoric and reality has to disappear' (Prodi, 2000: 7).

13 Certainly, these appointments also demonstrate Prodi's willingness to do so in a manner that would not necessarily go against the wishes of the large Member States. The appointments of Günter Verheugen and Pascal Lamy as Commissioners in charge of enlargement and trade respectively seems to confirm this view, not least because they came from the ranks of the then ruling German social democrats and French socialists.

14 Enlargement was a key part of this task and Prodi used it in his attempt to enhance the political role of the Commission (Prodi, 1999a: 3), whose role in enlargement negotiations is not infrequently seen to be technocratic.

15 The regular production of scoreboards which highlight 'leaders' and 'laggards' was a new example of the Commission's involvement in this process.

16 This is the natural result of their emphasis on comprehensiveness.

17 It is important to note Prodi's wise decision to define the portfolios first and then allocate them to individual Commissioners (Prodi, 1999b: 2) which arguably reflected his willingness to rationalise the operation of the College.

18 For interesting accounts of why 'Commissioners matter' see Smith (2003) as well as Joana and Smith (2002).

19 The proposal must be relatively modest so as to be supported by a number of Member States that is large enough to achieve qualified majority (QMV).

PART I

The Commission
as an organisation

John Peterson

1

The Prodi Commission
Fresh start or free fall?

One of the great challenges of studying the EU is that it rarely stands still for very long. We would be challenged to think of any other system of government whose governing 'constitution' was amended five times in seventeen years, and at times quite radically, as occurred in the EU beginning in 1987.[1] It has not been hard to justify sticking with the same introductory line to the first introductory lecture given to undergraduates starting a course on the politics of the EU: 'Well, we are fortunate that we will be studying the EU at a *particularly* interesting moment in its evolution'. One of the only things that does not change about the EU is that it is always changing (see Peterson and Bomberg, 2000).

Yet, with an intergovernmental conference (IGC) about to agree reforms of the Treaties *and* radical enlargement of the EU's membership set to occur almost simultaneously in 2003–4, the Union really did appear to be approaching a true crossroads (Devuyst, 2002), or what Ackerman (1991) has called a 'constitutional moment': a time ripe for fundamental choices about the future evolution of a political system. Asked how long the 'constitutional treaty' the EU appeared to be moving towards would last, the chairman of the grandiosely titled Convention on the Future of Europe – convened ahead of the IGC – Valér/ Giscard d'Estaing, boldly predicted: 'fifty years'.[2]

Any analysis of a changing European Commission has to begin by acknowledging that a lot was up for grabs in the period between the convening of the Convention in 2002 and the (scheduled) conclusion of the IGC in 2004. The approach of the EU's own constitutional moment helps explain why the Commission under Romano Prodi embraced several high-risk strategies to try to advance the Commission's institutional position in the EU, or make it work better, in the first half of his presidency (whose full term was 1999–2004).[3] However, Prodi's dogged determination to reform the Commission, raise its profile and defend its traditional role sometimes smacked of desperation. Dissatisfaction with the way the Commission worked was widespread among EU member governments, especially those of its largest and most powerful states. To be fair, the Prodi Commission handled a busy policy agenda mostly well. It did much to renovate the Commission internally, even if there was still far to go. To an extent that often went unappreciated, the Commission under Prodi recovered from the nadir it reached under the previous President, Jacques Santer, when the entire college of Commissioners was induced to resign amidst charges of mismanagement and nepotism.

Moreover, the jury was still largely out on the overall performance of the Prodi Commission as it neared the end of its term.[4] Even the Commission's most fervent critics could not deny that there were many very able and formidable Commissioners in Prodi's college. Ultimately, the Prodi Commission was likely to be judged largely on the success (or not) of two long-term projects: its internal reform programme and enlargement. But an equally crucial litmus test was its own contribution to the Convention and IGC, and particularly its success (or not) in shaping the views of member governments about the future role of the Commission. Potentially crucial in determining the Prodi Commission's success was the timing of its intervention into the EU's quasi-constitutional debate, and particularly its skill in building coalitions with its traditional best friends among Member States: namely, small EU states. Looking ahead, it was worth remembering that all of the twelve applicant states closest to membership – leaving aside Poland (and arguably Romania) – were small states.

This chapter's central argument is that the Commission's future could well end up being brighter than appeared possible during the Prodi Commission's rather grey and dismal first few years.[5] However, it was unusually difficult at the time of writing to gauge the Commission's future, and how it would emerge from the Convention and IGC. What was clear was that its role was being fundamentally re-evaluated, in ways that made it likely that its future position might end up fundamentally different from its familiar, past role.

The analysis which follows identifies the most important factors that will determine Prodi's legacy, and proceeds in four parts. First, it considers the record of Prodi himself as President. Second, the performance of the college of Commissioners under his Presidency is evaluated. Third, the problems and prospects of the 'rest' of the Commission – the personal advisers to individual Commissioners, or *cabinets*, and its permanent Directorates or services – are considered. Fourth, some thoughts are offered on the Commission of the future, before the chapter concludes.

President Prodi: disaster or diesel engine?

More than once, Romano Prodi suggested that future historians would view his Commission as analogous to a 'diesel engine' (see, for example, Castle, 2002: 10). In other words, this Commission took some time to get started and then to warm up. But once it got going, it became something like a powerful, clean-burning, efficient machine. It got where it was going more economically than via any alternative mode of 'transport'. After reflecting on Prodi's allegory, three observations seem apt.

Presidentialism

First, there is no question that the Commission has become both more presidential *and* more ministerial under Prodi. At first glance, it seems counterintuitive that these two qualities could both be embraced at the same time, as they appear to be two opposite ends of a continuum. In fact, Prodi has managed to push the Commission in both of these directions at once (see pp. 21–4).

The shift towards a more ministerial Commission is analysed in the section that follows. Here, it suffices to note that Prodi's Commission was generally more presidential – that is, subject to political direction by its President – than most Commissions of the past. For one thing, Prodi kept no portfolio for himself, unlike Santer, who retained overall responsibility for European monetary union (EMU) and external relations. Thus, Prodi was free to present himself as the political figurehead at the top of the Commission, putting forward his own 'macro', political message about what the Commission was doing and where the EU should be heading. Prodi's presidentialism was also reflected in his appointment of his own hand-picked operatives to pivotal positions within the services. For example, David O'Sullivan served as Secretary-General, or the top permanent Commission official, after previously heading Prodi's own *cabinet*. Ricardo Levi – Prodi's former press spokesman – was appointed head of what used to be called the Forward Studies Unit, the Commission's in-house think tank, which itself was rebranded under Prodi as the 'Group of Policy Advisers', and clearly brought within the orbit of the President's office.

Unfortunately, the Commission's increased presidentialism often seemed as much a liability as an asset under Prodi. A central problem was that Prodi was often a poor communicator, both politically and interpersonally. Officials reported leaving meetings with him not only unsure of what he wanted, but actually unsure of what he even had *said* in the meeting. One senior *cabinet* official admitted that he and his counterparts each had their own impersonation of Prodi, all of which involved them talking into their ties (interview, Brussels, 7 November 2000).

In terms of more general political communication, Prodi had some good moments in the first half of his tenure. During his very first press conference as President, he offered sound-bites in five major European languages, thus ensuring widespread media coverage. By the latter part of 2002, he was able to claim – with some justification – that the Convention on the Future of Europe had been launched because member governments realised that they had made a hash of the Treaty of Nice, just as Prodi had insisted after it was agreed in December 2000. Despite the aversion of much of the London-based press corps to all things European (and his ill-judged Oxford University speech in spring 2002),[6] Prodi actually succeeded in charming a good slice of the British press corps on his visits to the UK. To the relief of the Brussels-based press corps, Prodi eventually stopped speaking his broken, often rambling and discursive, English and French in his press conferences, and instead spoke his native Italian, which was translated for the assembled hacks.[7] Occasionally, Prodi spoke truth to power in ways that others dared not to when the truth was awkward for the EU. The best example was Prodi's description of the Growth and Stability Pact, which limits how much Eurozone members may spend and borrow, as 'stupid', in an off-the-cuff remark to French journalists, a sentiment widely shared but unspoken among EU member governments. Most welcomed Prodi's subsequent proposals to apply the Stability Pact with 'more intelligence and authority' (quoted in the *Financial Times*, 28 November 2002: 12), such as by cracking down hard on states that went on unfunded public spending binges but allowing states to borrow more for investment in infrastructures.

But there was no question that Prodi had a lot of bad moments of political communication, too. One was early in his presidency when he proposed inviting Libya's Muammar Al-Qadhafi to Brussels. Another came later when, against the grain of what the Commission and the Irish Government were pleading, Prodi publicly suggested that EU enlargement would not be delayed even if Irish voters rejected the Treaty of Nice in a second referendum. Perhaps *the* most notorious communication gaffe was the *Frankfurter Allgemeine* incident, when stories appeared in the German broadsheet alleging that a palace coup was underway in the College, apparently led by the two British Commissioners, Neil Kinnock and Chris Patten, to try to purge Prodi. Prodi's response was to call an extraordinary meeting of the College without officials or interpreters, which went on for hours and thus kept the story alive. He then sent Levi, then his press spokesman, to address the Brussels press corps (which is, by some measures, the largest in the world). However, Levi spoke only in Italian without interpretation, thus giving the impression that Prodi had something to cover up.

The allegations never surfaced again and Prodi trundled on. In any event, Prodi's attempts to 'presidentialise' the Commission mostly succeeded in the sense that his Commission bore his own personal and political stamp. But by no means was the close identification of the Commission with Prodi himself without costs.

Path dependency

A second observation prompted by the 'diesel engine' claim is that inertia has always been a very powerful force in the Commission, and might be best surmounted by a Commission that starts slowly and then comes to full speed gradually. For example, to be fair to Prodi, the Commission has *always* had a problem of political communication. Take the case of a Commission event put on in Prague in 2001, when a journalist noticed that there was none of the usual pro-integration literature, of the sort the Commission usually provides, available at the event. A Czech national working for the Commission office in Prague said that this was intentional, not accidental: the Commission's literature reminded Czechs too much of the pro-Soviet literature that used to be widely distributed in Prague during the Cold War.

More generally, the Commission retains a muscular attachment to the status quo (see Stevens and Stevens, 2001). Its resistance to radical change, such as those mandated by the reforms piloted by Kinnock, Vice-President and Commissioner for internal reform (see pp. 25–7), often seems ingrained. The idea of 'path dependency' that features so prominently in institutionalist theory – the notion that institutions often get stuck on well-trodden paths from which they cannot escape (March and Olsen, 1989; Olsen, 2002) – is very powerful within the Commission. It is perhaps better illustrated here than in any other EU institution.

In this context, Prodi made several moves that arguably reinforced resistance to the new breeze that was meant to be blowing through the Commission. In particular, by blatantly insisting on the placement of his own cronies in plum jobs, Prodi seemed to undermine the effort to create a new, more meritocratic Commission. In a way that both recalled the ruthless tactics of Jacques Delors (President from 1985 to 1994) *and* exasperated Kinnock, Prodi *pistonnered* O'Sullivan into the Secretary-General's job. He did much the same when Levi's position as chief spokesman became untenable following the *Frankfurter Allgemeine* incident, shuffling Levi sideways into a job as head of the Commission's Group of Policy Advisers. In short, for all the talk of transforming the Commission into a new and different type of institution, there seemed much about the bad old days of cronyism, as was alleged to have occurred under Santer, in the Prodi Commission.

Snubbed by the giants

A third response to the claim that Prodi's Commission started slowly and then shifted into gear is to acknowledge that, even in his first months and years, Prodi himself occasionally led from the front on big issues and in a way that was nothing if not 'presidential'. For example, despite losing credibility with some member governments in his first months by pushing for actual target dates for enlargement, he at least added to the political momentum behind an ambitious, early expansion of the EU's membership. This momentum appeared to culminate in a firm political commitment to enlargement at the December 1999 Helsinki summit. Subsequently, in the weeks and months immediately after 11 September 2001 when enlargement suddenly began to seem like a dimension of security policy, the groundwork was already laid for taking the next step towards a 'big bang' enlargement of ten Member States or more.

Enlargement was by no means the only big issue to which Prodi gave a perceptible and effectual steer. Together with the German Foreign Minister, Joschka Fischer, Prodi was well ahead of the curve (even before he was confirmed as President) in insisting that the EU's policy in the Balkans had to be radical, expansive and truly regional in the aftermath of the war in Kosovo – as indeed it eventually became. Moreover, the Dehaene report , a Commission-sponsored reflection paper by three 'Wise Men', designed to set the agenda for the pre-Nice IGC, was very much Prodi's own project. The paper's ambitious, integrationist proposals were trashed by European leaders at the Helsinki summit . But the paper at least gave ammunition to member governments that wanted to widen the Nice IGC beyond just the narrow 'Amsterdam left-overs'.[8] Besides, the Wise Men's chair, former Belgian Prime Minister Jean-Luc Dehaene, ended up being appointed as Vice-Chairman (along with former Italian Prime Minister, Giuliano Amato) of the Convention on the Future of Europe. The failure of the Nice summit to agree very much that was substantial, and the subsequent decision to launch the Convention, could be viewed as exonerating Prodi's decision to convene the Wise Men and then to back their plans. More generally, Prodi showed himself adept at identifying long-term themes, even if he, in the words of one official, has been better 'at getting things right ahead of time . . . [than] managing to get credit for it' (quoted in Castle, 2002: 12).

In this context, Prodi followed one of the key recommendations of the Dehaene Report and submitted a full blueprint for institutional reform in the name of the Commission to the Convention in May 2002.[9] To the eyes of many in numerous national capitals, the Commission's blueprint seemed to embrace a maximalist agenda: it proposed to quash national vetoes over all issues except defence, give the Commission far more prerogative over Justice and Home Affairs policies, and (especially) make the Commission the new 'centre of gravity' in the making of EU foreign policy. It clashed, at times violently, with rival proposals backed by the UK as well as Spain and France to give far more power to the Council, notably through the creation of an elected President. The Commission's proposal to the Convention could be defended as putting down a marker, giving small states something to rally around, and bidding high so that the Commission could later retreat to defending the status quo (plus) in terms of its institutional position. Still, tabling such a bold proposal appeared counterproductive in the prevailing political climate. Prodi himself sometimes seemed to forget that 'the Commission has historically been most influential when it makes less grandiose claims and acts quietly and efficiently' (Cram, 2001: 783).

Ultimately, Prodi's main political problem was that he lacked the absolutely crucial resource that Delors had, and the one that may matter more than any other: the respect and/or backing of key members of the European Council. Delors was seen as a political equal by Kohl, Mitterrand and even Thatcher (although she would never admit it). In fact, insiders during the Delors years concurred that several heads of government were positively afraid of Delors, for at least two reasons. First, Delors was such an incredibly hard worker that he almost always had a far better command of the dossiers than anyone else in the room. Especially in the absence of technical help from absent national officials, Delors was very difficult to contradict or oppose in a policy argument. Second, Delors repeatedly threatened to leave European Council summits when they were deadlocked and go to the press to tell them that European leaders left behind in the room were short-sighted, narrow-minded, pettifogging politicians with no vision or idea of what Europe was about. The press loved it and generally believed what Delors told them (in contrast to the situation under Santer or Prodi).[10]

It may be unkind to observe that no European leader was ever afraid of Prodi or, for that matter, Santer. But it is notable that even though both were former Prime Ministers, neither was ever treated as a political equal within the European Council. Both contrast on this score with Delors in a way that is striking, and politically important.

The Prodi College: treading water or 'big stars'?

Squaring the two analytical claims that the Prodi Commission was both more presidential *and* more ministerial starts by acknowledging that the College of Commissioners under Prodi was an unusually professional one. Moreover, it faced a policy agenda more buoyant than any previous Commission had ever handled. Perhaps above all, Prodi's team was selected in unusual circumstances.

Despite claims by past presidential nominees, such as Roy Jenkins , that they shaped member governments' choices about who was appointed to the College, Prodi probably had more actual influence on both the composition of his College, and who ended up doing what, than any previous President. For one thing, member governments in spring 1999 were unusually agitated about the state of the Commission after Santer's resignation, and keen to restore its credibility. For another thing, Prodi was able to seize on a new Treaty article, inserted via the Treaty of Amsterdam (art. 219, ex art. 163) and for which Santer had argued strenuously, which stated clearly and for the first time, that the College worked 'under the political direction of the President'.

To be clear, Prodi was by no means free to select his own College, and there is no evidence to suggest that he vetoed the choices of any of the EU's 15 member governments. But he clearly did lobby hard to shape choices about who was appointed and, crucially, what their portfolios would be. Thus, for example, he dismissed concerns about whether a former German Minister for Europe, Günter Verheugen, should take over the enlargement portfolio, in light of Germany's particularistic interest in enlargement. He also pushed for the re-appointment of Mario Monti, one of the most competent of Santer's disgraced team, and the assignment to him of the powerful competition policy portfolio.

More generally, few in Brussels denied that Prodi's economics team was the best that the Commission had ever had. Along with Monti, the Commissioner whose portfolio gave them real power in a hard sense was Pascal Lamy, formerly Delors' head of *cabinet*, who took over external trade. Extraordinarily hard working and able, and with a background in the private sector, Lamy also knew Brussels and the Commission intimately from his previous tenure under Delors. His propensity to dive into debates about issues far removed from his portfolio – such as the Common Foreign and Security Policy (CFSP) or the Stability Pact

– and close relationship with Prodi sometimes made Lamy seem to be the President's second-in-command in practice, although officially only Kinnock and Loyola de Palacio, Spanish Commissioner for transport, energy and relations with the European Parliament, were officially designated as Vice-Presidents.

The rest of the economics team revealed how, to an extent previously unseen, expertise was matched closely to portfolio in Prodi's Commission generally. Despite having his hard defence of the Stability Pact undermined by Prodi, Pedro Solbes – a former Spanish Finance Minister – showed *gravitas* in wielding the Commission's new prerogatives related to the euro. Erkki Liikanen showed grip and imagination in his role as Commissioner for Enterprise. Frits Bolkestein, despite occasional lapses in his command of the complicated internal market portfolio, gave little quarter to Member States when they veered towards protectionism.

Elsewhere, the College contained talented and energetic Commissioners in areas where the Commission was far busier than it ever had been before (see table 1.1). Chris Patten came to the ferociously hectic external affairs portfolio fresh from his post as Governor of Hong Kong, and gave the Commission both new ideas on EU-Asian relations and credibility in Washington of a sort that only a British Tory could. David Byrne generally made the best of a very difficult job (particularly concerning genetically modified foods and British beef) in consumer protection. Antonio Vitorino, a former Deputy Prime Minister in Portugal, presided competently over the Commission's rapidly expanding (especially after 11 September 2001) duties in justice and home affairs. Vitorino, widely thought to have 'perhaps the sharpest mind in the College of Commissioners' (Dombey, 2002: 10), also served, together with Michel Barnier (responsible for institutional reform), in the 'praesidium' of the Convention on the Future of Europe. In the main, then, the College under Prodi was a highly professional, committed College. Perhaps not coincidentally, many officials with experience of both the Santer and Prodi Commissions stressed how much less pompous and self-important Prodi's College was compared to Santer's (despite having four members in common): the Prodi Commission basically just got on with its work.

To his credit, Prodi usually stayed out of the way of his Commissioners and let them get on with the execution of their policy responsibilities. While pledging to 'offer leadership' to the College, Prodi also insisted: 'I want each Commissioner to be a star, a big star, in his or her own policy area' (quoted in Peterson, 2002: 83). To reinforce the point, Prodi decreed that each Commissioner would locate his or her own office physically in the same building as the Commission service, or Directorate-General, for which they were responsible, instead of the College being collected together in one building as in the past. One result was to reinforce the ministerialism of Prodi's Commission, with Commissioners and their *cabinets* literally sitting on top of the services *à la* ministers presiding over ministries.

This mode of working was not entirely without costs. For one thing, the College under Prodi was not a very collective or collegial Commission. There

Table 1.1   The Prodi Commission

Commissioner (nationality)	Portfolio(s)	Relevant previous post
Romano Prodi (I)	President (without portfolio)	Italian Prime Minister
Neil Kinnock (UK)	Administrative reform (Vice-President)	UK Labour Party leader
Loyola de Palacio (E)	Relations with EP; transport; energy (Vice-President)	Spanish Agriculture Minister
Franz Fischler (A)	Agriculture and fisheries	Austrian Minister of Agriculture
Erkki Liikanen (FIN)	Enterprise and information society	Finnish Finance Minister
Mario Monti (I)	Competition	Economics Professor
Michel Barnier (F)	Regional policy; institutional affairs	French Minister for Europe
Frits Bolkestein (N)	Internal market	Chair of Dutch Liberals
Philippe Busquin (B)	Research	Belgian Minister of Education
David Byrne (Ir)	Consumer protection	Irish Attorney-General
Anna Diamantopoulou (Gr)	Employment and social affairs	Greek Industry Ministry (top official)
Pascal Lamy (F)	External trade	Head, private office of Jacques Delors
Poul Nielson (Dk)	Development and humanitarian aid	Danish Development Minister
Chris Patten (UK)	External relations	Governor of Hong Kong
Viviane Reding (L)	Education and culture	MEP
Michaele Schreyer (D)	Budget	Environment Minister, (Senate of) Berlin
Pedro Solbes (E)	Monetary affairs	Spanish Finance Minister
Günter Verheugen (D)	Enlargement	German Minister for Europe
Antonio Vitorino (P)	Justice and home affairs	Portuguese Deputy Prime Minister
Margot Wallström (S)	Environment	Swedish Social Affairs Minister

were no more or fewer conflicts between individual Commissioners, especially ones whose policy responsibilities were so close as to engender turf battles, than in previous Commissions. Collective responsibility for the decisions of the Commission was not noticeably any less difficult for Prodi to enforce on his College than it had been for his predecessors, even though Prodi made it clear that he would expect any Commissioner to resign if he asked them to.[11] But the Commission often struggled to agree common lines on issues related to the Convention, institutional reform and its own future role.

One interesting upshot was that a very powerful culture of avoiding votes emerged in the College under Prodi. Under the Commission's internal rules, any proposal may be put to a vote of the College, with positive approval by a simple majority (eleven of twenty in the Prodi Commission) after which all Commissioners must publicly support the decision, or else resign. Under Prodi, there appeared to be considerably fewer formal votes in the College than under Santer or Delors, perhaps because Prodi feared exposing the Commission's potential for discord.

At more than one point, the twin trends towards presidentialism and min-isterialism in the Commission clashed. One was when Prodi unveiled plans for a new inner cabinet of ten vice-presidents to push through policy more quickly and forcefully, and the relegation of all other Commissioners to second-class status. Under the proposals, the College as a whole would meet only once or twice a month (compared with its present weekly meetings) to set political strat-egy, while the inner cabinet would meet weekly. Despite having the apparent endorsement (and even the fingerprints) of Lamy, the plan was widely and openly attacked by a number of other Commissioners, including Kinnock and Patten (Black, 2002). Eventually, it was quietly dropped.

While by no means a very cohesive College, Prodi's Commission managed to keep most of its dust-ups away from the headlines after the *Frankfurter Allgemeine* flap. Fears of major internal disputes at the end of the pre-accession negotiations with the applicant states proved to be unfounded. There remained speculation that Prodi's experiment with ministerialism in the Col-lege would be abandoned under his successor, and that all Commissioners would be reunited in one building when the Commission's long-time head-quarters, the Berlaymont, re-opened in or after 2004.[12] Nevertheless, regardless of Prodi's legacy, and any secular decline in the institutional position of the Commission, it was clear that the Prodi College would be remembered for its competence and diligence as much as or more than anything else, thus doing much to restore the Commission's credibility after the crash of the Santer Commission.

The *cabinets* and services: relaunch or relapse?

Under Santer, or perhaps only after his presidency, students of the Commission came to grips for the first time with how the administration had become dys-functional, in a variety of ways, over time. In particular, the *cabinets* – collecting together the personal advisers of individual Commissioners – had become too closely associated with the interests and priorities of member governments, thus violating the putative commitment of the Commission to the 'common Euro-pean good'. *Cabinets* were originally intended to act as the eyes and ears of Com-missioners, who after all were *collectively* responsible for everything the Commission decided. They were also meant to act as a bridge between the Com-mission's political and administrative layers and duties.

Yet, complaints were rife in the Commission's permanent services, under both Delors and Santer, that the *cabinets* had become outposts for member gov-ernments, and interfered far too aggressively and directly in the work of the DGs (see Donnelly and Ritchie, 1997: 48–9, Peterson, 1999: 56–7). An oft-cited claim of one senior official, made during the Delors era, was that 'intergovernmental-ism begins when proposals hit the *cabinets*. They're mini-Councils within the Commission' (Peterson, 1999: 56).

The role of *cabinets* was transformed in crucial respects under Prodi. First, the *cabinets* became more truly 'European'. One of Prodi's first injunctions after his appointment as President was that all Commissioners would be required to appoint a *chef* or deputy *chef* from a Member State other than their own. Unsurprisingly, most (fifteen of twenty initially) appointed one of their own nationals as *chef* and a non-national as deputy. However, insiders conceded that a more diverse range of views than in the past tended to be reflected within individual *cabinets*. A weekly lunch of all deputy *chefs*, most of whom did not share the nationality of their Commissioner, provided an interesting forum for debate and brain-storming about the work of the Commission generally. Moreover, all *cabinets* under Prodi had officials of at least three nationalities, marking a significant break from the past, when each *cabinet* was required to include only one non-national (who were often marginal players within *cabinets*).

Second, the *cabinets* featured a lot of new faces, in contrast with the pre-Prodi era when officials often served in multiple *cabinets* of multiple Commissioners and thus effectively remained in post for long periods of time. Under Prodi, only about a third of all *cabinet* officials had previously served in *cabinets*. Almost 40 per cent of all *cabinet* officials were women. Both represented big increases on past totals.

Third, *cabinets* were smaller under Prodi: six for each Commissioner instead of as many as nine previously (although Prodi himself retained a *cabinet* of nine for himself). One important implication was that *cabinet* officials were often ferociously overworked. Moreover, the move of all Commissioners' offices (except Prodi's) out of the central Breydel building, combined with the smaller size of *cabinets*, meant a lot less contact between them, and more direct contact between *cabinets* and the services. Whether these were good or bad things, the ministerialism of the Prodi Commission was certainly enhanced.

What was considerably less clear was whether *cabinets* – smaller, more European, and more like ministers' private offices – were any less of a line of direct input into the Commission for national capitals. The fact that relatively few *cabinet* officials had previous *cabinet* experience also meant that few could compare present with past practice. Generally, however, it was difficult to find either Commission or national officials who thought that very much had changed on this front, especially on personnel questions. For his part, Prodi often seemed to do little or nothing to challenge national capitals on personnel matters. A common view in Brussels was that Prodi would have been hypocritical if he did, given the way that he manoeuvred his own people into top jobs.

Nevertheless, there was no denying that, at the level of the Commission's services, significant changes were taking place as a consequence of the Kinnock reforms (see Ch 2 Kassim, this volume). A wide series of 'reforms to personnel policy, structures, and operating practices [sought to] ... make the services more management-focused and, it is hoped, more efficient' (Nugent, 2002: 162). In particular, internal Commission selection procedures underwent significant change. The role of the staff trade unions, traditionally a major barrier to administrative reforms, was transformed. A new path for career progression within the Commission – far more sensible and flexible than the one it replaced – was developed.

At the same time, there was no question that significant costs were involved in trying to systematise the work of the Commission.[13] The first months of Prodi's Commission were often chaotic, not least because of the implementation of the President's injunctions that Directors-General should be rotated to new posts periodically and could not share the same nationality as the Commissioner responsible for their service. Thus, the existing heads of the Commission's Agriculture, Budget and Economic Affairs DGs all moved to new jobs at the same time. Meanwhile, as a new DG for Enlargement was being created, the Commission's top official on enlargement, the talented and experienced Klaus van der Pas, was forced to move to another post, because both he and the Commissioner for Enlargement, Günter Verheugen, were German. A flap over the removal of the Danish-born Director-General for Fisheries, Stefan Smidt, allegedly after pressure from Spain (and the Spanish Commissioner, de Palacio), who fiercely opposed fisheries reform plans backed by Smidt, smacked of the bad old days of national capital interference in personnel decisions. Kinnock was forced to apologise for mishandling the incident, while also dismissing claims that he had acted under external pressure as 'pernicious' (quoted in *European Voice*, 23–29 May 2002: 1).

There was also significant disruption at lower levels in the services, as nearly 10 per cent of all Commission staff were redeployed from over-resourced to under-resourced DGs. Many motivated, hard-working Commission officials complained that reforms designed to make the Commission more accountable and systematic in its work had negative and demotivating effects. To illustrate the point, many Commission officials spent several days each year working on the newly required UMP (Unit Management Plan) which was eventually inserted into their Directorate's AMP (Annual Management Plan), which itself formed part of their Directorate's ASP (Annual Strategy Paper). In parallel, the UMP elements needed to be translated into individual man/months and inserted into the Directorate's activity tree in the IRMS (Integrated Resource Management System), which often seemed to be considered at the top of the Commission as the cure for all of its management, budgetary and resource ills. Once all of this was done for (say) 2003, each Directorate had to generate a 2002 AAR (Annual Activity Report) and prepare for its Director-General's signature a declaration that all of its Service's work had been done correctly in the past year. All the while, the Commission was switching to Activity-Based Budgeting (ABB) and Activity-Based Management (ABM), which involved significant transactions costs for some Directorates. Many officials moaned that they were justifying their existence rather than actually doing the job they were paid to do, all so that Kinnock would be able to produce a list of all the improvements that he had introduced during the Prodi Commission.

In general, what the Kinnock reforms (see Kassim, Ch 2 this volume and Cini, Ch 3 this volume) seemed to highlight most clearly was how shambolic many parts of the Commission had become *before* Prodi came to office. For example, there was no doubt that the credentials of candidates seeking posts in the Commission were being examined far more thoroughly under Prodi than ever before. But just how lax, or even non-existent, previous scrutiny had been was exposed by the *cause célèbre* surrounding the suspension of Marta Andreasen, a senior accounting officer in Budget Directorate, in spring 2002. Soon after Andreasen was appointed to the post at the beginning of the year, she wrote first to her Director-General and then (months later) to Prodi himself, alleging that the Commission's computer-based book-keeping system was vulnerable to fraud. When neither replied, Andreasen wrote directly to the EU's Court of Auditors making the same claims: an act ostensibly in violation of the EU's Staff Regulations. Regardless of the veracity of Andreasen's claims, which few in the Commission sought to deny outright, it became clear that the Commission had not bothered to seek references from Andreasen's previous employer, the Organisation for Economic Co-operation and Development (OECD), before appointing her. If they had, they might have learned that she had been dismissed from the OECD for making similar claims about its own accounting system. In any event, despite claims that the Andreasen story attracted little media attention outside the UK, where Conservative MEPs sought to use it as a stick with which to beat Kinnock (a former leader of the British Labour Party), the saga was, to say the least, unhelpful to Prodi's and Kinnock's efforts to claim they had transformed the Commission as an administration.[14]

Despite the pathologies associated with internal reform, the spirit of the exercise within the Prodi Commission was undeniable. One very senior Commission official close to Prodi admitted that internal reform was, inevitably, a long-term project, but estimated that 'the job will be about seventy-five per cent done' by the end of the Prodi Commission (interview, 20 November 2002). There was at least some evidence that, after all the turmoil arising from 'forced mobility' within the Commission in Prodi's first year, the changes were beginning to bed down, yielding a better-organised Commission that was far more effective in its work than in years past. The effect was to lend some degree of credence to Prodi's claim that his Commission was, indeed, a diesel engine that was slowly but inexorably coming up to speed.

Beyond Prodi: the Commission of the future

By the time that the Prodi Commission reached the middle of its term, it was still debatable whether the Commission had recovered its institutional position in the EU system after the nadir of the Santer Commission's mass resignation. All of Prodi's and Kinnock's efforts, and the diligent professionalism of most in Prodi's College, were not enough to compensate for the Commission's most important political weakness: its lack of support in large state national capitals. Rather than debating where the Commission was on its road to recovery, it became plausible, at least as a thought exercise, to argue about whether the Commission had reached a plateau or was in a state of decline (see Peterson, 2003).

Meanwhile, it gradually began to seem as if the Commission had both the most to gain and the most to lose from the process by which the Convention/IGC produced and agreed a new 'constitutional Treaty' for the EU. That the stakes were extremely high for the Commission was revealed in bold relief when Prodi tabled another Commission paper (European Commission, 2002b) on the future 'institutional architecture' of the EU in late 2002. The paper was almost shockingly maximalist: calling for a far more powerful and independent Commission (elected by the EP), with extensive new powers in economic and foreign policy, and free of the shackles of national vetoes following the scrapping of unanimous voting. In presenting the paper, Prodi poured scorn on the idea of creating a new and powerful President of the European Council, which was favoured by the UK, France and Spain, asking 'What would this President be doing for the other 360 days of the year when the [European] Council is not meeting and George Bush is not calling?'.[15]

The Commission paper's staunch defence of the 'Community method' of decision-making, whereby the Commission retained its monopoly on the right of initiative, was very much in keeping with the Commission's past pronouncements under Prodi. This emphasis reflected, not least, the Commission's unease about the increasing ubiquity of the so-called Open Method of Co-ordination (OMC), in EU governance (Hodson and Maher, 2001). Although mainly confined to areas outside the EU's own competences, OMC became an increasingly favoured mode of policy co-operation after its early application to employment strategy, justice and home affairs and monetary union in the 1990s. For example, it was deemed central to the so-called 'Lisbon agenda', according to which EU Member States loosely committed themselves in 1999 to a range of economic reforms designed to make the Union the 'most dynamic economy in the world' by 2010.

OMC involved systematic comparisons of national policies, and the dissemination of 'best practices' in areas such as employment and social protection. The aim was usually to agree and apply non-binding European guidelines to national and regional policies, while still respecting national and regional differences. The role of the Commission under OMC was fundamentally different than under the traditional Community method, not least because OMC fastidiously avoided actual Community legislation *per se*. Instead, the emphasis was on peer review, 'benchmarking', and the voluntary convergence of national policies (although often convergence was not even sought). Under the OMC, the Commission became a mere scrutiniser and critic of national policies, and lost the clear policy lead that flowed from its monopoly on the right of initiative. In its submission to the Convention, the Commission cagily suggested that 'the Union must have at its disposal a range of instruments to implement its policies' and conceded that the OMC deserved mention in the constitutional treaty. Yet, it also insisted that the OMC was only appropriate for certain areas which lay outside the Union's legislative powers.

It was difficult to judge the extent to which the Community method (and thus the Commission's policy lead) was under threat from OMC and new forms of 'co-regulation', which involved quasi-voluntary agreements with industry and (usually) no EU legislation. But the Commission's monopoly on the right of initiative within pillar I, its trump card in inter-institutional terms, certainly did not seem unassailable in the long run. Fear of losing it, overlapping with more general concerns that a powerful Council presidency would, in future, effectively set the agenda, led Prodi to argue that the Commission should become subject to some kind of new, democratic underpinning such as the election of the Commission President. Thus, the Commission's December 2002 submission to the Convention called for the election of the President by a secret ballot of the European Parliament, with a two-thirds majority required, and the choice then ratified by the European Council.

There were clear virtues to the proposal. If nothing else, it would induce something that almost never happens in the EU: a truly pan-European media story about the EU every five years. Generally, the only EU stories that ever are covered across the fifteen national medias are negative ones – such as the resignation of Santer – or gladiatorial ones about who won and who lost at each European summit. As Timothy Garton Ash (2001) has argued, a basic brake on European co-operation is that there is nothing approaching a pan-European media: the best way to reach a truly European audience may be via the *New York Review of Books*.

Yet, in a sign of how ministerial and only loosely 'collective' the Commission had become under Prodi, the proposal to elect the President via the EP was reportedly fiercely opposed by Kinnock, Palacio, Vitorino and Monti (the latter according to some reports) amidst acrimonious exchanges within the College just before the Commission paper's publication. In another sign of how *presidential* the Commission had become, some in the College – including Vitorino and Barnier – complained bitterly that the paper had been prepared by Prodi's own operatives with little input from anyone else. It was unclear whether future Commissions would replicate the Presidentialism and ministerialism of the Prodi Commission, especially given that it was set to expand in size after enlargement to at least twenty-five members. But it *was* clear that the Commission had reached a crossroads in its institutional history, and difficult to imagine that its role would not be different – and perhaps radically so – after 2004.

Conclusion

To summarise, alarm bells were going off in Commission corridors by the end of Prodi's tenure. Several proposals floated in the Convention in 2002 proposed blatantly to emasculate the Commission and shift much of its power to the Council. The Commission's longstanding problem of poor political communication seemed to worsen under Prodi, who often came across in the media as either too combative or discursive. The spirit of internal reform was considerable, but it was also undermined by allegations of inadequate spending controls as well as Prodi's own cronyism. Meanwhile, Commission officials reported themselves to be overwhelmed with onerous new reporting and control systems championed by Kinnock.

Whether the Commission was just going through a bad patch or was in a permanent state of decline was a matter of considerable debate (see Spence, 2000; Cram, 2001; Cini, 2002; Nugent, 2002b; Peterson, 2002). However, it was widely agreed that the Commission under Prodi had become rather inward-looking, because of its quite radical internal shake-up, and very edgy and twitchy, largely because of the dramatic way in which things ended for the Santer Commission. At times, it seemed politically marginalised. One former Commissioner with experience of multiple Presidents lamented the Prodi Commission's 'astonishing weakness' (quoted in Peterson, 2002: 89–90). No member government of any large EU state was prepared to spend any real political capital defending the Commission (see Kassim and Menon, ch 5 this volume). On the contrary, several seem determined to demonise, isolate and even humiliate the Commission. In retrospect, the idea that Prodi might prove to be 'another Jacques Delors', and match the record of the dynamic and politically powerful Commission President of the 1980s, which seemed possible when Prodi was first appointed, sometimes seemed like an ironic joke.

Yet, to write off the Prodi Commission as unable to stem the steady decline of the institution that had actually begun under Delors (see Peterson, 2002: 77), and then accelerated dramatically under Santer, seemed premature. The convening of the Convention and the dramatic enlargement of the EU encouraged traditionally *communautaire* countries, particularly small ones, to revert to the comfortable position of backing the Community method, a strong Commission, and a generally more united Europe, particularly in external policy. In particular, the Commission's proposal for a new 'Secretary of the European Union' (see Cameron and Spence, Ch 7 this volume), who would be 'double-hatted' and combine the roles of the Commissioner for External Affairs *and* High Representative for the CFSP (who was also Secretary-General of the Council after 1999), already attracted widespread support. Whether the 'Secretary' would end up as a Vice-President of the Commission with special status, and an administration to back him/her composed of Commission, Council and national officials, as Prodi's submission to the Convention suggested, remained to be seen. But widespread support for the notion that the EU *had* to become a more effective international actor, together with the considerable financial, personnel and organisational resources already wielded by the Commission in external policy (see Nugent and Saurugger, 2002; Peterson, 2003), gave credibility to what seemed, on paper, to be a radical proposal. One delegate to the Convention put it succinctly: 'People may not agree with all of the Commission's proposals. But a majority is sympathetic to their argument' (quoted in *Financial Times*, 24 May 2002: 18).

Moreover, most of the more *communautaire* states were small states, who faced strong incentives to work together if they were to avoid being marginalised in the Convention and IGC. Many of Prodi's ideas for institutional reform were supported by what became known as an 'open conspiracy' of small states (numbering at least seven of the EU–15: Ireland, Luxembourg, the Netherlands, Greece, Austria, Finland, and Sweden), which began meeting openly to plan strategy during the Convention.[16] The bloc of 'smalls' was not without internal divisions: for example, the Netherlands and Belgium found it hard to agree on whether the Council's rotating presidency system should be abandoned or whether an empowered Council presidency should be created. Still, all realised that they were nearly powerless unless they acted together, and that they were soon to be joined by a gaggle of (nine or ten) new, small EU Member States. The key strategic task for the smalls was to attract support from Germany, traditionally the most *communautaire* of the large states and represented in the Convention by German Foreign Minister Joschka Fischer, by far the most popular politician in the EU's largest Member State, *and* the most *communautaire* political heavyweight in the EU (see Fischer, 2000). The future fate of the Commission hung in the balance.

Notes

I am grateful to five senior Commission officials and two UK Foreign Office officials who granted me non-attributable interviews in connection with research into this chapter in November 2002. Thanks also for their comments to participants at the Oxford University Centre for European Politics, Economics and Society workshop, at which an early version of this paper was initially presented, in May 2001. This chapter draws on both Peterson (2002) and (2003).

 1 For various sides of the argument that the Treaties had become, by the late 1990s, the equivalent of a 'constitution', see Weiler, 1999.
 2 See interview with Giscard in *Financial Times*, 7 October 2002: 8.
 3 Precisely when and how Prodi's term would end was complicated by the setting of May 2004 as the date of the EU's next enlargement. What was certain was that ten new Commissioners, one from each accession state, would join the Prodi Commission in May 2004. The ten new Commissioners would be given full voting rights but no portfolios until the end of Prodi's term in November 2004. This timing allowed the procedure for appointing the next Commission to take place between May and October 2004 involving the newly elected Parliament, which would vote first on the candidate for President (probably in July) and then, after the customary hearings, on the College as a whole (probably in October). As laid down in the Treaty of Nice, the new Commission would be composed of one Commissioner per member state. There was still much debate as to the formula for the composition of subsequent Commissions after 2009.
 4 For a useful mid-term evaluation of the Prodi Commission, see Castle (2002). For the views of leading MEPs, see Banks (2002).
 5 Grey and dismal are more than metaphors in this case. During the twelve-month period spanning April 2000 and April 2001 (when the Prodi Commission was settling in and much of the research for this chapter was conducted), it rained in Brussels almost exactly one hundred days more than during the previous twelve months.

6 Prodi spoke at Oxford on 29 April 2002 and infuriated the Blair Government and British diplomats with an attack on the UK's 'special relationship' with the United States. Prodi mused: 'I wonder what makes this great nation so confident when dealing with a vastly more powerful nation over three thousand miles away, but afraid to play a full part in shaping the future of the continent to which it belongs'. Graham Watson, a UK Liberal MEP, later lamented: 'A quieter type of diplomacy is sometimes preferable and it would have been better if, on this occasion, he'd had this conversation in private' (quoted in *European Voice*, 27 June–3 July 2002: 3).

7 It mattered, particularly in terms of how Prodi was received in Paris, that he was the first non-francophone since Roy Jenkins to hold the Commission presidency.

8 The Amsterdam left-overs were rebalancing (national) voting weights under QMV on the Council, the size of the Commission, and the extension of QMV to more types of decision (Peterson and Jones, 1999).

9 The Commission later – in December 2002 – submitted a paper to the Convention on the future operation of the Commission itself, the timing of which seemed far more astute given that smaller Member States (including accession states) were starting to find something like a collective voice in the Convention, and opposition appeared to be mounting against the proposal for a powerful, elected European Council President.

10 I am grateful to Philippe de Schoutheete, a vastly experienced and senior Belgian official with intimate knowledge of the European Council, for sharing his insights on this point (see de Schoutheete, 2002).

11 Prodi reportedly extracted a commitment in 1999 from each member of his College, before they were appointed, that they would resign if the President ever asked them to (see *Financial Times*, 12 July 1999: 17).

12 Actually, while still a remarkably small administration, the Commission probably could not all physically fit into the Berlaymont even if it wanted to after 2004. If the College was reunited, it would almost certainly be into two buildings: the Berlaymont and the neighbouring Charlemagne building, the former home of the Council, where the external relations Commissioners – Lamy, Patten, Verheugen and Poul Nielson (Commissioner for Development Aid) – were already placed together under Prodi.

13 Here I draw on Peterson (2003).

14 On top of the Andreasen affair, separate fraud allegations were made at approximately the same time by Dougal Watt, an official in the Court of Auditors, and Dorte Schmidt-Brown, an official in the Commission's statistical agency, Eurostat (see *European Voice*, 20–26 June 2002: 1, 3; *Financial Times*, 3–4 August 2002: 11).

15 Quoted in *Financial Times*, 10 December 2002.

16 Convention representatives from each of these states held a series a working dinners in late 2002, to several of which Joschka Fischer, Germany's delegate to the Convention, was invited ahead of a Franco–German declaration on the Convention to be unveiled in January 2003 (see *European Voice*, 28 November–4 December 2002: 2; *Financial Times*, 6 December 2002: 10).

Hussein Kassim

2

A historic accomplishment
The Prodi Commission and administrative reform

Whatever it accomplishes in other fields, future judgements of the Prodi Commission will almost certainly be based on its success in bringing about administrative reform. Following the mandate it received from the Heads of State and Government, and commitments made to the European Parliament, the Prodi Commission has embarked upon an unprecedented programme of modernisation. Its ambition bears comparison with any project of administrative reform anywhere in the world in terms of the order of change that it aims to bring about and the short time-scale set for its implementation. Indeed, no other public-sector organisation at national or international level, to paraphrase a senior Commission figure, has designed and implemented a radical programme involving the simultaneous modernisation of its whole financial system, planning structures and processes and staff regulations within a four-year period and without additional resources for this purpose (private correspondence, 3 June 2003).

This chapter has more modest ambitions. It offers a critical analysis of administrative reform, which proceeds in four stages: after looking at the Commission's record on reform, it documents how the demand for Commission reform came about, examines the content of the reform programme and strategy, and offers a reflection on what has been achieved. It advances three arguments. The first is that the moment and, to a large extent, the content of reform were externally imposed, but that the reform programme echoes to some degree an internal reform agenda that had developed within the Commission from the late 1970s, but which it had been unable to implement. The second is that, by contrast, the reform *strategy* was formulated by the Commission. The reform Vice-President, the former leader of the British Labour Party, Neil Kinnock, who has been the main architect of the strategy, drew very explicitly on his and the institution's experience and sought consciously to avoid the pitfalls encountered by previous reform efforts. Third, although there have been problems and setbacks, the reform has been remarkably successful both in responding to the problems highlighted by the 1999 crisis and in implementing change, even if the extent to which it accomplishes its goals can finally be judged only in the long term (see e.g. Brunsson and Olsen, 1993).

A short history of Commission reform before 1999

Until Prodi's appointment, the Commission had not undergone any major programme of administrative reform. For just over forty years, during which time its functions and responsibilities expanded dramatically and its 'task environment' (Metcalfe, 2000: 826) altered considerably, the Commission's basic structures and procedures concerning aspects of staffing, financial management and control, and decision making, had remained largely unchanged. The absence of reform over such a period contrasts not only with national administrations and international bodies, but with organisations more generally, which 'are characterised by gradual evolution and sudden revolution' (Metcalfe, 2000: 826). In contrast with national administrations, moreover, the Commission had not experienced retrenchment, but known only growth and expansion (Shore, 2000: 174) – even if the enthusiasm with which the Member States have multiplied its responsibilities was never matched by a preparedness to grant it commensurate resources.

It would be mistaken to conclude, however, that the procedures and structures that had been crucial to establishing the Commission as an independent administration in the late 1950s were necessary or appropriate decades later, or that there had been no prior awareness of its shortcomings within the organisation. What was true was that reform had rarely made its way on to the Commission agenda and, when it did, the initiatives taken were generally modest and ran into serious opposition.

An internal reform agenda
The first comprehensive analysis of the Commission as an administration was not carried out until the late 1970s.[1] Produced by an independent review body in 1979 at the Commission's request, the Spierenburg Report identified a number of failings, including: a lack of cohesion within the College; poor inter-departmental co-ordination; a lack of management skills; inefficient staff deployment; and a flawed career structure.[2] Reducing the number of Commissioners and streamlining Commission services, a greater emphasis on management, and expanding the role of the Director-General, as well as 'Better staff discipline, greater staff mobility, clearer job descriptions, better staff reporting, and improved recruitment procedures were amongst the reforms which the report advocated' (Stevens and Stevens, 2001: 183–4). However, opposition both in the Council of Ministers and from the staff unions – as well the intrusion of issues such as enlargement and the budgetary crisis – led the Commission to the abandonment or dilution of most of its recommendations by the then Commission President, François-

Xavier Ortoli. Despite the failure of the reform effort, the report came to be regarded as the definitive organisational critique of the Commission.

Internal reform was not a priority during the Delors era, but administrative issues were not completely overlooked. A modernisation programme was launched by the Commissioner for Personnel and Administration, Henning Christophersen, in 1985, which aimed to improve management skills and give greater responsibility to Directors General. An Inspectorate General was created to evaluate staff deployment in the Commission, a 'screening exercise' launched to examine the use of human resources within the organisation, and an anti-fraud office – UCLAF – was established at the insistence of the European Parliament.[3] However, not only did these initiatives fall far short of a comprehensive overhaul but, more importantly, they ignored the organisational implications of major changes in Commission competencies and responsibilities that took place in the late 1980s and early 1990s.[4] Instead of refusing additional tasks when it lacked the capacity to carry them out, the Commission improvised.[5] 'Mini-budgets' – the use of operational rather than administrative budget lines to pay for temporary staff or consultants, the recruitment of detached national experts from the Member States, and, most damagingly of all, the creation of technical assistance offices (TAOs) – consultants to which the Commission delegated responsibility for implementing Community programmes – provided means by which the Commission sought to close the gap between tasks and resources (see Laffan, 1997; Committee of Independent Experts, 1999a; 1999b). A report on the state of the administration and its effectiveness commissioned by the then Commission President found that many of the problems identified by the Spierenburg Report still remained (Stevens and Stevens, 2001: 186).[6] At the same time, Peter Schmidhuber, departing Budget Commissioner, prepared a memo for his successor, in which he identified defects in financial management, including: lack of attention on the part of departments to administrative matters compared with their concern for policy content; inadequate preparation in the implementation of the budget; over-dependence on the Financial Controller; and inadequate evaluation of funding programmes (Laffan, 1997: 181).

Somewhat ironically in view of its ultimate fate, the Santer Commission was the first to prioritise administrative questions. Under the heading 'Tomorrow's Commission' it undertook a number of initiatives that attempted to introduce greater financial awareness, to decentralise responsibility for budgetary and personnel matters,[7] and to adapt the Commission to the task of handling a budget that had grown exponentially over a relatively short period. It included two main programmes. The first, Sound and Efficient Management (SEM 2000), aimed to modernise financial management and improve planning and control throughout the organisation, including: the development of better procedures at departmental level; the decentralisation of financial responsibility to line managers; and overall improvement in the management of EU funds (Stevens and Stevens, 2001: 187–92; Levy, 2002: 74–6). The second, Modernisation of Administration and Personnel Policy (MAP 2000), sought to devolve greater responsibility to the services, introduce greater cost awareness and to simplify internal procedures. Directors-General were to be given greater control over their budgets, personnel and the organisation of their departments. A major screening exercise, Designing Tomorrow's Commission (DECODE), was also begun, the aim of which was to give the Commission a detailed analysis of the full range of its activities, resources, and working methods with a view to rationalising the organisation. Meanwhile, DG IX, responsible for personnel and administration, started to look at ways of updating the Staff Regulations.[8]

Although it addressed the right questions, Tomorrow's Commission was far from successful.[9] It lacked an overall strategy and was not based on a systematic diagnosis. Initiatives were launched piecemeal, with no clear final ambition, proper co-ordination or sufficient forethought.[10] The management of the reform was little short of disastrous. There was little attempt to prepare the ground by explaining the purposes of proposed changes to relevant constituencies. A climate of secrecy surrounding the reform enabled the staff unions to exploit anxiety among Commission personnel. When, for example, the 'Caston report' – containing proposals for replacing the existing four-category career structure (A, B, C, D) with one based on two broad categories, reforming the staff reporting system in an attempt to end grade inflation, making merit the main consideration in promotion and changing working conditions – was leaked, the unions called a widely observed strike that led to the abandonment of the proposals. The decision to create a group, composed of equal representatives of staff and management, and chaired by former Commission Secretary-General, David Williamson, resolved tensions and restored peace, but only at the cost of retreat on the part of the administration.[11] Thereafter, the unions argued that the 'Williamson report' made further change unnecessary.[12]

Explaining the non-reform of the Commission

Despite their ineffectiveness, weaknesses in the design and strategy of these reform efforts offer only a partial explanation for the non-reform of the Commission. If organisational reform is problematic for any administration, it is especially difficult in the case of the Commission, where policy conception and initiation have traditionally been regarded by its staff as prestigious and noble functions, while management has been seen at best as a matter of secondary importance (see, e.g., Abélès *et al.*, 1993; Cini, 1996; 1997, Laffan, 1997; Hooghe, 2001; Stevens and Stevens, 2001).

A second obstacle is the perception on the part of its staff of the special nature of the Commission, the uniqueness of its mission and the idea that it and it alone represents the common European interest. Any suggestion that it might change is interpreted as a challenge to the organisation's independence and a threat to the inheritance of Monnet and Schuman (Shore, 2000: 177–8). In a multinational institution, moreover – particularly, one whose hybrid culture is considered an essential ingredient of its uniqueness – administration and management are culturally loaded concepts, and hence, divisive. Taking an example cited by Shore, 'Practices of "staff appraisal" or "performance review" accepted in the Danish, Dutch and British civil services, are "anathema" in most Mediterranean countries. For a Spaniard, the very suggestion of performance appraisal would be considered an insult' (2000: 198).[13] It has not been lost on the staff unions that Commission reform has been advocated primarily by Member States whose commitment to the European Union is most open to question.[14]

Organisational factors are also relevant. Experience at the national level suggests that strong leadership is necessary to achieve fundamental reform.[15] However, power and authority are fragmented in the Commission. At the political level, the College lacks cohesion, while the Commission President, even after the Treaty of Amsterdam, is little more than *primus inter pares*, lacking the authority to impose far-reaching change and the institutional resources to oversee it. At the level of the services, meanwhile, Directors General enjoy considerable autonomy, which they are keen to preserve.[16]

A further problem is the Commission's lack of independence. As the Spierenburg Report noted, the Council and the Parliament 'authorize, not an overall appropriation for staff expenditure, but *a specific number of posts at different levels*' (1979: 3, emphasis added).[17] More generally, while the Member States have enthusiastically delegated more and more functions to the Commission, they have been less willing to match these with the appropriate resources. The Commission's ability to act to introduce reform is also limited by its dependence on other institutions. Changes to financial control and management and staff policy require legislative action, involving the Council and the Parliament, to amend the Financial Regulation and the Staff Regulations respectively. In the case of the Staff Regulations, the staff unions are also involved through their representatives on the *Comité du Statut* which must agree on any changes.

The Commission's latitude for action is also limited by the Member States. Their insistence that the larger Member States should nominate two Commissioners and smaller countries one has with successive enlargements led the College to become unwieldy. In addition, the 'geographical balance' historically applied to A1 and A2 positions, and more recently to appointments at A3 and A4, not to mention Member State support for dubious practices such as *parachutage*, has limited the Commission's ability to pursue an independent promotions policy based on merit.[18] The willingness of national governments, acting through their permanent representations, to intervene in defence of their nationals has, moreover, imposed restrictions on other aspects of personnel policy.[19] The divergent outlooks of the Member States, their contrasting visions of Europe, and different expectations of the Union, as well as their differing administrative traditions, poses obvious problems in negotiating any movement away from the status quo.

Any would-be reformer is also likely to face opposition from the staff unions. Though EU institutions have not been strongly unionised, historically the European civil service is based on an 'ideology of social partnership' (Stevens and Stevens, 2001: 56) that gives staff unions a formal role in the internal management of the institution.[20] They sit as staff representatives on the Commission's Joint Committee, which decides on recruitment, put up candidates for election to the Staff Committee, and oversee the selection of members for the various commit-tees that manage promotions, reports, disciplinary matters, training and the selection boards for recruitment competitions.[21] An agreement of 1974 granted the unions representative status and extends them a number of privileges, while the administration agreed in 1988 to pay the salaries of officials to work full-time for the unions.[22] Aside from their formal status, the staff unions have been increasingly prepared to resort to strike action in defence of the '*acquis of the Statut*' (Stevens and Stevens, 2001: 61).

Collectively, these obstacles create a formidable barrier to change. The imped-iments are such that reform is likely only under exceptional circumstances.[23]

A mandate to reform: from the Santer to the Prodi Commission

The circumstances leading to the appointment of the Prodi Commission are crucial to understanding why reform is different this time. The role played ini-tially by the European Parliament and the Committee of Independent Experts in events that led to the resignation of the Santer Commission, and the responses of the European Council and the European Parliament were decisive and far-reaching.

The downfall of the Santer Commission

The soundness of the Commission's administration of Community finances came increasingly into question in the 1990s. Concerns were raised with regard to the 1995 Year of Tourism programme,[24] humanitarian aid in 1998 and, in the same year, the French press published allegations of cronyism in the education and training department of Commissioner Cresson relating to the Leonardo programme.[25] A pile of documents delivered by a disaffected official employed in the Commission's Financial Control unit to the leader of the Greens Group in the European Parliament gave apparent substance to these suspicions.[26] Follow-ing a threat by Green MEPs to table a censure motion, the Commission Presi-dent promised to establish an independent investigation office outside UCLAF. Dissatisfied by the Commission's response, the Parliament voted on 17 Decem-ber 1998 not to discharge the 1996 Budget and threatened to dismiss the Com-mission. A motion of censure was moved, but failed by a margin of 293 to 232 when it took place a month later. On the same day, the Parliament called for a Committee of Independent Experts to investigate the allegations of fraud, mis-management and nepotism to be delivered in a first report by mid-March and to prepare 'a more wide-ranging review of the Commission's culture, practices and procedures in a second report within the context of issues arising in its first' (Committee of Independent Experts, 1999a: 1.1.7). It asked the Commission for a set of detailed proposals on the 'far-reaching' reform of its 'administrative culture'.[27] The creation of the committee was welcomed by the Commission, and its members, including two former Presidents of the European Court of Auditors, approved by the Parliament and the Commission.

The Commission was deeply divided on the issues raised by Parliament (*Agence Europe*, 3 March 1999; 4 March 1999). It was similarly split on how to respond to the Committee's first report, published on 15 March, deciding eventually to resign rather than face a further vote of censure. Although the report found no evidence that any member of the Commission had benefited from fraudulent dealings, individual Commissioners were singled out for criticism and the Committee concluded that there were 'instances where Commissioners or the Commission as a whole bear responsibility for instances of fraud, irregularities or mismanagement in their services or areas of special responsibility' (Committee of Independent Experts, 1999a: 137).[28] It reported that three of the programmes it investigated – tourism, MEDA, and Leonardo da Vinci – had been poorly managed and found evidence of problems in the award of contracts and the operation of TAOs. In the case of Leonardo, poor audit control and a failure to respond to 'known serious and continuing irregularities over several years' were also cited. With respect to ECHO, the Staff Regulations had not been properly observed, and in the case of the security office, the Commission President – the member responsible – was found not to have taken action even after an audit had revealed the existence of a 'state within a state'. In its much-quoted last line, the report concluded that 'It is becoming difficult to find anyone who has even the slightest sense of responsibility'. After a tense debate the Commission tendered its resignation, although its President made clear his bitterness about the circumstances surrounding the decision.[29]

The appointment of the Prodi Commission

The Parliament continued to press for reform after the Commission's resignation, passing a resolution in which it called for a radical reform of financial control and management.[30] In a climate of crisis[31] the Heads of State and Government agreed in March to nominate Romano Prodi, a former Prime Minister of Italy, as President-elect of the Commission – the first former premier of a larger Member State to be chosen. The incoming Commission was entrusted with a mandate to carry out reform and to restore confidence in the organisation as a matter of urgency.[32] It was also agreed that parliamentary hearings would be held following the June elections,[33] that the Commission would take office in autumn 1999 – until which date, the Santer Commission would remain in office in a caretaker capacity, as the Treaty provided – and that the new Commission would serve until 2005.[34]

From the outset, Prodi made clear his commitment to reform.[35] As well as announcing his intention to appoint a Vice-President specially to manage reform – an indication of the importance he attached to the task – he gave notice of specific measures that he planned to introduce. These included: locating Commissioners in the same building as their departments, a new system of senior appointments, a code of conduct for Commissioners, reducing the size and increasing the multi-nationality of *cabinets*, and insisting that his colleagues pledged to resign, if he requested them so to do.[36] In addition, he undertook to abide by the Committee of Independent Experts' second report, due in September – a commitment also made by the reform Vice-President.

The Prodi Commission was appointed at a time when confidence in the institutions was at an all-time low. Unlike any previous Commission, it took office with an explicit mandate from the Heads of State and Government to enact far-reaching reform. The European Parliament, before and after the June elections, made clear its intention to follow the Commission's efforts closely and subjected the President- and Commissioners-designate to particularly close scrutiny in the summer hearings.[37]

The reform programme: content, strategy and implementation

The commitment to accept the recommendations of its second report effectively delegated to the Committee of Independent Experts the task of deciding the content of reform. The reform strategy, by contrast, was largely determined by the Commission, with the reform Vice-President, its principal architect, concerned to avoid or pre-empt the problems that had beset previous reform efforts.

The second report of the Committee of Independent Experts
The CIE's second report (Committee of Independent Experts, 1999b), published on 10 September 1999, set out a long list of detailed recommendations that touched virtually every aspect of the Commission's organisation and operation. It called for a comprehensive overhaul of financial management, control and audit arrangements and put forward recommendations that echoed reports of the Court of Auditors (Levy, 2002). The Commission's centralised system of *ex ante* financial control, which, in the Committee's view, served only to relieve 'Commission managers of a sense of personal responsibility for the operations for the operations they authorise, while at the same time doing little or nothing to prevent serious irregularities of the sort analysed in the Committee's First Report (Committee of Independent Experts, 1999b: 12), was to be replaced by procedures that put financial responsibility in the hands of authorising officers. The Committee's second report recommended the creation of a new audit system with an audit capability in each DG and an independent central audit service, which would be responsible for establishing minimum standards, monitoring audit functions across the Commission and providing advice to the department. A similar model was recommended for financial control: decentralisation of responsibility to DG level with a central body responsible for formulating procedures and exercising oversight. Separating financial control and auditing, hitherto located in the same DG – namely, Financial Control – would end any possible conflict of interest.

The Committee also called for a recasting of the Financial Regulation to make explicit the responsibilities of authorising officers and to allow for expenditure by policy, thereby replacing the problematic distinction between administrative and operating expenditure. The introduction of clearer rules governing contracts – a point of particular concern – strengthening protection of the Community's financial interests against fraud,[38] and a more rigorous treatment of the claims submitted by Member States in areas where the management of spending programmes was shared between the EU and governments, were also strongly recommended.

In the longest section of its report – 53 pages out of a total of 146 – the Committee called for an 'in-depth reform of staff policy'. As well as proper application of the Staff Regulations and 'vigorous enforcement' of the merit principle, the report recommended that less emphasis be placed on maintaining a balance between nationalities in senior positions. It called for greater mobility of, and better training, for officials, reform of the promotions system, an overhaul of disciplinary rules and procedures, an end to irregularities in the recruitment of temporary staff, and limiting the power of the staff unions – in short, a new personnel policy.

Finally, among measures calculated to improve responsibility and accountability, the Committee recommended a strengthening of the Commission presidency, as well as a stronger role for the Secretariat-General in inter-departmental co-ordination and enforcement. It called for the creation of an independent Committee on Standards in Public Life, and appealed to the budgetary authority – the Council and the Parliament – to take into account the resource requirements of the Commission when entrusting it with new responsibilities.

These were radical recommendations. Some, particularly those relating to personnel, echoed an internal agenda of the Commission, but across the board the Committee's recommendations went beyond previous initiatives in terms of both the depth and scope of the changes that it called for.

The reform strategy

The Prodi Commission began introducing changes at its very first meeting on 18 September 1999 – a week after the second report was published. Some reaffirmed decisions taken by the Santer Commission after its resignation – for example, new codes of conduct for Commissioners – or built on work begun during the previous Commission, such as the code of conduct on relations between Commissioners and their departments and the re-organisation of the Commission's administrative structures.[39] Others put into practice ideas that Prodi had discussed informally with his colleagues soon after his nomination. The College also set about the broader task. It announced that strategic guidelines would be approved in December 1999 and that a White Paper, setting out the measures to be taken, would be presented by March 2000. Although in devising the reform strategy, Kinnock sought to avoid the failings of previous reform attempts, it also where possible, incorporated or built upon elements of previous initiatives, notably DECODE, SEM 2000 and MAP 2000.[40] Its main characteristics were as follows:

- *The creation of a task force to draft the reform blueprint and to assist in the development of concrete measures.* A Task Force on Administrative Reform (TFAR) was created on 14 September 1999, composed of ten Commission officials of varying levels of seniority, from different departments and of different nationalities, and headed by an experienced, senior French official. Its first task was to draft a reform White Paper; its second to assist in translating the proposals into concrete measures.[41] The creation and composition of the task force was premised on the belief that reform could only be successful if it drew on inside knowledge of the house. A series of Planning and Co-ordinating Groups (PCGs), working groups looking at financial circuits, human resources, and externalisation, as well as the ABM Group – also drawn from across the Commission – broadened the circle of officials involved and ensured that the reform programme would be informed by experience from all parts of the Commission. Directly responsible to Kinnock, as reform Vice-President, the TFAR could not be identified with any particular departmental interest, and as a sunset body, destined to expire after two years, would have no long-lasting impact on the organogram.
- *Learning from the experience of other organisations.* Proceeding from the assumption that a belief in its uniqueness had led the Commission hitherto to ignore developments in other administrations, the reform Vice-President sought to gather 'best practice' from other institutions. The TFAR consulted with experts from national administrations and international organisations, such as the World Bank and the OECD, as well as professional organisations, such as the International Institute of Auditors.
- *The early development of a comprehensive plan of action with a detailed schedule and identification of responsible bodies.* The Commission gave itself seventeen working weeks to formulate an action programme. Strategic guidelines were approved by the College on 8 December 1999, a consultative document adopted on 19 January 2000 and the White Paper on Reform in March 2000. The short time-scale served not only to demonstrate its commitment to reform, but also to make it easier to sustain momentum and to make possible the completion of reform within the lifetime of the Prodi Commission. A timetable and detailed attribution of responsibilities to departments enabled progress to be measured and monitored.
- *Transparency, staff consultation and preparing the ground.* Kinnock was aware that poor communication and secrecy had derailed previous reform attempts, and that reform could be accomplished only if staff were persuaded of its merits and did not feel insecure.[42] An extensive communication strategy was devised, characterised by extensive campaigning to explain the reform, openness and direct contact with staff – a step that was denounced by at least one union member as 'total demagoguery'.[43] As well

as formal consultations with the staff unions and the *Comité du Personnel*, input from all DGs via reform correspondents, and regular attendance at the weekly Directors-General meetings, Commission employees were invited to offer their comments on reform at various stages in the development of the programme. The call for comments on the consultation document, for example, was answered by thousands of officials, and feedback was relayed to the Directors-General and the College the following month. In addition, in 1999 and 2000, Kinnock visited each DG in turn. He addressed mass meetings – there were two during the pre-White Paper consultation – held breakfast meetings with officials from all levels, and invited staff to e-mail him personally with their queries and concerns. Direct contact enabled the administration to convey the message that reform was not a transatlantic import that would ruin the character and mission of the engine of European integration or betray the inheritance of Monnet and Schuman, but an attempt to create an efficient independent institution that was trusted politically and by the public (interview, Brussels, 17 January 2002). Moreover, all reform-related documents (working papers, as well as final proposals) were made available to staff on Europaplus, the Commission intranet, where an ideas bank was set up to enable staff to contribute suggestions. Reform was covered regularly in the weekly staff newspaper, *Commission en Direct*. Furthermore, progress reports were published regularly (for example, in July 2000, February 2001 and spring 2002) and Kinnock appeared in the Parliament at six-monthly intervals and in the Council to keep MEPs and governments informed of developments. In addition, management was at pains to emphasise the benefits of reform, pledging that working conditions would be improved and stressing that there would be no material loss to staff.

- *The collective ownership of reform*. Whereas previous reform efforts have been largely personal projects, Prodi and Kinnock sought to ensure that the post-Santer programme was owned by the entire College. The reform Vice-President may be the member of the Commission most closely identified with the process, but reform was regularly discussed by a reform group of eight Commissioners, which was habilitated to adopt draft proposals for consultation,[44] and by the College at its weekly meetings. The College was kept informed about reform proposals and took decisions relating to reform in the same way as it does with other subjects. The Commission President spoke in support of reform on a number of occasions, and was personally involved in the Peer Group exercise. Moreover, draft communications on the various aspects of reform submitted to the College for its approval were drafted by Directors-General to ensure their participation as stakeholders.[45]

- *A willingness to confront the staff unions*. In the past, reform had been blown off course by the unions (Stevens and Stevens, 2000: 192–3). The Kinnock strategy has been to engage the unions in dialogue, while at the same time not being afraid to confront them, curtail their powers – for example, by reducing the number of staff granted to the unions – or talk over their heads to staff.[46] A move to modernise the Social Dialogue was made as early as October 1999, when the Commission agreed orientations on a new framework to replace the 1974 agreement. An early success included agreement between the Commission and five out of the six union organisations in January 2000 to streamline concertation arrangements within the Commission and to limit the number of union officials involved in official bodies.[47]

The Commission's reform strategy was thus consciously developed to avoid repeating the mistakes of earlier would-be reformers and to deliver results within a short time-frame.

The White Paper

The College adopted the White Paper on 1 March 2000. The first part set out a series of strategic guidelines; the second outlined an action plan, specifying the ninety-eight measures necessary for its implementation, the deadline for each and the actors responsible. It emphasised the radical nature of the task in hand, and noted that action has already begun. The document was intended not only to map out action, but also to mobilise staff in support of the reforms. Thus, it stressed the high quality of Commission personnel, but argued that their ability to the job is inhibited by the system. Similarly, it placed 'a strong, independent and effective Commission' at the centre of 'the functioning of the European Union as a whole and its standing in the world', but observed that 'Working practices, conventions and obligations that have accumulated over decades now inhibit [its] effectiveness'. Almost a half of Commission officials 'are fully occupied in executive tasks', which is 'not an efficient use of scarce resources', and 'detracts from the Commission's role as defined in the Treaties'. Administrative reform, or 'modernisation', as the White Paper re-branded it, would enable the Commission 'to fulfil its institutional role as the motor of European integration' and to return to its core functions: 'policy conception, political initiative and enforcing Community law'.

That reform has been imposed on the Commission from without has been omitted from the narrative presented by the White Paper. The document did acknowledge the influence of the two reports submitted by the CIE, but it was the internally generated reflections that were highlighted. The importance of staff input was emphasized.[48]

The proposals of the White Paper were listed under four headings.

1   A CULTURE BASED ON SERVICE

The first chapter identified the five key principles – independence, responsibility, accountability, efficiency and transparency – that informed the reform and that would form the foundations of a culture based on service (see Cini, Ch 3 this volume). Although 'the whole reform process will contribute to developing this culture' – cultural change can be brought about only by deliberate and coherent actions – specific measures are also necessary. These include a code of conduct for relations with EP, rules to improve public access to EU documents, and prompt payment of monies owned by the Commission.

2   PRIORITY SETTING, ALLOCATION AND THE EFFICIENT USE OF RESOURCES

The White Paper acknowledged that better use of the limited resources at the institution's disposal was necessary. After noting action already underway to achieve this objective,[49] it proposed the introduction of Activity-Based Management (ABM) to integrate priority setting and resource allocation across the organisation, enable activity to be monitored from the centre, and make management and evaluation easier at all levels.[50] To ensure that the planning of activities and the use of resources is more policy driven, a system of Strategic Planning and Programming (SPP) would be introduced. SPP would be centred on an annual planning cycle, beginning in December. Following discussion in the College, based on submissions from the departments, the President would adopt an annual policy statement, that informs the work of each official in every DG. An SPP function would be located in the Commission's Secretariat-General under the authority of the President to assist the College in setting priorities and allocating resources. Each DG would be required to submit an annual activity report, identifying the extent to which it has met the objectives specified in its field of responsibility.

A new more systematic approach to externalisation – 'the delegation by the Commission of all or part of its tasks or activities' (Commission of the European Communities, 2000b: 6) – was also proposed. Responding to the criticism levelled against the chaotic way in which contracting out had been handled hitherto, the White Paper proposed a new framework that distinguished between, and set out principles covering, three possibilities: devolution to Community bodies, decentralisation to national public bodies, and contracting out (outsourcing) to private sector bodies. Particular attention was paid to external aid, which accounts for two-thirds of the external assistance offices used by the Commission. The delegation of non-core functions would allow Commission staff to focus on the institution's core responsibilities. A variety of proposals were brought together under the 'performance-oriented working methods' subheading. Performance-oriented working methods would be introduced throughout the organisation, decision-making and administrative procedures simplified, inter-service co-ordination, and the keeping of archives improved (Shore, 2000: 187–8), progress made towards the e-Commission, and quality-management techniques introduced.

3   HUMAN RESOURCES DEVELOPMENT

Emphasising the calibre of Commission staff, the White Paper argued that an integrated human resources policy was necessary to enable staff to fulfil their potential. The 'modernisation of human resources policy from recruitment to retirement' would benefit staff of all grades. It would enable the Commission to work effectively and 'an independent, permanent and high-quality European civil service' to be maintained. Consultative documents covering all aspects of personnel policy 'based on analysis of best practice in Member States civil services and in other international organisations' would be brought forward to form the basis of consultation with staff.

Among the specific aspects that it addressed, management skills, particularly in relation to senior positions, received special emphasis. Improvements in training, career development and mobility were outlined and a commitment was made to a more vigorous approach to gender equality. At its core were proposals to replace the existing four-category career structure with a linear system, and, linked to a new promotions system, the introduction of a new merit-based system of appraisal designed to give a more accurate assessment of an official's abilities and which would be less prone to 'grade inflation' than the existing system. Further measures included: support for under-performing staff, a review of arrangements relating to non-permanent staff, improving the Commission's disciplinary procedures, guidelines for officials wishing to report alleged wrongdoing, a consolidation of the Staff Regulations, and the integration of research staff into the mainstream of Commission personnel policy (Stevens and Stevens, 2001: 19–20).

Pay and pensions were also addressed. The White Paper stressed that reform would not result in the deterioration of the terms and conditions of employment of existing staff. It indicated that a way would have to be found to manage two sets of negotiations with the Council – the first, in relation to the Method for the annual adjustment of staff salaries, due to expire on 1 July 2001;[51] the second, concerning amendments to the Staff Regulations that reform would entail – both of which had budgetary implications and each of which had implications for the other.

4 ORGANISATION OF FINANCIAL MANAGEMENT

The White Paper declares as a central aim the creation of 'an administrative culture that encourages officials to take responsibility for activities over which they have control – and gives them control over the activities for which they are responsible'. It observes that Commission systems are 'no longer suited to the type and number of transactions which they have to deal with',[52] calls for the overhaul of the financial management, control and audit system, a clearer definition of the responsibilities of authorising officers and managers, and better protection of the Community's financial interests. The recommendations contained in the second report of the Committee of Independent Experts (1999b) are incorporated more-or-less wholesale. The main challenge was to ensure that the requirements of the Financial Regulation, such as centralised *ex ante* control, continued to be met, while the new architecture was being introduced and pending formal amendment (see p. 49).

Implementing the reform programme

The volume and range of the measures set out by the White Paper and the short time-scale proposed made implementation a formidable task, and inevitably there was some slippage. Nevertheless, the Commission was able to announce in January 2003 that eighty-seven of the ninety-eight measures specified in its reform blueprint had been enacted (Commission of the European Communities, 2003). By May, the reform of the Staff Regulations effectively completed the implementation phase. Though each chapter encountered particular problems, human resources proved, perhaps unsurprisingly, the most difficult.

A CULTURE BASED ON SERVICE

The rather disparate measures grouped under this heading were implemented steadily from March 2000. By the end of 2000, the Commission had: adopted a Code of Conduct, binding on all Commission staff; put in place improvements to the Commission's disciplinary system; adopted a communication intended to reduce payment delays; created a Customer Panel to advise the Vice-President on the quality of services provided for personnel and administration; and introduced measures to simplify working methods.[53] Other changes took longer to accomplish. The whistleblower's charter, proposed in November 2000, which required strong input from the Legal Service, was not adopted until 4 April 2001 and measures to introduce an electronic system for administering and archiving documents in January 2002. Meanwhile, the Commission's proposal of December 2000 to create an independent Advisory Group on Standards in Public Life covering all EU institutions was rejected by the Parliament and Council. In total, nine of the eleven actions specified under this chapter of the White Paper had been implemented by January 2003.

STRATEGIC PLANNING AND PROGRAMMING

The first task – mapping the full range of Commission activities and human resources – drew on the DECODE exercise and was completed in July 1999. This made it possible to produce a description of the work and the objectives of each post (adopted on 24 May 2000). The peer group exercise, carried out in the spring and summer of 2000, also provided important input. A steering group of Commissioners, chaired by the Commission President, reviewed Commission activities and personnel deployment with a view to identifying 'the tasks it can accomplish, additional personnel it may require, and, "possibly", activities that "should be reduced or interrupted if resources are inadequate" ' (*Agence Europe*, 18 July 2000). It concluded that there was a shortfall between tasks and resources of 1,254 posts,[54] and that though two-thirds of the deficit could be met by redeployment, productivity gains and early retirement, an application to the budgetary authority was the only way to meet the remainder.

The introduction of ABM was the centrepiece of this part of the reform. The following elements were put in place progressively from September 1999.[55]

1   An annual policy strategy (APS): the College adopts policy objectives for the coming year in February, following discussions the preceding November or December on a proposal made by the President. The APS, which sets out the Commission's policy priorities, the actions necessary, and the resources required, is presented to the Council and Parliament.

2   Annual management programmes: the APS is translated into mission statements and work programmes for each Commission service, setting out specific objectives for the coming year. Commission departments are assisted by IRMS[56] an information technology management tool designed to provide data on human and financial resources, scheduling, and job descriptions, and to assist the writing of monthly reports.[57]

3   An Annual Commission Work Programme: this programme aggregates the annual management programmes and specifies the operational decisions to be taken by College to execute the APS. The programme includes monitoring, evaluation and reporting. The Commission's Work Programme is presented to the Parliament and the Council after its adoption, and updated each month, allowing the Commission to inform the Parliament each month of its plan for the following four months, and mid-term and final reviews are presented to the Parliament in June and November respectively.

4   Annual activity reports: the Director-General of each service is required to submit a report covering the previous calendar year by 1 May, which includes a strategic evaluation of its activities and expenditure, an assurance declaration that resources have been spent properly, and provides feedback for future planning and programming. A synthesis report based on the reports is presented to the Council, the Parliament and the Court of Auditors, which enables them to see how departmental operations are assessed.

5   SPP located in the Secretariat-General of the Commission to support the President and the College in identifying priorities, monitoring the implementation of the annual programme, and representing the Commission in the inter-institutional dialogue.

Although an *ad hoc* test of the system was carried out in 2000,[58] the first cycle ran in 2001, and the work programme for 2002 was the first to be approved under the new system.[59] The first annual activity reports – and the synthesis report – were submitted in July 2002, and debated by EP Committees two months later. The system did not, however, become fully operational until 2003 when the amended Financial Regulation enabled the priority-setting system to be synchronised with the budgetary process.[60] The new Financial Regulation introduced Activity-Based Budgeting (ABB), a tool used to identify the administrative resources necessary for each budget line. The first full budgetary exercise in ABB began in 2003 for the preparation of the 2004 budget.

Most measures relating to externalisation envisaged in the White Paper were put in place without much difficulty. The main package was adopted by the College on 13 December 2000. Creation of a new type of body to implement

Community programmes – the executive agency – was agreed by the Commission in December 2000. Agencies are established by the Commission, expire on completion of the programme that they are responsible for running, and receive an annual subsidy. Though headed by a Commission official, they are separate legal entities. Measures covering offices – a second new category – that perform duties linked to a Commission department on a permanent basis, were introduced in May 2002. Three have since been created.[61] The system for managing Community aid to third countries has also been reformed. The process began in 2000, but the major steps were taken the following year, when the EuropeAid Co-operation Office was created and a three-step process begun to decentralise the management of external assistance by the end of 2003. Other measures include a new policy on decentralising tasks to networks of public agencies designated by the Member States, the adoption of a *vade mecum* for programme managers on contracting out administrative and technical assistance to the private sector, which includes a standard contract, and agreement on guidelines covering management of Community programmes by networks of national agencies. It also announced plans to phase out half of the 199 TAOs. A prototype database for contracts came into use on 30 June 2001.

FINANCIAL MANAGEMENT

The process of separating financial control and audit functions began in April 2000, when three new structures were created. The role of the Audit Progress Committee is to monitor the quality of audit work in the Commission.[62] The Central Financial Service, set up in the Budget DG with a staff of sixty-five and accountable to the Budget Commissioner, was charged with responsibility for defining financial rules, procedures, common minimum standards that departments must observe in their internal controls, and advising the finance units created in each DG as part of the move towards decentralisation. The third – the Internal Audit Service – was entrusted with evaluating and controlling the management and control systems created in each DG from September 2000, improving systems of administrative and financial management and internal control, and advising DGs on systems for managing human and financial resources.[63] The IAS was not able to exercise all its designated functions until the Council gave its approval to the separation of financial control and auditing (see p. 50), but pending this decision the Commission adopted a charter governing the operation of IAS in October 2000, and the new body began to recruit and to train staff,[64] develop methodological tools, and assess the internal audit capacity of the services. During the transition period, the IAS operated as a Directorate in DG Financial Control (DG FC).[65]

The planned reform of the Financial Regulation would end the requirement to obtain prior approval from the Financial Controller before committing or authorising expenditure and the *ex ante* control of transactions would be fully decentralised to the authorising DGs, but in the interim – following a communication adopted on 25 April 2000 – some officials were re-located to the services, where they continued to perform their traditional function,[66] while about a hundred remained in DG FC. DG FC also offered advice to the DGs on financing decisions, as they began to improve their internal financial management systems.[67] The Commission proposed an amendment of article 24 of the Financial Regulation to allow the separation of internal audit from *ex ante* financial control in May 2000, and the Council gave its approval in April 2001 with effect from July.[68] This enabled the Commission formally to create two separate DGs – the IAS and DG Financial Control – to confirm the appointment of the Director-General of the IAS – the Commission's internal auditor – and to appoint a new Financial Controller.[69] *Ex ante* control became an internal responsibility of each service.[70]

In December 2000, the Commission drew up a charter on the responsibilities of authorising officers, standards for internal monitoring and general guidelines on financial circuits and the role of financial units. The Commission's internal rules on budget implementation were adjusted in April 2001 to bring the charter into force, and the responsibilities of authorising officers spelt out in a memorandum of 27 June 2001, clarifying the content and scope of the annual reports and declarations that Directors-General were required to make. It required Directors-General to include their services' annual accounts in their annual activity report, as well as a formal declaration of assurance that adequate internal controls have been put in place and resources managed properly.[71] The new system was put into partial operation in 2001.[72] Full implementation took place in 2002, when Directors-General presented their first statements of assurance, signalling that each DG is now responsible for the organisation of its management and control systems, under the responsibility of its senior manager. In annual activity reports, submitted in July 2002, thirty-one services expressed reservations, with half indicating that financial controls needed to be more vigorous.

The process of reforming the Financial Regulation began with a general discussion by the College of a strategy paper in April 2000, which formed the basis of the formal proposal adopted three months later. As well as providing for the creation of new and separate systems for financial control and auditing, it sought to write the responsibilities of authorising officers into the Regulation, and to end the division between administrative and operational spending in favour of budgeting by policy areas. These measures were part of a general attempt to revise the Financial Regulation. However, agreement was not reached in the Council until June 2002 and the new Financial Regulation became effective only on 1 January 2003. In the interim, the Commission set out a comprehensive Accounting Reform Project to modernise EU accounting, which included the plan to move from cash-based accounting to accrual accounting.

The fraud office, OLAF, was strengthened. Its staff was doubled in size (to three hundred) and a former German prosecutor appointed to head the organisation. In June 2000 the Commission set out its strategic approach to combating fraud. It advocated action on four fronts: developing a coherent anti-fraud policy, by in particular making legislation more fraud proof, improving detec-

tion, monitoring, follow-up and penalties; creating a new culture of co-operation with the Member States; developing an inter-institutional approach to prevent fraud; and enhancing the legal protection of Community interests. The
following year, an action plan set out priority measures to be implemented by
all its departments. Towards the end of 2001, it adopted a memorandum on the
fraud-proofing of legislation and contract management, and a Green Paper on
the legal protection of the Community's financial interests and the establishment of a European prosecutor who would investigate cases and lead action
in national courts.[73] The Convention on the Protection of the Community's
Financial Interests finally came into force in 2002. The first protocol under the
convention – on active and passive corruption – also became effective.

HUMAN RESOURCES

Human resources has proved the most difficult chapter of the reform. The trade
unions made their views clear during consultation before the publication of the
White Paper. They argued variously that reform was unnecessary, wrong-headed
and inspired by a desire on the part of the Council and the Parliament to undermine the Commission's independence, and that the envisaged changes in personnel policy threatened the status, pay and privileges of staff.[74] The proposed
reform of the social dialogue, which would reduce their presence and power, was
also contested. The process was destined to be lengthy, given the Commission's
commitment to consultation on each aspect of the reform. Whether the Council
would agree to an extension of the Method – and, indeed, whether the Member
States and the Parliament would support the Commission more generally –
added a further complication. Given these difficulties, the deadlines set out in the
White Paper – most fell in summer or winter 2001 – proved somewhat opti-
mistic, even if by late January 2003, the Commission could report that thirty-
eight out of the forty-two actions identified in the White Paper had been
implemented (Commission of the European Communities, 2003).

A new framework for the organisation of social dialogue was among the
first actions. In January 2000, the Commission and five of the six staff unions
agreed on the system with a new forum, better delineated levels of concertation
and clearer procedures.[75] Other measures included the Code of Good Administrative Behaviour for officials in their dealings with the public, adopted in
September 2000, proposals on working conditions the following month covering family holidays, flexible working, part-time work for parents with young
children, tele-working, the e-Commission and staff temporarily on leave, and
consultative documents on equal opportunities, better perspectives for the
disabled, concerns about serious wrongdoing, and the introduction of a new
disciplinary system – which had also to be discussed with other EU institutions,
since it involved a reform of the Staff Regulations – in November. Dialogue
with other institutions also began in early 2000. DG ADMIN started work
on proposals to extend the method by two years, which bore fruit when the
Council agreed to an extension until 30 June 2003.[76] Work on a common

recruitment office, involving representatives from the Council and Parliament was also begun.

The main human resources package was adopted by the Commission at its meeting on 28 February 2001.[77] It included several radical proposals along the lines set out in the White Paper (linear career structure, promotion linked to annual appraisal etc.), which were balanced by a commitment to continuation of the method and by the pledge that there would be no overall reduction in pay and allowances. The unions stepped up their criticism of the content and method of reform in advance of the February meeting, and expressed particular dissatisfaction at what they saw as an attempt to limit their input – a view strenuously denied by the President, reform Vice-President and other senior officials. At their instigation, a General Assembly of Commission personnel was convened for 2 March, where a strike warning for action on 19 March was issued and a resolution adopted. The latter called on the Commission to state that the decisions of 28 February would not be binding, to set up a High Level Group (HLG) of representatives drawn from the administration and unions to discuss the most controversial areas of reform, and to adhere to the terms of the 1974 framework agreement.

Facing the threat of a strike, the administration sought and succeeded in achieving an agreement with the unions to create a HLG which would bring representatives of the two sides together to discuss the proposed changes in human resources policy. Composed of eleven representatives from each side, the group was chaired by Niels Ersbøll, a former Secretary-General of the Council. It proved a very effective forum and union opposition was effectively quelled.[78] At the end of the process, only one trade union (*Renouveau et Démocratie*) remained opposed. The HLG discussed the consultation papers agreed by the Commission, and presented its conclusions to the Commission in May and July. Agreement was reached on several issues, allowing the College to adopt revised orientations in July. Outstanding differences on career structure, appraisal and promotion, and temporary staff required discussion over the summer months, but agreement was eventually reached, and the College adopted its revised orientations on 30 October (SEC (2001) 1697).[79] The new policy was structured around a more precise and transparent system of assessing staff performance, and also aimed at modernising and improving working conditions, including: more training, better management training, flexible working and parental leave, strict but equitable procedures in cases of professional incompetence. The proposals fell under two categories, as follows:

Changes that require no change to the *Statut*:

- Recruitment: improvements to procedure and staff to be recruited according to need.
- Training: increased opportunities with quadrupling of the budget to allow each official to have ten training days a year.
- Appraisal: merit to be recognised and rewarded with evaluation taking

place annually in the form of a consensual dialogue between each official and his or her line manager and performance scored out of twenty.

- Promotion: to be used to reward merit with officials to be promoted automatically on achieving particular number of points.
- Mobility: to be increased with officials expected to change posts after a fixed period of between two and five years.
- Probation for middle management: job of Head of Unit to be redefined with management requirements specified and training provided, with trial period to ensure equal opportunities, professional rigour, disciplinary procedures, whistleblowing rules, and overhaul of regime for temporary agents.

Changes requiring modification of the Staff Regulations:

- Career structure: introduction of two categories of official – Administrators (A) and Assistants (through a merger of B and C and the progressive disappearance of D), simplification of the salary scale with two categories and sixteen grades, each with seniority steps, easier and greater movement between categories and more promotions; individual guarantees that no official disadvantaged during the transition and the promotion of officials 'blocked' at B1, C1 and D1.
- Early retirement: preservation of existing system except for removal of fiscal penalties for officials opting for early retirement and standard treatment for officials taking early retirement in the interest of the administration, all officials aged 55–60 to have the right to work part-time and temporary officials similar pre-retirement conditions provided that served more than ten years and aged over 50.
- Social reform: rights to work part-time for officials with young children, better maternity and paternity leave, introduction of parental leave and family leave.
- Disciplinary procedures.

It was also agreed that the Method would be incorporated into the Staff Regulations.

Following conclusion of an agreement with the staff unions and further consultation in the *Comité interinstitutionnel du Statut*, the proposal to amend the Staff Regulations was adopted by the Commission on 20 December 2001.[80] It took more than a year, however – until 19 May 2003 – for the Council to reach agreement on the package.[81] The new Staff Regulations, which are due to become effective in 2004 in advance of enlargement (on 1 May 2004), endorse the Commission's policy of career development and promotion based on merit.[82] Other points are as follows:[83]

- A new career structure is introduced in a two phase transition period with two main groups – Administrators and Assistants – and a linear pay scale with sixteen grades, each with five seniority steps, with an automatic pay rise of 13.1 per cent over eight years in every grade. Average career profiles are guaranteed equivalent to the current system, but the new structure increases the possibility of enhanced final salaries for current staff.

- Overall levels of pay are secured and net pay guaranteed.
- The existing Method applies from 1 January 2004 for eight years with a review after four.
- A special levy on staff is introduced (the temporary contribution ended on 30 June 2003) to help finance social policy measures and the European Schools.
- Resources will be available to finance promotions.
- The system of allowances is overhauled.
- The statutory pension age for new officials is raised to 63.
- A new category of non-permanent staff, contract agents, is introduced with five-year contracts to work on non-core tasks in Agencies and Executive Offices and replacing local staff in Delegations and Representations, and up to three years to replace Auxiliary Staff. Temporary agents occupying permanent posts, including in research, to have maximum six-year contract.
- Working conditions are enhanced with expansion of opportunities for part-time work, the possibility of job-sharing, improved family-related leave, and family allowance and sickness insurance for same-sex partnerships. Social policy is written into the Staff Regulations.
- Rules governing discipline and 'whistle-blowing' have been clarified, freedom of expression guaranteed, and equal opportunities anchored in the Staff Regulations.

Some of the changes not requiring legislative change became effective in January 2002, but the new appraisal and promotions system came into operation on 1 January 2003.

Reform of procedures relating to the appraisal, selection and appointment of senior officials was agreed independently of the above. The College agreed on a number of changes in December 2000. The main objective was to end the system of national flags. Recruitment was opened up and limits imposed on the length of time Directors-General can remain in one post. Several rounds of appointments and re-appointments have taken place, subsequently, the most important of which announced in January 2002 saw twenty senior officials switch job or take early retirement under article 50. By the end of 2002, with only one exception, there were no Directors General or Deputy Directors-General who had been in the same post for longer than seven years. An increase in the number of women in A1 and A2 positions rose from 22/262 in 1998 to 35/276 in 2002 (or from 8 to 13 per cent).

Concluding assessment

The above discussion has examined the circumstances under which the demand for reform arose, how the content of the reform programme was determined, and how the reform strategy was influenced by the experience of earlier attempts to introduce change. It has put the Kinnock reform in historical perspective, underlining precisely how it differ from previous initiatives, not least in its success in translating proposals put forward in the White Paper into concrete measures. Though it is still early days – and there is insufficient space here to undertake a detailed examination – no account would be complete without an evaluation of the reform and a brief discussion of problems that have arisen.

In terms of its content, there can be little doubt that the reform has identified and sought to address many long-standing failings of the institution, as well as more recent problems, that have been documented by observers both inside and outside the institution (see, for example, Sasse *et al.*, 1977; Spierenburg, 1979; Stevens and Stevens, 1996; 2001; Laffan, 1997; European Court of Auditors, 1998; 1999; 2000; Metcalfe, 2000; Shore, 2000; Levy, 2002). Personnel policy – or the lack of it – has been a serious problem, which has prevented the institution from making effective use of its human resources and made it difficult for talented staff to be appropriately awarded, while the lack of emphasis on management skills within the organisation has been a long-standing problem.[84] The introduction of more robust financial management, control and auditing systems, and the emphasis on personal responsibility, represent a response to problems that have emerged in the more recent past, when the inadequacies in procedures designed to handle a small budget across a modest range of activities became increasingly evident as the EU budget multiplied and the Commission accumulated management tasks. A systematic approach to externalisation was also clearly necessary, given the lack of any policy on what responsibilities could be delegated or procedures governing the awarding of contracts. In addition, the Commission has sought to address well-known deficiencies in its internal functioning – such as poor horizontal coordination, the lack of archives, and the requirement that an official should collect the signature of the full line of command even for routine business – that are inefficient or time-consuming.

With respect to strategy, the reform has been a great success. An overwhelming proportion of the measures proposed by the White Paper have been implemented in a very short space of time. A small number have been blocked (for example, inter-institutional ethics office) or were delayed, but the overall strike rate is impressive. The momentum has been sustained and opposition from the staff unions, which has in the past thwarted reform efforts, has been overcome. The canvassing campaign and the communications element of the strategy are at least partially responsible. Although it would be a drastic overstatement to say that the 'hearts and minds', or even the active support of a majority, of staff were won, the transparency of the reform process certainly reduced the levels of anxiety and to an extent checked the feelings of insecurity that had in the past allowed opposition to be easily mobilised. However, the fact that so much has been achieved in such a short space of time, and that the reform has had such a direct and immediate impact on them, demonstrates a high level of adaptability on the part of Commission staff and in itself might be regarded as a significant achievement. Close to 30 per cent of officials, for example, have changed jobs within three years. Nearly all staff have undergone extra training, over 3,500 been trained to enable them to operate the new financial management and control systems, and since 1 January 2003 all officials have gone through the new Career Development Review.

Administrative reform is never a comfortable process, and complaints that that there had been too much consultation – that officials were drowned in paper or diverted from their 'real' work, or calls to 'reform the reform process', or that consultation was too little and too late were entirely predictable. Others concerning, for example, the scope of the reform programme – 'too many bonfires on too many hills' – that may have had some resonance when the White Paper was first published, seemed less well founded two years' later, when most of the proposed new structures and procedures are in place.

This is not to suggest, however, that the reform programme or the process has been unproblematic, or that the long-term success of the reform is assured. Some elements of the reform raise important questions. Considerable faith is put in ABM, for example, as a mechanism for matching resources to activities, orchestrating policy within an overarching programme, and evaluating action at all levels of the Commission. However, while ABM may suit an organisation with a strong central authority, it is unclear how well it will fit the Commission as a collegial body, where the Commission presidency has yet to acquire the institutional resources or the formal powers that effective directive co-ordination requires. Moreover, the suitability of a mechanism designed to introduce predictability over the medium-term for an institution whose strengths include flexibility and the ability to respond to sudden or unforeseen demands will need to be demonstrated. Furthermore, it remains to be seen whether the Commission will in practice be willing to drop tasks designated as 'negative priorities' or, indeed, whether the Council will allow it do so, and whether the budgetary authority will be responsive to the Commission's requests for additional resources.

The new policy on externalisation could also prove problematic. As in the case of ABM, the diagnosis of the problem is sound, but the appropriateness of the prescription needs to be demonstrated. As Levy (2002: 81–2) observes, three out of four EP reports on the White Paper express reservations about the impact of the Commission's new approach on the operation of the EU system as a whole. The main fears are that decentralisation risks a confusion of responsibilities, that it may restrict transparency, making control difficult, and that it may not be compatible with the principle of subsidiarity, since financial management with regard to EU competencies is a function best exercised by and from Brussels. In addition, it is not clear that the Commission has yet evolved the capacity for outsourcing, described by Metcalfe (2000: 827) as the ability to take 'make–buy' decisions, which requires clarity in what core functions can and cannot be delegated.

Beyond these questions of design are concerns with the implementation or unforeseen consequences of the reforms. Will the new promotions system prove sustainable? To what extent does the use of outside consultants with little knowl-edge of the 'house' to conduct management training courses for Commission officials undermine the credibility of the new approach to human resources?

If the administrative burden falls on heads of unit, who as middle managers are expected to assume many new responsibilities, will the post continue to be attractive? Will national governments accept mobility and merit in senior posi-tions, if their nationals are not well represented?

Some, by contrast, have argued the reform does not go far enough.[85] More serious, however, are concerns about the efficacy of new systems of financial management, audit and control. The new financial management and control architecture raises at least two questions. The first is the cost of decentralisation. Essentially similar bodies charged with roughly the same functions have now been created in all Commission services, when previously they were handled centrally. Although control may improve, economics of scale have been lost. Second, operational DGs with differentiated functions and a relatively small budget may find the cost of putting in place and maintaining the apparatus required for management and control purposes disproportionately high. The new audit system has also not been without its problems. The creation of the IAS, which was envisaged as a 'motor of reform',[86] disseminating new disciplines and instilling a sense of responsibility, was not given a universal welcome. Not only was there disappointment in some quarters of the Commission at the abolition of the IGS, but the wishes of the IAS that it should be seen less as a watchdog and more as a friendly adviser or friend have not been fulfilled.

Difficulties surrounding the 2001 budget have highlighted further prob-lems. Criticisms made by the Court of Auditors were given apparent weight by Marta Andreasen, the former chief accountant suspended after claiming that the Commission's accounting system was severely deficient, who suggested that the Commission's budget department was 'severely under-resourced' and bud-getary control systems 'a source of "major concern" ' (Parker and Buck, 2003: 12).[87] In the same connection, in a leaked memo, the Internal Auditor apparently expressed concern with respect to assurance statements submitted with the annual activity reports that there were few checks made on their quality of the documents, thereby leaving the Commission open 'to a high level of reputa-tional risk' (Parker and Buck, 2003: 12).

However, to concentrate on what may prove to be teething problems should not be allowed real achievements to be overshadowed. In the same report in which it expressed its concerns, the ECA stated that it 'must acknowledge that the Commission is fulfilling its commitment to work hard at improving its administrative and control practices' (cited in Commission of the European Communities, 2003). Moreover, commenting in March 2003, the Internal Audi-tor emphasised the great strides made by the Commission towards greater responsibility and accountability, noting that 'Last year, for the first time, 35 directors-general had to sign off the E100 billion that we spend. They had to certify the integrity of the numbers and the regulatory of the expenditures . . .

It was the first time they had to put their signature to the money they sent out of the door ... it was very salutary, the supreme wake-up call' (cited in *European Voice*, 6–12 March 2003: 3). Although they withheld their assurance in a total of 155 areas, they have generated a risk profile for expenditure made by the organisation.

Although these are real concerns, reform is always intensely problematic and attracts criticism more easily than praise. They should not be allowed to diminish an extremely significant, even historic, accomplishment.

Notes

I am greatly indebted to the two members of the Commission, the thirty-five Commission officials and the three national officials, who agreed to grant me non-attributable interviews during the research for this chapter. Thanks are due to the participants of the Oxford workshop for their comments on an earlier version of this chapter, to Anne and Handley Stevens for many helpful conversations and help, to Anand Menon for encouragement and remarks on an earlier draft, and to the British Academy and Birkbeck College for research grants that made the fieldwork possible.

 1 There had been occasional reviews of some aspects of its organisation and functioning and a major exercise in advance of the institutional merger in 1967.
 2 The functioning of the *cabinets* was also strongly criticised (1979: 19).
 3 Action was also taken on equal opportunities, training and recruitment. The Method was re-negotiated and extended, and a social contract signed by the administration and the unions.
 4 These include the 1992 project, assistance to the countries of Central and Eastern Europe, and programmes in education and culture.
 5 As Stevens and Stevens have observed 'When the shoe has pinched the Commission has been adept at devising stop-gap solutions' (1996: 13).
 6 It could be argued that the *modus operandi* of the Delors presidency, described by Ross (1995) and Shore (2000), represented an acknowledgement of the administration's excessive rigidity.
 7 For example, to end the centralised deployment of *huissiers* and leave arrangements for staff.
 8 In the continental tradition, the Staff Regulations (the *Statut*) set out the rights, duties and obligations of officials (Shore, 2000: 194–5; Stevens and Stevens, 2001: 28–9, 43–7).
 9 An evaluation of SEM 2000 referred to 'a lack of coherence in its objectives, a failure to identify problems exhaustively, a focus on inputs rather than outputs, and huge complexity' (cited in Levy, 2002: 75).
10 For example, the proposed decentralisation of financial and managerial responsibilities to line managers was not accompanied by a plan to provide the officials concerned with the resources necessary to carry them out.
11 The Williamson report was seen on the administration's side as 'a social peace deal' (interview, Commission official, 16 January 2002). For discussion of its content see Stevens and Stevens (2001: 192–3).
12 See, for example, the comments of Giovanni Sergio, President of *Union Syndicale Fédérale*, the largest staff union, reported in *Commission en direct*, no. 192, 16–22 February 2001.
13 Although how much evidence there is for this view is contestable.

14 An episode in the 1980s appeared to confirm the association between reform and national interest, when a Danish commissioner organised training seminars for the entire Commission staff and the contract was won, in open competition, by 'a Danish firm with a particular emphasis on time management using methods which require the purchase of a good deal of associated proprietary stationery' (Stevens and Stevens, 1996: 17).

15 See also Metcalfe (2000: 823).

16 To quote one of the leading figures involved in the reform 'the bureaucracy is a collection of baronies that are loyal to their subjects, generally supportive to the Institution, and often considerate to their Commissioners – but hardly any of these to the President' (interview, 17 January 2002).

17 Though dependence on other institutions offers only a partial explanation for non-reform.

18 For contrasting perspectives see Spence (1997), Shore (2000) and Stevens and Stevens (2001).

19 Discipline for poor performance becomes difficult, since 'when I fire someone, I am not firing him, but a nationality' (German official, cited in Shore, 2000: 196).

20 Union membership is estimated at between 18 and 35 per cent.

21 Stevens and Stevens (2001: 57) report that in the early 1990s there were twenty-five committees overall, seventeen of which were permanent.

22 In 1999, the main trade unions were the *Union Syndicale, Renouveau et Démocratie*, and the *Fédération de la Fonction Publique Européenne*.

23 With the exception of the ECA – the least powerful – none has exhibited sustained interest in the internal operation or management of the Commission.

24 The ECA found irregularities in respect of the Year of Tourism programme, which led Parliament to refuse to discharge the 1995 budget.

25 It was alleged that the Commissioner had employed friends with official money in the pursuit of private political purposes (Spence, 1997: 19).

26 For a profile of Paul van Buitenen see *European Voice*, 21 January 1999. His allegations were investigated by the Commission in 2001–2.

27 For the Committee's mandate, see OJEC C104, 11 April 1999.

28 It reported 'a loss of control by political authorities over the administrations they are supposed to direct . . . [which] implies a heavy collective and individual responsibility of the Commissioners' (cited in *Agence Europe*, 15 March 1999).

29 See *Bulletin of the European Union* 3, 1.10.12 for Santer's response.

30 See *Bulletin of the European Union* 3, 2.3.1.

31 For example, it was unclear how long the Santer Commission could remain in office in a caretaker capacity. Also, the Treaty requires, in the event of the College not serving out a full term, the appointment of a team to serve out the remainder of the mandate. This being the case, it was not clear whether another set of commissioners would have to be appointed, when the Santer Commission's original term of office came to an end formally.

32 'The Commission should speedily put into effect the necessary reforms, in particular for the improvement of its organisation, management and financial control. In order to do this, the next Commission ought to give urgent priority to launching a programme of far-reaching modernisation and reform. In particular, all means should be used in order to ensure that whenever Community funds, programmes or projects are managed by the Commission, its services are suitably structured to ensure highest standards of management integrity and efficiency' (*Bulletin of the European Union* 3,1.39 I.).

33 It had initially been unclear whether the hearings would be conducted by the outgoing or the incoming Parliament. The Parliament insisted on the early use of the investiture powers granted under the Amsterdam Treaty.

34 See *Bulletin of the European Union* 7/8.
35 In a speech to Parliament in July 1999, he declared his aim to 'transform the Commission into a world-class administration that leads by example. Our watchwords at every stage will be transparency, accountability and efficiency' (*European Voice*, 2 December 1999).
36 The Santer Commission, which remained in Brussels in a caretaker role, introduced two codes of conduct – on the conduct of EU Commissioners and on relations between Commissioners and Commission departments – and promised a third (on the professional conduct of Commission officials). The creation of a Fraud Prevention Office and a draft agreement on its operation were also agreed (*Bulletin of the European Union* 3–1999).
37 The hearings are available at www.europarl.eu.int/pressroom/com/default_en.htm.
38 The Committee called for OLAF to be strengthened, the creation of a new legal framework to protect the Community's financial interests, and stronger commitment on the part of the Member States to protect the financial interests of the Community.
39 The re-organisation of the Commission was informed by the DECODE exercise, published in May 1999. The number of departments was cut from forty-two to thirty-three. Two new DGs were created.
40 As one of the architects of the reform put it, this information would be helpful so as to know 'what rocks and reefs to avoid, what tides and winds to use' (interview, 17 January 2002). The Commission stated that it would take full account of an assessment of SEM 2000 in drawing up its reform programme, while an internal report on MAP 2000 was presented to the new Commission in September 1999. It is worth noting that the new Secretary-General, David O'Sullivan, who was briefly Prodi's *chef de cabinet*, was a team leader in DECODE.
41 Once the White Paper was published, responsibility was transferred to the relevant DGs.
42 Commission Vice-President Kinnock, cited in *Commission en Direct*, no. 192, 16–22 February 2001.
43 'Cette démocratie totale se transforme en demogagie totale': Giovanni Sergio, President of *Union Syndicale*, cited in *Commission en Direct*, no. 192, 16–22 February 2001.
44 The reform Group of Commissioners was supported by a steering committee, composed by the Secretary-General, the Financial Controller, the Director-General of DG Budget, and various *cabinet* members serviced by senior officials, which reviewed suggestions submitted by the TFAR. The management and delivery of external aid was reviewed by RELEX Commissioners.
45 All director-generals in the PCG Financial Circuits had to defend the internal financial procedures of their DG before their peers.
46 See n. 41.
47 Representation on these bodies was to be in proportion with the votes cases in elections to the *Comité du Personnel*.
48 Annex II lists the changes introduced following staff contributions.
49 An overall assessment of activities and resources, based on the Williamson Report and th DECODE exercise, was already underway. Data from the latter was used to identify policy priorities, and to decide on the departmental distribution of resources.
50 ABM echoed the attempt to integrate resources and priorities in SEM 2000 (Interview, SEC (2000) 382, SEC (2000) 1051 to 1051/3, SEC (2000) 1744/5).
51 The Method is a mechanism for the annual adjustment of pay and conditions of Commission staff each year in relation to salaries paid to officials in national administrations and spending power in Brussels. When Member States contested the method in 1991, staff went on strike. A compromise was reached, whereby pay was brought down, but pensions increased, and the Method would expire in June 2001.
52 The document notes that financial transactions have doubled over the preceding five years and external trade tripled over the preceding ten.

53 A new deputy secretary-general was appointed in June 2000 to work on the latter. The measures included sub-habilitation, allowing decisions to be taken at the right level – i.e. by director-general or Head of Service – rather than the Commissioner.

54 See General Report 2001, 1266.

55 See *Bulletin of the European Union 7/8–2001*, 1.9.10.

56 IRMS was in use in fifteen DGs and across the board by July 2002.

57 These will become more detailed in time.

58 Though ad hoc, it led to staff redeployment and a reduction of staff working on low-priority tasks.

59 See *Bulletin of the European Union 7/8–2001*, 1.9.01.

60 The new categorisation of expenditure by policy rather than administrative and operational will make the process more transparent.

61 A Paymaster's Office, and Infrastructure and Logistics Offices in Luxembourg and Brussels were set up in November.

62 Members include the Budget Commissioner, the Vice-President for Reform, two other Commissioners and an external appointee. Its Charter was adopted on 31 October 2000.

63 For example, contracts, training, recruitment, organisation of activities, and risk evaluation.

64 Its first head, appointed in December 2000, was an experienced auditor, who had recently completed a five-year term as Vice-President and Controller of the World Bank, where he oversaw reform. He was formerly a senior partner with Ernst and Young.

65 To avoid any conflict of interest, the Financial Controller reported on internal auditing to the Reform Vice-President, not the Budget Commissioner, during the transition period.

66 About eighty officials remained in DG FC, where they continued to monitor high-risk areas.

67 A financial management handbook was circulated to all officials, and training organised for managers, officials working in financial units, and authorising officers.

68 Council Regulation EC, ECSC, Euratom, No. 762/2001 of 9 April.

69 Jules Muis was appointed to the former post; Edith Kitzmantel, a senior Commission official, to the latter.

70 The Commission refined the concept of *ex ante* financial control the following April to strengthen internal control systems and maximise error detection. Relocation of financial controllers to the departments was completed in December. A user network, bringing departmental representatives together, began operations on 31 Janury.

71 To assist them in these tasks – they would be scrutinised by the IAS, DG Budget and the Task Force – directors-general were assisted in carrying out a thorough self-assessment of financial circuits in their departments.

72 The latter became effective on 1 January 2001, though with interim measures in operation for the first year. In June, the Commission approved the report for 2000 on internal audits. Thirty-four reports were submitted by services.

73 It also reported a reduction in the number of cases of irregularity notified by the Member States and a decline in the amounts involved.

74 Among other contentions were claims that the reform proposals were out of step with the conclusions of the CIE, that there was no need to reform staff regulations radically and the removal of one stone was likely to bring down the whole edifice, that the reforms were trying to change the 'DNA behind the building of Europe' and were the front to a political agenda underlay reforms, and the reform Vice-President was seeking to 'transform the Commission into light, monolingual organisation, at the beck and call of the Member States and powerful lobbies' (cited in *Commission en Direct*, no. 178, 13–19 February 2000).

75 The new system was formalised in December 2000. The Peer Group proposed a reduction in the number of officials working full time for the staff unions from twenty to twelve.

76 CM Reg 2805/2000 OJEC L 326, 22.12.2000. A consultants' report showed that EU officials were paid more than their counterparts in national administrations, but less than staff in the UN, NATO or the Permanent Representations.

77 Early initiatives included the creation of an office for career guidance in DG ADMIN and drafts on the working environment, equal opportunities, external staff, whistle blowing and unprofessional conduct. In July and September, further proposals were brought forward relating to voluntary retirement, mediation, simplification and transparency.

78 Less controversial issues – equal opportunities, disabled, working conditions, personnel services and equipment, training and mobility – were dealt with under the normal arrangements for consultation, leaving the HLG to handle the more controversial issues.

79 See *Commission en Direct*, no. 220, 9–15 November 2001, for details. On 21 November proposals for overhauling policy on research staff and reform of the unified external service were agreed.

80 Much of the HR package was formalised. Communications on the Translation Service and the Joint Interpreting and Conference Service were improved.

81 Other measures including changes to allow auxiliary staff to be recruited for up to three years rather than one, and an early retirement scheme had been agreed earlier.

82 The EP must give its formal opinion and the *Comité de Statut* must also approve the new regulations before they are adopted definitively.

83 See Commission press release IP/03/710 of 2003 and European Commission (2003c).

84 'There is no personnel policy. Or rather, the policy is to have *no* policy. What we have instead are the "Staff Regulations" The concepts of "career development" and human resource management are absent from the Commission' (Shore, 2000: 198).

85 Why, asked one *cabinet* member, not decentralise recruitment to the level of DGs. Why could DGs not operate as recruiting centres? (Interview, 17 December 2002).

86 See *Commission en Direct*, no.183, 24–30 November 2000.

87 A leaked memo from the Internal Auditor seemed to give further substance to these concerns.

MICHELLE CINI

3

Norms, culture and the Kinnock White Paper
The theory and practice of cultural change in the
reform of the European Commission

Since the summer of 1999 the European Commission has been engaged in a
process of internal organisational reform. The reform was initiated as a response
to criticisms from, among others, the Court of Auditors, the European Parliament and the Committee of Independent Experts, whose reports have been
particularly influential. One of the most interesting effects of the events
surrounding the resignation of the Santer Commission on 15 March 1999 has
been the attention it has drawn to the many cultures that define the Commission as a distinctive bureaucracy. But to what extent are references to the cultural
characteristics of the Commission more than just catchy buzzwords? What
follows below is a first attempt at addressing this question by looking at the way
the word 'culture' has been used in the Commission's reform documentation.
But before doing so, the chapter questions the extent to which models of cultural
change exist within the organisation theory literature, in the hope that such
models can help to provide a theoretical context to explain the Commission's
approach to planned cultural change.

Thus the chapter begins with a brief introduction to definitions and models
of organisational culture and cultural change drawn from the organisation
theory literature. It then reviews the literature on organisational culture, as it has
been applied to the case of the European Commission. After providing a brief
overview of the current Commission reform agenda, the final section of the
chapter identifies key references to culture, in an effort to draw out Commission
thinking on this question.

Cultural change in organisations: a brief introduction
to the theoretical literature

Organisational culture is a concept drawn from the anthropological and organisational sociology literatures, the origins of which can be traced to Geertz

(1973) and Weber (1968) respectively. The disciplinary distinction more commonly made nowadays is that between anthropological approaches, on the one hand, and 'organisation theory' approaches on the other, the latter being closely tied to the management/business studies literature on corporate culture which became fashionable in the 1980s (see for example the seminal text by Peters and Waterman, 1982). However, cutting across these disciplinary distinctions lie deep epistemological and ontological cleavages that give rise to a host of different research questions, interests and methodologies (Smircich, 1983: 339). In some cases culture is treated as a meta-theory of corporate effectiveness (Linstead and Grafton-Small, 1992: 332); as an independent or dependent variable; or as an organisational attribute, allowing us to talk about strong and weak, or efficient and inefficient cultures. By contrast, in other cases, culture is taken to be a 'root metaphor', so that as Meyerson and Martin (1987: 623) state: 'Organisations are cultures'. From this perspective culture is what allows members of an organisation to interpret their experiences, at the same time constituting an expression of those interpretations. While anthropological studies have tended to focus on the symbolic or metaphorical aspects of organisational life, organisation theory has tended to be associated with a more hardheaded positivism, though the anthropological influence on organisation theory since at least the early 1980s has meant that a clear-cut distinction is no longer tenable.[1] Yet as Meek (1988: 459) notes, many anthropologists would still find ludicrous the notion that organisational leaders *create* cultures, as they believe that culture emerges from the collective social interaction of groups and communities, which is not open to the manipulation of (what organisational theorists call) change agents.

Allaire and Firsirotu (1984) chart these definitional differences in some detail, which might lead some to conclude that the search for an uncontested definition of organisational culture is a fruitless exercise. Definitions often amount to little more than lists of other related concepts: assumptions, values, beliefs, norms, symbols and artifacts, to name but a few. While some definitions see culture as an integrating mechanism, a social or normative glue (Meyerson and Martin, 1987: 624), others place more emphasis on the influence of diverse external cultural influences upon the organisation. In some cases, cultures are treated as distinct from the organisation's social structure.[2] They may be open to planned change, say as part of an organisational reform, or far beyond the control of organisational leaders.[3]

In general terms, researchers whose work is based upon positivist premises believe that planned cultural change is possible. However, even positivists differ in the extent to which they believe that leaders are able to control this process. There is also disagreement over issues such as the locus of change (or the level at which it occurs), the time-scale involved and which mechanisms explain cultural change. Just as public management experts fail to agree on the processes by which organisational reform should occur, there is no manual providing a route-map for cultural change within organisations – assuming that one accepts that such change is possible. Moreover, the bulk of the literature tackling this question refers to change within corporations, and sits a little uneasily with case studies of public administration and management.

The organisational culture of the European Commission: the state of the art

Since the early 1990s there has been a nascent interest in the Commission's cultural characteristics (see Abélès *et al.*, 1993; Bellier, 1995; Cini, 1996; McDonald, 2000; Shore, 2000). Although this does not amount to a substantial body of literature, it does add something new to the more conventional studies of the European Commission that focus on leadership, organisation and policy making (for example, Coombes, 1970; Edwards and Spence, 1994; Cini, 1996; Endo, 1999; Drake, 2000). What marks this small but fascinating literature on the Commission's culture is the dominance of the anthropological perspective.

In a first study, three anthropologists were asked to investigate 'the existence or not of a specific Commission culture, plus the weight of the different languages and national cultural traditions and their impact on working relationships, and how a European identity might emerge in such a context.' (Abélès *et al.*, 1993: 1). The Commission was thus treated as a sort of micro-society, even if it was recognised that 'the Commission does not exist in isolation' (Abélès *et al.*, 1993: 4). The study covers such aspects of Commission life as the use of language, the relevance of stereotypes and the importance of the social sphere (including the role of national associations and clubs). It also addresses organisational characteristics of the Commission, such as the impact that hierarchy, personnel policy and attitudes to management have on staff, as well as the relevance of the north–south distinction. The authors conclude that there is no one cohesive Commission culture, but a plethora of competing cultures constructed on the basis of nationality and language, but also at times built around departmental identities tied closely to specific policy areas or functions performed (Abélès *et al.*, 1993; see also Cini, 1996 and 2000b on this point).

In a second study too, a wide range of organisational themes are dealt with under the rubric of organisational culture. Shore argues that the Commission's cultural characteristics are a reflection of the rules, norms and the 'system of political bargaining and networking' that pervades the organisation (Shore, 2000: 173) as well as the 'stamp of the ideas and practices that prevailed at the time of its creation' (Shore, 2000: 177) and he focuses in particular on the informal network politics of the Commission. In Shore's work there seems to be much more of an implicit agenda – one which explores the nature of 'Europeanism', and which is, moreover, more openly critical of the European Commission and its culture, which is deemed to 'create conditions that are ideal for encouraging practices of fraud, nepotism and corruption' (Shore, 2000: 176).

Perhaps the most important distinction to draw between these two anthro-pological studies is that while Abélès *et al.* (1993) seem to imply that the culture *is* the organisation, Shore (2000), albeit implicitly, is suggesting a causal link between the organisation (its rule, norms, practices etc.) and the culture, and the culture and its potential effects (e.g. corruption). However, even here there is no suggestion of agency. As such the potential to apply this sort of approach to a project of planned change (or reform) would appear limited. It is only by drawing on positivist or symbolic (see Hatch, 1997) schools of organisation theory that 'planned cultural change' makes much sense. Yet as far as the study of the Commission is concerned, little use has been made of this literature (see Cini, 1996 and 2000b, however), even if the assumptions underpinning it can be found in studies of the Commission grounded in public administration and management (see Levy, 2000; Stevens, 2000).

The reform of the European Commission

Turning now to the case of Commission reform, it is clear that although the European Commission at the end of the 1990s was quite different to the EEC Commission in the late 1950s, no comprehensive reform of this organisation has ever taken place. This is not to say that reform was not needed: far from it. Indeed, many reports over the decades had identified organisational flaws, and proposed radical reforms. As Spence (2000) notes, perhaps the most compre-hensive of these reform proposals came from Dirk Spierenburg at the end of the 1970s (Spierenburg, 1979), though at the time the vast majority of these proposals were shelved. Where there were reforms, these were either driven by necessity as a consequence of the enlargements of the 1970s, 1980s and 1990s, or were responses to particular policy-related issues, thus not affecting the Commission as a whole.

It was not until the Santer era, from 1995 to 1999, that organisational reform became a Commission priority. This is easy to forget, given the bad press the then President of the Commission has since received. Yet, Jacques Santer arrived at the Commission committed to doing 'less, but better'. This is not perhaps the most exciting slogan around which to mobilise Commission staff, but it did reflect the fact that for once internal reform was being taken seriously. This was particularly important given that the previous Commission President, Jacques Delors, had done nothing to improve the internal organisa-tion and operation of the Commission (Peterson, 1999: 56). Yet one of Santer's main errors, it seems, was that his reforms were launched with more of a whimper than a bang. Outside the Commission, few were aware that they were taking place (Cram, 1999). This low-profile approach may well have been thought appropriate when internal reform was not seen as a legitimising device for the Commission. It was not really surprising that it was thought much more appropriate that the Commission should be ensuring a high profile for issues such as enlargement and EMU, on the EU's agenda at this same time (Peterson, 1999).

Santer's reforms were led in the main by two rather inexperienced Commissioners, Erkki Liikanen and Anita Gradin, and consisted in the first instance of two elements. The first of these became known as SEM 2000, short for Sound and Efficient Financial Management. The programme, which began in 1995, sought to improve the rigour of financial regulation and evaluation in Commission programmes and policy. It was at the second stage, MAP 2000 (Modernisation of Administration and Personnel Policy), initiated in 1997, that the implications of financial management reform were followed through in matters concerned with staffing and personnel. MAP 2000 sought to modernise personnel management by decentralising and devolving powers, simplifying procedures and identifying and applying new approaches in the administration and management of human resources.

Even though many of the objectives of the two programmes were implemented by the time Santer left office, they were far from constituting a comprehensive reform package. This is not to ignore the fact that after the resignation of the Santer Commission in March 1999, and the appointment of the new Commission, Romano Prodi, the new President, picked up where Santer had left off, repackaging the reform timetable that Santer had initiated, rather than initiating a brand-new Commission reform. Indeed, alongside SEM and MAP 2000 sat a third stage in the Santer reform strategy. This involved a whole-scale screening process, which would be used as the basis of a more comprehensive reform for the Commission and which was to be implemented by the Commission appointed in 2000 (which some say Santer had hoped to head). By the time the Santer Commission had resigned, and this project was put on hold, most of the screening exercise had been completed, allowing what is known as the DECODE project to be published in July 1999. DECODE, a French acronym translated in English as 'Designing Tomorrow's Commission', as has been pointed out by Metcalfe (2000), did not include 'designs' of any sort. But it did deliver a comprehensive review of the organisation and operation of the Commission at the end of the 1990s, identifying both problem areas and good practice within the organisation (Commission/ Inspectorate General, 1999).

This document provided a key resource from which the reform strategy of Romano Prodi, or more accurately his Vice-President, Neil Kinnock, could be developed. A second set of resources came in the form of the two reports published by the Committee of Independent Experts, set up under the auspices of the European Parliament, and in the case of the first report, of importance in triggering the Commission's resignation in March 1999. The first report dealt with questions of responsibility, mismanagement, fraud and nepotism at the level of the College (that is, the Commissioners and their staffs), while the second report, published in September 1999, dealt with management practices at the level of the Commission's services. Both were extremely influential in establishing the parameters and the substance of the reform strategy developed by Kinnock and his team in late 1999 and early 2000.

While indications of the approach likely to be taken in reforming the Commission came early (even before the Commissioners were formally appointed), the strategy to be adopted was set out definitively in a White Paper, published in March 2000. Some of what might appear as early initiatives of Prodi, such as the Codes of Conduct for Commissioners and the new Rules of Procedure, were already in the pipeline during the Santer Commission, and would probably have been introduced around the same time had the Santer Commission survived. The spin put on these new rules was, however, closely tied to the construction of a clean break from the past. It was politically important, on this basis, for Prodi to be seen to be taking the credit for acts that appeared almost impossibly early in his term of office. As noted, Neil Kinnock was given one of the two vice-presidential posts within the Commission. This was intended to highlight the high priority given to internal reform by Prodi. Taking a longer-term view, this may not have been the most rational approach to the nomination of new Vice-Presidents (Spence, 2000), but it did make sense at the time, given that reform provided practically the sole justification for Prodi's appointment. Kinnock was to spend the autumn and winter of 1999–2000 working up plans for the 'modernisation' of the Commission, a fundamental reform that, as Kinnock would frequently repeat, was to be 'a process not an event'.

The White Paper brought together the three strands of the reform package proposed by Neil Kinnock and his team. The first strand was summarised in the phrase 'the means to match our ambitions'. This was to involve a new approach to the setting of political priorities and the allocation of resources, to the extent that the Commission might in future refuse to take on new responsibilities should it not be given the resources to implement them. A new decision-making mechanism (known as 'Activity-Based Management' (ABM)) was to be introduced to ensure that responsibilities matched resources, and that the results were to be evaluated as a matter of course. The second strand concerned the reform of financial management. The justification here was one of empowering departments to establish internal control systems, by clearly and unequivocally identifying the responsibilities of all actors involved in financial management, as well as via systematic checks by the Commission's new Internal Audit Service. The third strand was the whole-scale reform of the Commission's human resources policy. The emphasis here was to be on 'performance, continuous training and quality of management, as well as on improving recruitment and career development' (Commission of the European Communities, 2000b: 6)

While Kinnock's approach was intentionally inclusive, there was also a clear acknowledgement from the very start that the Unions might attempt to sabotage the whole reform exercise (Kinnock, 1999a). While the Commission's six unions represent only 20 per cent of officials, they have in the past been able to mobilise a large proportion of the Commission's staff. Indeed, leaked proposals for the reform of the Staff Regulations during the Santer Commission had provoked a one-day strike with a 90 per cent plus turnout (*European Voice*, 7 May 1998; Cini, 2000b). Kinnock tackled this thorny problem by inviting the unions to participate and support the reform process. Reassurances were given by Prodi and Kinnock that they would fight for more (and not a cut in the number of) jobs, and that the reform process was not an attack on officials. However, Kinnock also proposed a reform of the Commission's system of 'social dialogue'. Though not proposing to change the system until after the reforms have been implemented, he is keen to get the Unions' agreement to a cut in the number of full-time union officials (by twelve people). By mid-January 2001, the unions were threatening to block reforms and were refusing to participate in negotiations over the Reform White Paper, to which Kinnock replied that though he would hope for their participation, if they did not see fit to negotiate, he would go ahead and introduce the reforms anyway (*European Voice*, 18 January 2001).

So how does this account of the birth of a Commission reform agenda justify this chapter's focus on cultural change? The answer lies in seeing Commission reform through the lens of the organisational culture literature. Emphasis in the literature on the importance of the process, as well as the substance of reforms draws our attention to the failings of the Santer reform project and to Kinnock's initial aim of inclusiveness. A second and related point draws on those theoretical accounts of cultural change, which emphasise the importance of strong leadership. Here, the literature frequently sees assertive leadership as one of the key prerequisites for successful reform. The elevation of the organisational reform to the level of a vice-presidential portfolio, together with Kinnock's apparent acknowledgement of the need to provide strong leadership during the reform process, suggests that this is another parallel development. However, taking these two features together implies a recognition, both in the theoretical and in the Commission's own reform texts, that what is needed is a leadership which is assertive but not elitist, one which encourages dialogue, the building of consensus and which recognises the importance of inclusiveness. However, moving beyond the rhetoric to achieve a balance between strong assertive leadership and consensus building is far from an easy task in practice. Moreover, this parallelism between reform strategy and the cultural change literature may be nothing more than coincidence. The next section considers this hypothesis in light of more explicit references to culture within the Commission's reform documentation.

The concept of culture in the Commission's reform proposals

Cultural change in the Commission is a theme that cuts across the current reform agendas proposed by Kinnock in the White Paper of March 2000. But this theme is not new. There are certainly references to cultural change in the SEM and MAP 2000 programmes that were initiated by the Santer Commission (Cini, 2000b), and the brief discussion of Commission reform in the Agenda

2000 Report also admits that 'Managing a high level of integration will require a thorough re-evaluation of the Commission's executive and management functions and a change in its administrative culture' (Commission of the European Communities, 1997: part 1/V), even if no clues are to be found as to what this might entail in practice. In some ways this is typical of an approach to organisational culture found within the Commission's documentation. While there may be frequent references to the concept, there seems to be little substance or coherence behind it. To what extent do more recent references to culture in the Commission's post-1999 documentation also suffer from this lack of specificity?

It is possible to trace much of the general framework of the Commission's post-1999 reform agenda to the criticisms in various reports published by the Court of Auditors, the European Parliament, and *ad hoc* groups and experts, such as the Williamson Report and the two reports of the Committee of Independent Experts (CIE) of March and September 1999. While the first CIE Report, which led to the resignation of the Commission, emphasised the need for Commissioners to take 'responsibility' for their departments, the second supplemented this criticism at the level of the services with a critique of something rather more abstract: the 'mentality' pervading the Commission administration. However, rather unhelpfully, the authors of the report suggested that while 'There are no specific ways of dealing with a problem of mentality . . . the Committee believes it should encourage a process of reflection and internal discussion in this respect' (Committee of Independent Experts, 1999b: point 8.3).

More explicit references to 'culture' in the reform documentation provide us with a starting point for analysing its usage. Indeed, there is a plethora of references to culture in the Commission's speeches and reports from mid-1999 on. Even before his formal appointment to the Commission, Kinnock was highlighting the importance of culture in the reform process. In written questions posed by the European Parliament's Committee on Budgetary Control before Kinnock's Hearing, the Commissioner-elect referred directly to the importance of modernising and reforming the *management culture* of the Commission. Developing further this management focus, references to 'culture' were frequently linked to the question of *propriety*. As mentioned above in the case of the Santer Commission, this was deemed a crucial part of the reform process, given that it would allow functions and responsibilities to be decentralised on a risk-free basis, enhancing managerial effectiveness by encouraging flexibility while at the same time maintaining a consistency of approach. In other words, a change in the management culture was assumed to be a prerequisite for decentralisation within the organisation. This, then, would solve one of the paradoxes of the reform process: how to decentralise this hierarchical institution, so as to create a real 'network organisation' (Metcalfe, 2000), without sacrificing accountability – also part and parcel of the reform strategy.

A recurrent slogan in the documentation refers to the need to construct a 'culture based on public service'. This is set out as a rationale underpinning reform in the 2000 White Paper, but appeared in more expansive form earlier on. Thus the European Parliament's Budgetary Control Committee asked Kinnock about the steps he planned to take to ensure 'a consistent *culture of impartial public service* of the highest standard across the entire Commission'. While this is something of a leading question, it did provoke from Kinnock one of his most detailed comments on the subject of cultural change:

> The general acceptance and practice of an administrative culture of efficiency, independence, transparency and accountability clearly cannot be achieved solely by drawing up rules. Implementation of Codes of Conduct like those recently agreed is a useful advance. But profound improvement also requires *inter alia* sustained staff training, organisational change, systematic auditing, investigation, and – where justified – penalising wrongdoing. I intend to reinforce such provisions in order that the highest standards of impartial public service will prevail throughout the Commission. That is necessary for good management, and the public has the right to expect such standards. (European Parliament, 1999: 15)

Here the language used goes beyond a rather specific notion of management culture to imply a more overarching definition of administrative culture. Indeed, this is the closest we get to identifying a Commission strategy for cultural change, in the sense of an injection of what Kinnock has called the 'fresh organisational ethos' which he has stressed must go hand-in-hand with improved practices in the Commission. Similar comments were made at the Press Conference in January 2000, which launched the Consultative Document (which formed the basis of the White Paper) in which Kinnock once again referred explicitly to the Commission's culture, noting that there have long been calls for a change in the 'culture' of the Commission. He went on to say that

> Obviously, in an administration, the 'culture' is not a matter of nature, it is the product of accumulated structures and systems. Reform therefore means modernising working methods and practices, creating new and more efficient systems, and setting and reaching fresh standards. (Kinnock, 2000: 2)

And in the Consultative Paper itself, Kinnock stated that though 'Many have called for a change in the "culture" of the Commission ... It is not by mere exhortation, but by modernising working methods, creating new systems and setting new standards that new habits will develop, new attitudes will be formed and a new culture will emerge' (Commission of the European Communities, 2000a: iii). This is perhaps the most definitive statement to be found on plans to change the culture of the Commission.

It is the White Paper, however, which provides the framework for reform. An introductory section entitled 'A Culture based on Service' spells out the principles which are to form the basis of the new culture: independence, responsibility, accountability, efficiency and transparency (Commission of the European Communities, 2000b: 7). More specifically, one of the key objectives of a new human resources policy is to 'create a common management culture across the Commission' (Commission of the European Communities, 2000b: 12). However, despite this emphasis on the creation of a common culture, reform will also involve 'training related to working in a multicultural environment and to managing diversity' as 'The legacies of the past mean that the organisation of work in the Commission tends to be rigid, with insufficient understanding of how the cultural diversity that characterises and enriches the Commission can affect working relationships'. Under 'Audit, Financial Management and Control' it is stated that 'One central aim of the Reform is to create an administrative culture that encourages officials to take responsibility for activities over which they have control – and gives them control over the activities for which they are responsible' (Commission of the European Communities, 2000b: 19). Finally, in the Conclusion to the White Paper, it is stated that 'This Reform is a once-in-a-generation programme. One of its purposes is to create a culture of continuous improvement and to ensure that the Commission is flexible enough to change itself in the future as new challenges confront it in an ever-changing world' (Commission of the European Communities, 2000b: 26).

It is interesting to note that in Part II of the White Paper, which comprises the action plan for reform, 'A Culture Based on Service' forms the heading of a chapter, distinct from those covering the three strands of reform identified in the section above. This chapter covers (i) standards of behaviour in public life; (ii) codes of good administrative behaviour; (iii) new rules to enhance public access to documents of Community institutions; (iv) improving dialogue with civil society; (v) framework agreement with the European Parliament; (vi) towards the E-Commission; and (vii) speeding up payments. This rather odd assortment of proposals which do not seem to fit under any other heading do generally have a bearing on the service provided by the Commission – whether to the citizens, other Community institutions, or clients. The focus would seem to be more on 'service' then, than on the creation of a new 'culture'. What is interesting, as in all of the references listed above, is what it tells us about the Commission's 'take' on this rather amorphous concept.

Conclusion

While there is no one authoritative statement on the cultural aspects of Commission reform, it is possible to make a tentative interpretation of the use of the culture concept in the Commission's reform documentation. This can be simplified by asking three (sets of) questions: (i) what is Commission culture, from where does it come and what does it do?; (ii) what sort of 'cultural change' is being referred to?; and (iii) how does cultural change occur?

'Culture' is defined only very loosely in the Commission's documentation, leaving the reader with a rather vague notion of what is being addressed. There are references to 'organisational ethos' and to 'attitudes', but these really leave us none the wiser as to how the concept is understood. There does seem to be an assumption that culture (in this organisational context) is the accumulated effect of systems and structures, and that cultures have effects – they cause things to happen. Addressing the type of cultural change at issue clarifies this somewhat. It becomes clear that the culture being alluded to in the documentation is generally 'administrative' or 'management' culture. Where an overarching culture is promoted it is to be one based on 'impartial public service', in the form of five general principles: independence, efficiency, responsibility, accountability and transparency. In other words, cultural change does not imply an undermining of the national or linguistic diversity to be found in the Commission, even if in practice this distinction is not so clear-cut, and national differences harbour particular administrative traditions. There is, all the same, a stated acknowledgement of the diversity that exists within the Commission. But this is tied to recognition of the limits of that diversity.

How, then, does cultural change occur, according to the Commission's documentation? Many of the references mention the importance of the planned introduction of new structures and systems (for example, organisational changes and the introduction of new auditing systems). Once implemented, these, it is noted on one occasion, will lead to new attitudes and to a change of culture. However, in one of Kinnock's quotes above, it is made clear that structures and systems are only two sources of cultural change. Others that are also important are introduced through such innovations as staff training and the penalising of wrongdoing. Thus, reading between the lines somewhat, it is possible to identify five general sources of cultural change: rules and standards; organisational/structural change; new systems (e.g. auditing); social learning/ socialisation; and sanctions (together with, one assumes, incentives). While these variables do not at this stage tell us much about the Commission's overall reform strategy, they may serve to inform or even to guide future research in this area. Moreover, they fit neatly with many of the key themes identified in the literature on cultural change. If this does not prove that Commission reform was influenced by this literature, it does suggest that it is in line with it, and that something more than lip service is being paid to cultural change as an element within the ongoing Commission reform.

Notes

1 There have, for example, been a number of studies from post-modern perspective. See Linstead and Grafton-Small, (1992), as an example. Note also that Smircich (1983) and Allaire and Firsirotu (1984) both seek to compare and/or unite cultural anthropological approaches with that of organisational culture/theory.

2 In other words, on the one hand we might ask of the effects of culture on organisations; on the other this question would be nonsensical, as organisations are collections of culture. See Allaire and Firsirotu, (1984).

3 It is not the aim of this chapter to provide a definition of 'organisational culture'; nor is it necessary to claim adherence to a particular epistemology or model, as the chapter aims only to explore the links between the Commission's conception of cultural change and that found in the organisational theory literature.

Véronique Dimier

4

Administrative reform as political control
Lessons from DG VIII, 1958–75

The aim of the current reform of the European Commission is to transform its administrative culture (Commission des Communautés Européennes, 2000a: 22; Cini, Ch 3 this volume; Kassim, Ch 2 this volume) and to render it less bureaucratic and more managerial (European Commission, 2001a: 27). Transparency, efficiency, accountability, performance, programming and evaluation are the keywords of what can be seen as a small revolution. That revolution was devised as an answer to the criticism that followed the financial scandals and the demise of the European Commission in March 1999, but also as an attempt to keep pace with the evolution of its tasks. From an institution that was initially meant to initiate policies, it has become increasingly involved in managing big budgets and programmes. However, it is argued that it lacked both the human and financial resources and the 'culture' required to carry out these tasks (Commission des Communautés Européennes, 2000a: 20). This is considered to be a source of 'bad practices', namely nepotism and inefficiency. Some of these practices concern the problem of management by DG RELEX (External Relations)[1] of the external aid programmes. The multiplicity of programmes, rules, procedures and external contractors involved in it – this 'time-consuming bureaucracy' (Commission des Communautés Européennes, 2000b: 9) – had rendered the system inefficient. As a consequence, DG RELEX became the flagship of the whole reform exercise and the testing ground for the new 'managerial culture' (Commission des Communautés Européennes, 2000b: 8). A new system of programming and evaluation was devised to measure the performance and efficiency of the programmes and a new division of tasks between the DGs concerned was put in place. The reform was presented as the only way to fight the evils of the past.

Nevertheless, one may consider that the past was not that evil. Rather, its vilification is part of a discourse on reform which has its own political logic. Indeed, it ignores that there has been, especially in DG Development, previously called DG VIII, a specific 'managerial culture', even though this culture is not of the sort desired by the current reformers. DG VIII was the first DG to directly run expensive programmes of the European Development Fund (EDF). Its institutional identity and management culture were built around this very task and may have survived until now.

This is why going back to the first years of its institutionalisation and the previous reforms may be of interest here. 'Institutionalisation' refers (Selznick, 1957) to the process whereby an organisation – and the officials who operate therein – develops its own identity or culture, by (a) defining its mission, e.g. aims, methods, principles, types of public action; (b) inserting this mission into a social structure through recruitment, socialisation process and a specific power structure; (c) legitimising this mission within a specific context; and (d) granting it a certain autonomy from its stakeholders. This process is led by strong leaders, but the identity itself stems from the balance of power between the senior officials who are the 'carriers' of different norms, methods and interests, and is defined within a specific environment (made up of the Member States, other EC/EU institutions, other international organisations). Building and maintaining a common identity in the context of a multinational organisation may be made more difficult by the very different professional and educational backgrounds of the officials, by the constant development of the wider institutional environment and successive enlargements. These elements also constrain the evolution of a given DG. Each enlargement changes the organisational environment and balance of power between Member States. At DG level, it leads to the recruitment of new officials with new norms and interests to defend; all in all it means new conflicts that must be regulated.

It is argued that reforms in the structure of the institution or policies and types of public action are the means to regulate these conflicts. Any administration, national or multinational, is a 'battlefield' where conflict takes place between diverse groups of senior civil servants. They seek to maintain their position, their power and access to various resources. The definition of reforms is part of this conflict for power or an attempt to control it. In that sense, it is highly political. It is all the more likely to occur in a multinational administration, for the very reasons presented above.

This chapter focuses on the first reform of DG VIII that followed Britain's accession to the European Community in 1973. It is argued that during the first fifteen years of its existence, DG VIII had a strong social cohesion, which limited conflicts of interests and norms. Strong leadership (former colonial administrators) allowed it to develop a strong *esprit de corps*, around an anti-bureaucratic identity, e.g. types of public action based on very personal relationships. These methods were essential for the efficient operation of the EDF and for building its legitimacy. Britain's accession was followed by a grand reform led by the newly appointed French Commissioner for Development, Claude Cheysson. It took the form of a campaign for efficiency, transparency and more rational approaches. Despite its ambition, this first reform did not lead to radical changes in the short term: the path taken by DG VIII (its

networks and methods) during the first years of its existence was likely to determine in the long run subsequent choices and trends, even though this reform
was, indeed, a window of opportunity (Kingdon, 1984) which, after subsequent
enlargements, has facilitated later changes towards more rational types of public
action. It will be demonstrated that this reform was mainly a way to regulate the
conflicts of norms and interests that occurred within DG VIII after Britain's
accession to the EC.

This chapter focuses on the first of these reforms, following Britain's accession to the European Community. Although the circumstances differ, the
objective of this chapter is to draw lessons with regard to current reforms.
Indeed, some interesting parallels can be highlighted right from the outset:
both reform efforts followed the enlargement of the EC/EU and they focused
on the need to increase 'efficiency' and 'transparency'. Previously legitimate
and effective methods of management came to be seen as pure 'nepotism'
whilst their proponent was branded a 'despot'. The rationalisation of management procedures, 'programming' and 'evaluation' methods became tools in the
quest for a new balance between different interests and groups within the
administration.

Managerial culture

The officials who played a major role in the institutionalisation of DG VIII were
former French colonial administrators (Dimier, 2001b). This role was promoted
as well as constrained by the *rapport de force* between Member States during the
negotiations for the Treaty of Rome and the wider framework set up with regard
to the status ('association') of overseas territories. For France, association was an
essential condition for the mere establishment of the European Economic Community. This had several consequences. First, association was mainly concerned
with those colonial territories which had 'specific'[2] links with France and Belgium. After the decolonisation process of the 1960s, this 'association' led to several five-year conventions (the Yaoundé and Lomé Conventions) negotiated
with the newly independent African states. This is why the mission of DG VIII
was defined along geographic and political rather than functional lines. This
mission, which includes trade agreements and foreign aid, was devised along the
lines of the French colonial regulations: what came to be called the European
Development Fund replicated the French Investment Fund for Economic and
Social Development (*Fonds d'Investissement pour le Développement Economique
et Social* – FIDES), created in 1946 to ensure the development of the French
overseas territories. The fund was mainly managed by DG VIII. It was responsible for selecting and analysing the development projects proposed by African
states and it became the intermediary between these recipient African states and
the Member States of the European Community (the Council) which decided
on the projects to be funded. Also, between 1958 and 1985, the Commissioner

in charge of this policy area was French, the first one being Robert Lemaignen, a former businessman who had worked in Africa.

As early as 1958, Robert Lemaignen asked a friend of his, Jacques Ferrandi, to become his *chef de cabinet*. Jacques Ferrandi, a former French colonial administrator in West Africa, had been the Director-General in charge of the economic services (1953–58) which oversaw the implementation of development projects (FIDES) in French West Africa. Thanks to his personal relationships, his knowledge of Africa, and his expertise in development policy, he was well placed to help the new Commissioner in making and implementing the policy supported by the EDF. In that task he was assisted by his 'clan' as he calls it, that is, his former collaborators in Africa whom he managed to place in strategic posts in DG VIII (Dimier, 2001b). This was made easier by the fact that until 1962 there were no regulations concerning the recruitment of senior civil servants (except a kind of balance between nationalities). When Robert Lemaignen left the Commission in 1962, Jacques Ferrandi left the Commissioner's *cabinet* after appointing his own successor, Jean Chapperon, a friend and former French colonial administrator he had worked with in Dakar. Jacques Ferrandi was appointed to one of the most important Directorates of DG VIII.[3]

As Director, he found himself in a place where only a small number of people could disturb his work (Dimier 2001b). This allowed him to accumulate enormous power. The Commissioners, Henri Rochereau, then Jean-François Deniau, were so preoccupied with their political career in France that they largely left their agenda in the hands of their *chef de cabinet,* Jean Chapperon. The first Director-General, Helmut Allardt, a former German Ambassador to Indonesia, was soon dismissed by his government after publicly criticising the EC's association policy. He was replaced by Heinrich Hendus, a former Ambassador to Algeria, who was more likely to understand French interests in Africa. The third person who could undermine Jacques Ferrandi's ambitions was the Director in charge of Directorate B, Jacques Lefevre, a Belgian with whom he had to share his power. Indeed, the two Directors had to agree prior to the submission of development projects to the Council of Ministers. However, they did not agree. Thus, the EDF management procedure was blocked. In 1963, Heinrich Hendus, backed by the Commissioner, decided to reform the administrative structure of DG VIII: the two directorates were merged into Directorate C. The new Directorate was headed by the man he trusted most, Jacques Ferrandi. Thankful for this confidence, the latter came to pay much respect to Heinrich Hendus and a kind of 'friendly pact' came to regulate their relationship, which gave Jacques Ferrandi even more freedom. Following that reform, a fourth Directorate (*Etudes de développement*) was established, which was supposed to provide advice on the development projects submitted by the African states and which could have become a testing ground for a more coherent approach to development policy (in terms of programming). However, as Jean Durieux, a young Belgian economist and the Head of this Directorate, conceded, it did not have any function or power (interview with Jean Durieux, 21 February 2001, Brussels).

Indeed, this reform went hand in hand with a simplification of the procedures of the EDF, which led to a further concentration of power in Jacques Ferrandi's hands and his 'clan'. After 1963 Ferrandi's role focused on the acceleration of these procedures: he was in charge of evaluating and reporting on each project proposed by the African states. Then, he would submit a 'financial proposal' to the European Development Fund Committee, composed of Member State representatives and chaired by a representative of the Commission. The Committee's final decision was based on his report. Following this reform, Jacques Ferrandi had effectively concentrated in his own hands the role of mediator and negotiator originally attributed to DG VIII. He was also in charge of awarding public works contracts to European firms. In other words, he was immensely powerful. These powers were further enhanced by the fact that the criteria for the evaluation of development projects were defined very slowly and remained very broad or even secret until the 1970s, thus allowing him a great margin for manoeuvre (Lister, 1988: 49). Only the EDF Committee could be seen as a check to his powers. Again, it seems that his experience and connections with African Heads of State, and his ability to forge coalitions, gave him a real superiority in his dealings with the representatives of the Member States. Most of the projects he endorsed were accepted by the Committee with little discussion. As he put it, 'I have never had so much power to dispose of public money. DG VIII was the EDF, and I was the EDF' (interview with Jacques Ferrandi, 26 August 1999, Porto Vechio), an assertion that none of the African Heads of State would contest.

The same expertise allowed Jacques Ferrandi and his team to gain some legitimacy within DG VIII itself and to impose their own methods drawn from their experience in Africa. Most of DG VIII officials did not have any practical knowledge of Africa (Lemaignen, 1964: 117). 'The French were the only ones who could manage a coherent action . . . We considered them as our master' (interview with Umberto Stefani, 22 February 2001, Brussels). The methods that they transferred to DG VIII (Dimier, 2001a; 2001b) were pragmatic and anti-bureaucratic, that is against any rationalisation and 'doctrine'. Individual projects were presented and adopted on an *ad hoc* basis, according to Jacques Ferrandi's political considerations and personal relationships with the African Heads of State.

These relationships were part of his system and power base. According to Jean Chapperon, no African representative visiting Brussels would miss the opportunity to have dinner with Jacques Ferrandi (interview with Jean Chapperon, 23 June 2000, La Garde-Freinet).[4] These personal methods became not only a way to run the EDF, but also a means to convince the African Heads of State, who were quite critical of the association scheme, that it was a *grande oeuvre de solidarité* and not the continuation of colonial policy (Dimier, 2001a). This personal network had become both a management tool, as well as an instrument for legitimisation and propaganda. Thus, they came to disturb the French Government: building his own networks in Africa and power within the DG VIII, Jacques Ferrandi began to grant DG VIII a certain autonomy from its main stakeholder, even though he went on serving indirectly French interests in Africa.

These methods were widely accepted at that time within DG VIII. Even those who later came to criticise them agree that they were 'efficient'. In a way, they became part of the DG's identity and what all officials interviewed for this chapter called its '*esprit de corps*'. Thus, the socialisation process led by Ferrandi and his team was quite – but not entirely – successful. Indeed, this 'harmonious' image was underpinned by conflicts of interests and norms. Some young civil servants working with Jean Durieux, trained in economics rather than in African affairs, had a more rational approach. Thus, they became increasingly irritated by Ferrandi's power. They were sceptical about his pragmatic and personal methods which eventually consisted in 'giving money to countries which needed it less'.[5] Those officials, however, had to keep silent and wait for better days. A major event, Britain's entry into the EC, proved to be a new opportunity for them.

In the name of efficiency and transparency

This event and the inclusion of some of the former British colonies in the family of associated countries had two consequences: it began to change the context in which the institutionalisation of the DG VIII was taking place, i.e. the *rapport de force* between Member States (Joly, 1991). States such as Germany and the Netherlands which supported the extension of the association scheme to other countries found in the UK, the other great former colonial power, a useful ally who supported their view. For DG VIII, it meant the recruitment of new civil servants with new ideas about development policy, new interests to defend, new networks in Africa to deal with. In short, new conflict was bound to arise.

As early as 1959, relations were explored between DG VIII and the British Government and academic institutions: trips to England by DG VIII officials and trips to Brussels by senior British administrators were continuously organised.[6] Briefings on the European Development Fund (EDF) were held by Jacques Ferrandi.[7] Thus, very quickly British officials became aware of the working practices and principles of DG VIII. They also presented their views as to the ways the association scheme ought to be reformed if the UK were to join. First, it had to be renamed because the word 'association' did not mean anything in English. Indeed, it was typically French.[8] But also, if Britain agreed to contribute to the fund, some kind of device had to be found to channel an equal share of the EDF funds to former British and French colonies, and British and French enterprises. Indeed, it became clear to the British that Ferrandi's system and network favoured the French interests and former colonies (Lambert, 1975).[9]

This explains in part their support for the rationalisation of EDF procedures (a) along the lines of the Commonwealth Development and Welfare Act and (b) through 'programming'. Aid ought to be linked to pre-determined programmes instead of relying on individual projects submitted and evaluated empirically, '*au coup par coup*'.[10] Besides, more precise, transparent and objective criteria reflecting 'the needs of the countries' would have to be used for the selection of the development projects, in an attempt to avoid any bias in favour of former French African colonies.

Clearly, these reforms were a threat to Jacques Ferrandi's power, methods and networks. More generally the mere inclusion of former British colonies disturbed the whole system he had set up: as Philippe Soubestre, *chef de cabinet* of Commissioner Claude Cheysson, noticed, Jacques Ferrandi did not have the same knowledge of English and of those territories. Therefore, his personal methods could not be extended there (interview with Philippe Soubestre, 25 February 2002, Paris). This is why he opposed the extension of the EEC's development policy to the British Commonwealth. It also accounts for the fierce British attacks against 'the small empire' that this 'Corsican' had built within DG VIII, for himself and 'his African friends' (Lambert, 1975). From being a 'Pope' he came to be considered by some officials of DG VIII (English and others) as a 'despot'. His pragmatic methods – previously seen as normal and efficient – came to be considered as pure nepotism (Lambert, 1975). In fact, an intense conflict of power, interests and norms arose in DG VIII from 1973, thus rendering necessary the definition of a new balance of power. Reform became the instrument for the resolution of this conflict. It took the form of a campaign for more efficiency and transparency. This reform effort was led by the new French Commissioner for Development, Claude Cheysson, and was backed by Hans Khron, the new German Director-General since 1970.

Unlike his predecessors, Claude Cheysson[11] had a strong interest in and precise ideas about development policy. They were similar to those of the British (Commission des Communautés Européennes, 1974). Moreover, he did not choose his *chef de cabinet* from former French colonial administrators: Jean Chapperon had to leave.[12] He was succeeded by Philippe Soubestre who was more in favour of a programme-based approach. The British press noticed (Lambert, 1975) that for the first time Jacques Ferrandi was confronted by a real boss. Claude Cheysson decided in 1973 to reform DG VIII, again 'in the name of efficiency', as a part of a wider reform of the EEC's development policy which was exemplified by the new convention signed in 1975 (Lomé Convention). Following this reform, the only Directorate in charge of the EDF was split again into two Directorates headed by a German and an Italian official. Two posts of deputy Directors-General were also created: one was responsible for co-ordinating the EDF (Jacques Ferrandi), the other (the English Maurice Foley) was in charge of the negotiations with former British colonies (protocol 22). As a result of this curtailment of his power, Jacques Ferrandi left the Commission in 1975.

The new Lomé Convention brought to the forefront the idea of 'programming', promoted by the British, and endorsed by some officials of DG VIII. It appears, however, that this idea could be interpreted quite differently by different people while its meaning evolved over time (Joly, 1991: 184; Ndoung, 1994:

285). Certainly, it was a first step towards some rationalisation of EDF procedures: from then on, national indicative programmes were set up for and by each ACP state immediately after the entry into force of the convention. These programmes indicated broadly the priorities of these states and the money that each could dispose of for five years. The distribution of funds between ACP states was to be decided according to clear criteria (GNP, size of the population). Within that framework, projects would still be selected one by one by the EDF Committee, but according to more objective criteria, which included efficiency and their relevance to the indicative programmes. A system of evaluation was set up.

Whether these changes were transformed into practice and modified the identity of the DG VIII, e.g. its types of public action, principles and methods, however, remains a matter of controversy. Although the interviewees were unanimous about Jacques Ferrandi's reign, they disagreed on subsequent developments. For some, authors or main reform actors, everything changed with the departure of Jacques Ferrandi and the signing of the Lomé Convention: 'it was the beginning of a real development policy, more efficient and transparent' (interview with Claude Cheysson, 23 June 2000, Paris) as opposed to the continuation of the French colonial legacy. Others tend to think that 'the period which left the most lasting mark on the DG VIII was Ferrandi's. . . . He left a style' (interview with Umberto Stefani, 22 February 2001, Brussels), that is practices which remained intact until well after his departure.

It is hard to draw a firm conclusion on this issue. 'Historical institutionalism' (North, 1990; Pierson, 1996) highlights the concept of path-dependent institutional development, thus favouring the latter view. The choices originally made by Jacques Ferrandi and his team, their networks and methods, were likely to determine subsequent choices. More importantly, they made reform difficult, at least in the short term. Thus, Jacques Ferrandi's methods were likely to resist any trends towards more programming. It is worth noticing here that Claude Cheysson used the same methods as his predecessor to build his own power: the reform allowed him to get rid of any potential competitor and to place his own people in strategic posts, Philippe Soubestre and Maurice Foley in particular. The latter was chosen because of his diplomatic skills and his political ties with British Tropical African elites.[13]

Most of the structures of the EDF and other instruments set up by Jacques Ferrandi were simply not modified by the Lomé Convention. Despite his departure, his team stayed: André Auclert, Ferrandi's main collaborator in managing the EDF, and a firm believer in the project-based system (interview with André Auclert, 16 May 1999, Tours), became in 1977 (and until 1986) head of one of the directorates responsible for the EDF (Finance et Administration). Their practices may have been forced to evolve had the British Government sent to DG VIII officials from the British overseas development administration. But, according to John Scott, Foley's main adviser (interview with John Scott, 22 March 2002, Maastricht), and to Claude Cheysson's disappointment, this did not happen. Indeed, the overseas development administration considered DG

VIII a potential competitor and chose to ignore it. This was clearly recognised later on by the British Parliament as the main reason for the poor number of EDF contracts awarded to British firms.

Thus, as noticed by another collaborator of Maurice Foley, Kaye Whiteman, the system as it existed was merely reproduced, with a new team guided by Claude Cheysson, and wider networks. These methods and networks may well explain the longevity of the Lomé Convention (Babarinde, 1995). They may also explain the very slow evolution towards programming and evaluation (Joly, 1991; Ndoung, 1994). For a long period it seems that programming did not mean more than the setting up of increasingly precise criteria in allocating funds for ACP states, even though the idea of building up coherent frameworks with clear priorities was supported by an increasing number of DG VIII officials, and gained ground when Dieter Frisch, a member of Jean Durieux's team, became Director-General (1982–92).

Towards bureaucratisation?

Palier and Bonoli (1999) highlight the fact that small changes can be introduced within an institution which in the long run, and following changes in its environment, may lead to more radical developments. The introduction of the idea of 'programming' and the concepts of 'efficiency' and 'transparency' could have been construed as a first move towards the rationalisation of procedures which, in turn, triggered the cycle of bureaucratisation described by Coombes (1970). In Coombes' view, Hallstein's Commission was largely non-bureaucratic: hierarchies were not set up in advance, authorities and initiatives could be easily delegated, and the system was based on very informal relations. This 'porous' organisation, as he calls it, was possible because within the Commission there were powerful leaders capable of (a) defining and enforcing its mission, and (b) maintaining a strong social cohesion among its senior officials based on mutual trust and shared beliefs as regards its aims and methods. However, this cohesion was fragile, because of the competition which was soon to appear between leaders bearing different interests and norms. This competition (facilitated by the multinational character of the institution) and the multiplicity of the Commission's tasks were to lead to its gradual bureaucratisation, that is, a growing rationalisation of its procedures: the porous organisation came to use (a) strict regulations regarding appointments and promotions, (b) rigid definitions of power and jurisdiction, and other 'bureaucratic tools' in order to ensure impartiality, neutrality, and balance between the various competing 'clans' and leaders.

Following Coombes, it seems that the ideas of 'programming' and 'evaluation' introduced in the 1970s paved the way for subsequent developments towards the increased rationalisation of procedures (Joly, 1991; Ndoung, 1994). In this sense, the current reform of external aid programmes and structures – emphasising programming, evaluation and efficiency – may be the result of a long process which was also influenced by external factors (e.g. the increasing collaboration with the World Bank). However, the fact that this reform, as also the overall reform of the Commission, is led by two British Commissioners, Chris Patten and Neil Kinnock, and is taking place right after a new enlargement, is probably not a coincidence. The current reform has exacerbated conflicts of interests and norms within the Commission: practices previously used with success by Jacques Delors for the implementation of his project, or by Philippe Soubestre and other DG VIII officials in managing the EDF, came under fire for they seem too despotic, too personal and too French (Shore, 2000). For the British, who have long been complaining about their lack of influence within the European Commission, the reform represents a new opportunity, while for the French it may be considered as a new Waterloo (*Le Monde*, 24 January 2002).

Either way, it can be seen again as a way to regulate conflict within the Commission at large and may lead to a new rationalisation of procedures. This, in turn, may produce unintended consequences both for DG VIII – a loss of identity and functions – and for the promoters of change (more bureaucratisation). The new system of programming which applies to ACP countries (Cotonou Agreement of 2000), and more broadly to all external aid programmes, includes the definition for each partner of a Country Strategic Paper, i.e. a coherent framework which will identify future priorities in several fields (economic, social and political) and shape clear objectives and a precise action plan. Common guidelines and standard criteria have been established to help the countries to draw up these papers. The programmes will be revised periodically and the funds can be re-allocated according to the progress made in meeting the clear objectives (human rights, governance). This constitutes a break with EU-specific principles, as it endorses the World Bank's concept of conditionality: funds will be disbursed according to the country's 'efficiency' rather than its needs, as was the case in the past. The whole system will be based on the logic of the 'stick and carrot', the very opposite of what the old style was based on: mutual trust and compromise with African leaders. It entails more rules and criteria as well as more central control, although the management of the evaluation and programming process will be left to the EU's local delegations. In fact, it is hard to see how these reforms will reduce red tape, i.e. the 'evil' it tries to fight. And the same comment applies to the new system of evaluation and programming used in the Commission at large (the setting of priorities, the new procedures for the budget) and the recent measures concerning the rotation and merit-based promotion of senior officials.

These tendencies towards rationalisation also led to another major change within DG RELEX, i.e. a move from a territorial to a functional division of tasks, which may lead to the unintended abolition of DG VIII. From 1998, some of the main functions of DG DEV (formerly DG VIII) were absorbed by two newly created DGs: DG Trade and the SCR (common service for external relations) which was directed by Philippe Soubestre for two years. Initially, his unit was only responsible for the implementation of all external aid, which had formerly been run by DG External Relations (concerning other countries as ACP) and DG DEV. In 2000, Philippe Soubestre was dismissed for 'nepotism' and another unit was created (Europ-Aid) which absorbed all DG VIII functions concerning the management of EDF (from project selection to project evaluation). DG DEV was left with a vague task of formulation of policy and programming for the ACP states. Battles with other DGs over the delineation of functions have re-surfaced, still proving the capacity of resistance of DG DEV. Deploring this state of affairs, Poul Nielson, the Commissioner for Development, proposed to merge DG Development and Europ-aid (*European Voice*, 28 February 2002) which will, in turn, be integrated in DG External Relations.

So, more reforms are likely to occur, in which DG VIII is most likely to dis-appear as a result of the new regulation of power relations within the Commis-sion at large. It will also disappear because, in its case, the long path towards rationalisation has undermined its very identity which was based on anti-bureaucratic types of public action, questioned its mission and *raison d'être*. In that sense, the case of DG VIII may be divided into two parts. The first, domi-nated by strong leaders such as Jacques Ferrandi, led to its institutionalisation, the development of a strong social cohesion around an anti-bureaucratic iden-tity which survived long after the first reform in the 1970s. The second began with Britain's entry into the EC and the battle between those who supported the old 'Ferrandian' style and those who promoted more rational types of public action. It has been argued here that the reform launched by the latter was a political means to regulate these conflicts and the new power relations within the DG. Despite its ambition, this reform did not produce immediate results but in the long run it triggered the cycle of bureaucratisation described by David Coombes (1970). The extent to which the case of DG VIII can be of use in analysing the history of the Commission at large will probably be a matter of debate in the future and must certainly rely on more detailed empir-ical investigation. However, as the recent reform of external aid may be seen as a new steps towards bureaucratisation, following the battles of interests and norms within DG RELEX in the 1990s, the recent reforms concerning the status of senior officials and the management of the EU budget can be viewed as the transformation of the Commission into a mature bureaucracy, following and preceding a new enlargement which inevitably bring new conflicts that must be regulated.

Notes

This chapter stems from a wider project on the institutionalisation and bureaucratisation of the DG VIII, which has been launched under the supervision of Marie-Christine Kessler and financed by the European Commission through a Marie Curie Fellowship and the EUSSIRF programme. The author is grateful to the thirty officials of DG VIII who have agreed to be interviewed for the purposes of this project.

1 DG Relex incorporated the following DGs: DG External Relations, External Trade, DG Development, DG Enlargement, Europe-id and ECHO. Prior to 1999, there were only two DGs in this policy area: DG Development (DG VIII) and DG External Relations (DG I).

2 These are terms used in the Treaty of Rome. Dutch Guinea and Italian Somalia were also included.

3 At that time, the DG VIII was divided into four directorates.

4 Archives de la Commission Européenne (ACE), IUE, Firenze, Bac. 25/1980/1503; Bac 29/1980/1493, for example note by Varenne on the trip to Brussels by the Senegalese delegation, 24 November 1960.

5 This is confirmed by the figures of the European Community (Lister, 1988: 50).

6 For reports on these visits: ACE, Bac 25/1980/1552; ACE, Bac 25/1980/1546. For example, ACE, Bac 25/1980/1552, programme of a visit to the Commission by a group of British civil servants, 14–15th February 1964.

7 Archives of the Colonial and Commonwealth Office (ACO), Public Record Office, London, Box 2104, Confidential telegram from the UK delegation in Brussels to the Foreign Office, 26 June 1962, refers to a meeting with J. Ferrandi (22 June 1960).

8 ACO, Box 852/2098, letter from J. W. Vernon (Colonial Office) to G. Barnes (Colonial Office), 17 October 1961.

9 ACO, Box 852/2104, memorandum by J. W. Vernon to L. Pliatzky (Treasury), 28 June 1962. This is largely confirmed by the figures given by the European Commission and regularly published in the French journal *Les Marchés Tropicaux*. In 1966, the share of the public works financed by the EDF was as follows: France: 43.85 per cent; Belgium: 3.49 per cent; Germany: 9.14 per cent (*Marchés Tropicaux*, 11 March 1967: 3).

10 ACO, Box 852/2104, Minutes of the Common Market Steering Committee, 6 March 1962, note by Sir H. Poynton; ACO, Carton 852/2104, memorandum by J. W. Vernon to L Pliatzky (Treasury), 28 June 1962.

11 Cheysson had worked in Lagos as Secretary General of the Commission for Technical Co-operation in Africa (1957–62). This had exposed him to British elites and ideas.

12 Philippe Soubestre was a graduate of a Parisian business school.

13 A former Labour politician (Foreign Office, 1967–69) and trade unionist, he had been a member of the Young Christian Workers. Thus, he had links with NGOs and heads of state in British Tropical Africa. His collaborators, especially John Scott (a former UN and Foreign Office official) had also first-hand experience of Tropical Africa.

PART II

The Commission as an actor

HUSSEIN KASSIM AND ANAND MENON

5

EU Member States and the Prodi Commission

The relationship between Member States and the European Commission is a core element of the institutional system of the European Union. The extent to which the Commission is an obedient servant of the Member States, acting only and always in their interests, and subject at all times to their control, or an autonomous actor, able to exercise an independent influence over the direction of European integration and policy outcomes at the European level, is a key concern (See Cram, 1993; Moravcsik, 1993; 1998; Pierson, 1996; Pollack, 1996; 1997; Matlary, 1997; Doleys, 2000). No less important, but often overlooked, is the way in which the relationship has changed over time, reflecting and reinforcing the shifting balance between supranational and intergovernmental bodies, methods and procedures at the EU level (see, for example, Kassim and Menon, 2003; Menon, 2003).

The appointment of Romano Prodi, formerly Italian Prime Minster, to the post of Commission President was widely held to represent a desire on the part of the Member States to rejuvenate the institution by providing it with the firm leadership lacking under his predecessor, Jacques Santer. For some academic observers, this high-profile appointment – the first former Prime Minister from a large Member State to be appointed to the office – implied that the Member States had chosen to equip the Commission with the resources necessary to carry out its existing tasks rather than to downgrade it. That Prodi became the first incumbent to enjoy the enhanced powers of the Commission President following the reforms introduced by the Amsterdam Treaty was a further cause for optimism among supporters of a strong Commission.[1] In practice, however, these hopes have been confounded.

This chapter examines the dynamics of the relationship between national governments and the Commission since the appointment of Romano Prodi.[2] After discussing developments up to September 1999, it looks at how the relationship has developed since the Prodi Commission assumed office. The argument presented below can be simply stated: the decline of the Commission, evident before Prodi took office, has continued apace and has been evident in development in both policy-related and institutional developments. This decline can be attributed largely to the assertiveness of the Member States, (excessively) concerned to entrench their autonomy and limit that of the Commission, but is due also to failures on the part of the institution itself.

Prodi's inheritance: the Commission under pressure

Prodi took office as President of the European Commission at what could euphemistically be described as an inauspicious moment in the organisation's history. His appointment followed the resignation of the entire Santer Commission in the face of accusations of fraud, mismanagement and nepotism (see Spence, 1997; Committee of Independent Experts, 1999a). No Commissioner was accused of committing fraud, nor of benefiting financially from the irregularities and instances of mismanagement allegedly engaged in by officials in the services. However, the resignation, following months of seemingly endless allegations of scandal and corruption, escalating conflict with the European Parliament, and the publication of the first report by the Committee of Independent Experts, brought the reputation of the institution to an all-time low.[3] It revealed serious weaknesses in the internal management and administration of the organisation (see Kassim, Ch 2 this volume). Moreover, although the Commission was not actually brought down by a formal vote of confidence, the circumstances of the resignation vividly illustrated its accountability to Parliament – a message that was conveyed loudly and clearly to the President-designate and his nominees during the parliamentary hearings that took place over the summer of 1999.

The Santer debacle was but the latest stage in an ongoing process under which the Commission had seen its influence within the EU institutional system decrease. Some challenges have been direct. The Member States have limited the Commission's power and responsibilities in new areas of EU competence, restricted the Commission's monopoly over the initiation of legislation, refused to make available to the Commission the human resources necessary for it to carry out its existing responsibilities, and challenged how it exercises its prerogatives. The three-pillar structure, as well as the principle of subsidiarity, introduced at Maastricht, were intended to rein in Commission ambitions and to establish Member State control over policy formulation in the new – and politically sensitive – areas brought within the scope of the European Union (Menon, 2003).[4] The fiction of the common institutional framework did little to disguise the erosion of Commission powers.[5] In a radical departure from the Community method, the Commission did not obtain its traditional monopoly over policy initiation in the new pillars and Member States (acting in the Council) acquired the formal right to bring forward proposals for the first time. The General Affairs Council and the European Council, operating by unanimity, became the main decision-making bodies in the second pillar (CFSP). The third pillar (JHA), meanwhile, 'formalized the network of inter-governmental cooperation among national ministries of justice and the interior, and among related national agencies' (Den Boer and Wallace, 2000: 494). The Council was the key body, serviced by the K4 Committee, a special committee that co-ordinated the work of a complex network of working groups (Hayes-Renshaw and Wallace, 1997: 96). The Commission's legislative role was shared with the Member States in some areas of JHA. In others, the Member States were granted exclusive competence. Determining the visa regime for third country nationals was the only area within the heterogeneous subject matter of the third pillar where the Commission was given its traditional monopoly over policy initiation.

The Commission's status in the institutional system has also been altered indirectly, as a consequence of the attribution of new powers and responsibilities to other bodies, and the introduction of new methods and procedures. The functions of the European Council have grown and its remit expanded, new 'modes of governance' (Devuyst, 1999 ; Wallace, 2000; Wessels, 2001) – institutional and procedural alternatives to the Community method – have been introduced, and the European Parliament has been strengthened at successive IGCs (Hix, 2002a; Majone, 2003). The effect of the greater power of the Parliament over the Commission threatens, it has been argued, to turn the latter from a non-majoritarian institution, capable of independent action, into a majoritarian body, concerned about its short-term survival and placating parliamentarians rather than the delivery of the objectives set by the treaties and serving the general interests of the Union (Majone, 2002, 2003).

More broadly, throughout the decade, the Member States asserted their authority and institutionalised their leadership over the direction of integration. IGCs became more frequent. Their agendas were longer, the level of detail greater, and their expansion into policy more extensive. The Commission was relegated to a secondary role. The greater frequency and detail of IGCs were not, however, the sole sign of growing Member State assertiveness, only the most visible. The volume and scope of business transacted at European Councils also increased. In policy matters, Heads of State and Government no longer concentrated only on high politics, nor limited their attention to troubleshooting. Instead, there was evidence of 'creeping competence'.

The post-Maastricht climate, and the changing status of the Commission, was reflected in the attitude of the Santer Commission, which took office in 1995.[6] Under the slogan of 'do less, better', it set out not to look for more responsibilities or to expand its competencies, as its predecessors had done, but to consolidate and concentrate on its existing functions. It is somewhat ironic that an introspective Commission, which made internal reform a priority (see Kassim, ch 2 this volume), and which boasted such modest ambitions should have been brought down amidst allegations of impropriety.

At the time of the appointment of the Prodi Commission, therefore, the authority and influence of the institution were in decline. The Member States had become wary and suspicious of the Commission, and were re-orienting the Union in an intergovernmental direction. Through a process of 'learning', Member States had become increasingly wise to the Commission's ability to exploit possibilities of expanding EU competencies (see Cram, 1993). Since Maastricht, they have shown far greater vigilance in institutional matters, limiting opportunities for entrepreneurial expansionism on the part of the Commission. The re-emergence of Europe as a salient domestic issue ensures that political leaders keep on top of their game. Growing popular suspicion of, and scepticism towards, further integration followed the French, Irish and Danish referenda on the ratification of the Treaty of European Union, and the Commission came to be seen as representative of what was increasingly perceived as a distant and undemocratic Union. Moreover, a decrease in solidarity among EU states (Devuyst, 1999) and leadership changes in France, Germany and Spain has brought into office heads of state or government that are less instinctively supportive of ever closer Union, less ready to recognise the achievements of integration, and prepared to challenge the Community method with the Commission at its heart (Devuyst, 1999; Wallace, 2000).

The Member States and the Prodi Commission: continuing intergovernmentalisation

The decline of the Commission, evident throughout the 1990s, has continued since the Prodi Commission took office in 1999. The Member States have consolidated their power across a range of key policy areas, most notably, EMU, the CFSP and the emergent Common European Security and Defence Policy (CESDP). They have also considerably enhanced their role in domains, such as social policy, not previously been considered an area of 'high politics'. Institutionally, the strengthening of intergovernmental institutions, most notably, the European Council, has continued, while the Commission was again a peripheral presence at negotiations over the future of Europe at the 2000 IGC. New methods and techniques, such as the OMC, moreover, have enhanced Member State power, while further downgrading and displacing the Commission. The Prodi Commission, despite the abundance of talent of its members, rivalling that of the first Delors Commission, has not succeeded in re-asserting the institution's authority and influence. This can be explained, partly, by the agenda it inherited – internal reform is an introspective exercise not likely to fire the imagination, and enlargement, where the Commission does the technical work, but decisions are taken by Heads of State and Government – and, partly, by the realisation of many of the goals specified in the original treaties. However, the Commission has also, to a significant extent, been the author of its misfortune (see pp. 99–101).

Policy areas

Member States have asserted their control, while marginalising the Commission (and the European Court of Justice) in a number of policy areas. Economic and monetary union offers one illustration. The passage from the convergence criteria stipulated by the TEU to the birth of the euro was undoubtedly one of the greatest triumphs of the integration process. However, that transition has been marked by the increased predominance of ECOFIN as an arena for managing the euro, marking a clear break from the entrepreneurial role played by Delors – and indeed the Commission more generally (Jabko, 1999) – in the early stages of the project. The Commission plays a somewhat limited, though not unimportant, role in the complex institutional architecture created to manage economic and monetary union. It is represented in only two of the three decision-making systems or 'sets of policy rules' (Jones, 2002) that govern economic and monetary union – economic and employment-related – where it performs a 'watchdog' function (Tsoukalis, 2000: 162), while the European System of Central Banks and ECOFIN are the key actors in the third, monetary policy (see Jones, 2002: 35–57).

The economic rules commit the Member States to ensuring that their economic policies are consistent 'with Community objectives, with each other, and with EMU' (Jones, 2002: 47), and establish two accountability procedures. The first, multilateral surveillance, is designed to ensure Member State compliance with broad economic policy guidelines that are adopted annually by ECOFIN and form a common frame of reference for governments. The second, the excessive deficit procedure, concerns the budgetary situation and government debt in the Member States. ECOFIN is the central actor in both. As Jones (2002: 48) observes:

> The basic model for oversight on economic policy is that the Council establishes the terms of reference, the Member States provide the basic information, the Commission and the EFC audit and analyze that information in order to prepare recommendations for the Council, then, finally, the Council decides as to whether the Member States have lived up to their obligations . . . If the Council determines that a particular Member State is not in compliance, it will instruct the Member State to reform its policies and, if necessary, it will apply relevant sanctions.

The enforcement rules relating to employment, by contrast, are far looser (see discussion of OMC, p. 95) and the position of the Commission much weaker. Although it performs a similar function to its role with respect to the economic rules, its criticisms of performance by national governments are not translated into sanctions. As Jones has contended (2002: 50–1), because 'the employment-related rules are process-centred, compliance has more to do with participation than with the outcomes of participation per se . . . The employment-related rules more closely approximate a form of self help than a form of delegation . . . The institutions of the European Union are primarily just concerned intermediaries'.

The dominance of the Member States and the marginalisation of the Commission have been even more marked in relation to the Common Foreign and Security Policy. Although always intergovernmental (Forster and Wallace,

2000), developments since autumn 1999 have further strengthened Member State control, as Heads of State and Government have sought to establish a capacity for autonomous action in internal crisis management (see Cameron and Spence, Ch 7 this volume). Although the Commission is fully associated with the work carried out in the CFSP, and shares the right of initiative with the Member States and the High Representative, it is not a key actor.

A further danger for the Commission inherent in the development of the European Security and Defence Policy (ESDP) has been the tendency on the part of certain Member States to use the EU's defence ambitions as a pretext for inter-governmentalising more and more areas of foreign policy. During the French presidency of the second half of 2000, Paris was quick to attempt this, arguing in favour of passing control over the EU's initiatives on land mines from the Commission to the Council on the ground that it represented part of the EU's security policy (interviews, European Commission, Brussels, June 2001). In a similar vein, the Franco-German contribution to the Convention on the Future of Europe, presented in January 2003, showed a flagrant disregard (as predictable from Paris as it was surprising from Berlin) for both the Community method and the independence and effectiveness of the Commission with, notably, its proposal for the creation of an EU Foreign Minister who would simultaneously be based in the Council and the Commission.

The assertion of Member State control is evident beyond these, admittedly, areas of 'high politics'. In adopting, at the Lisbon European Council in March 2000, the strategic goal of becoming 'the most competitive and dynamic knowl-edge-based economy in the world, capable of sustainable economic growth with more and better jobs and greater social cohesion for the first decade of the new century', the Heads of State and Government laid claim to leadership across a broad swathe of existing policy areas. Objectives were set under two headings – preparing the transition to the new economy and modernising the European social model – in relation to a wide range of specific projects, programmes or policies. These included: the information society, the creation of a European Area of Research and Innovation, the development of a friendly environment for starting up and developing innovative businesses, especially small and medium-sized enterprises (SMEs), economic reforms to complete the internal market and make it fully operational, efficient and integrated financial markets, coordinating macro-economic policies, education and training for the knowl-edge society, the development of an active employment policy, modernising social protection, and promoting social inclusion.

The European Council has not only defined the aims, but will also orches-trate their realisation. It has assumed 'a pre-eminent guiding and coordinating role to ensure overall coherence and the effective monitoring of progress towards the new strategic goal' (European Council, 2000a: 8). Progress towards the achievement of these aims will be reviewed annually at a special spring meeting of the European Council.[7]

Institutional developments

Institutional developments within the Union have also served to enhance Member State control and to limit the influence of the Commission. The further strengthening of the European Parliament (through the extension of co-decision to seven new areas) in the Nice Treaty is one example. The continued refusal of the 'masters of the Treaty' to reform comitology is another, despite repeated calls for change on the part of the Commission – most recently in the White Paper on Governance (European Commission, 2001) – particularly in relation to management and regulatory committees (Wincott, 2001).[8]

Three other developments during the Prodi presidency are also significant. The first is the introduction of the OMC as part of the Lisbon process.[9] Formally introduced as a new form of EU decision-making at the Lisbon European Council (European Council, 2000a: 8), the method has been applied to macro-economic policy, the employment chapter of the Treaty, social policy, and structural policy. The objective of the OMC is 'not to establish a single common framework, but rather to share experience and encourage the spread of best practice' (Wallace, 2000: 33) through the setting of guidelines, the establishment of performance indicators, the translation of targets from European to national and regional levels, and periodic monitoring, peer review and evaluation (Hodson and Maher, 2001). It is highly decentralised in line with the principle of subsidiarity, and marks a rejection of both the 'Community method' based on the adoption of binding legal and non-legal instruments in Brussels, where the Commission plays a key part in 'policy design, policy-brokering and policy execution' (Wallace, 2000: 28) and the 'regulatory model', where the Commission has played the role of 'architect and defender' (Wallace, 2000: 30). The 'desire of the EC to control outcomes, as manifest in the directive as the rule of choice in the single market, with its emphasis on common outcomes if not methods, is overcome by recognition of the importance of diversity at the national level in relations to policy formation, legal frameworks, ideational references and popular perceptions and relations to either the European project generally or the specific policy being coordinated' (Hodson and Maher, 2001: 731).

The Commission has little influence where the OMC is concerned. Its agenda-setting and policy leadership functions are redundant, since the European Council sets strategic priorities, monitors progress and, with the Council under the Luxembourg, Cardiff and Cologne processes, decides what action is relevant. Neither does it play a co-ordinating role. Indeed, co-ordination 'can arise only when there is support from the European Council . . . [Its] central role also underlines the intergovernmental nature of co-ordination and ensures that processes remain open in terms of outcomes, such that there is no attempt to centralise policy formation or to introduce top-down methods of integration' (Hodson and Maher, 2001: 739). While some of the characteristics of the policy areas where the OMC has been introduced suggest that the method may be difficult to apply to other sectors, it nevertheless marks an important evolution in the relationship between Member States and the Commission, and a significant illustration of how Member States perceive multilateral cooperation within the EU framework.

A second development is associated with the incorporation of new policy sectors, which has led to the introduction of new forms of policy making, designed, at least in part, to ensure effective intergovernmental control at the expense of the 'supranational' institution. Developments in the foreign and defence policy fields have been emblematic of these trends. The EU's foreign policy has always been intergovernmental, and the formal structure introduced by the Nice Treaty for managing the EU's defence capacities remain consistent with that constitutional principle. The Council Secretariat has been given a key role, within which a significantly increased staff will be responsible for defence policy matters.[10]

Certainly, the Commission has managed to co-operate quite effectively with the Council Secretariat, which has emerged as a central actor in the EU external policy system (Christiansen, 2001a). Yet it is important not to overstate this. While some scholars are anxious to stress the collaborative nature of the relationship, (Christiansen, 2001a), based on what they see as shared allegiance, a common bureaucratic culture, and the emergence of an epistemic community amongst external policy specialists in Brussels, there is still significant scope for tension. For one thing, the emergence of the Council Secretariat as a significant and, for the first time, high-profile actor, confronts the Commission with a potential rival. Second, the relative harmony that has characterised relations between the two to this point may owe much to purely contingent factors — the relatively good personal relationship between the High Representative, Javier Solana, and Commissioner for External Affairs, Chris Patten (see Cameron and Spence, Ch 7 this volume) — or the fact that the military elements of the EU's external policy have not as yet been seriously tested. Finally, it should be noted that a large proportion of the staff recruited to the Secretariat General to work on ESDP are not Community officials but detached national experts from national administrations. At the very least this provides room for doubt as to whether any shared allegiance exits between the Commission and Council staff. Indeed, a more compelling characterisation of the development of decision-making structures in the defence policy sphere is perhaps Helen Wallace's (2000) notion of 'intensive transnationalism', as national officials in the permanent representations, along with colleagues from the Council, develop habits of co-operation and approaches to common problems that distinguish them from both the Commission and, potentially, their home governments.

More broadly, recent institutional initiatives have led to an effective downgrading of the Commission's status in terms of the external representation of the Union, as the Commissioner for External Relations has now *de facto* accepted subordinate status to the High Representative (at press conferences attended by multiple EU representatives, the trend has been for the Presidency to speak first, followed by Solana and then Chris Patten). In keeping with practice in the second and third pillars, the Commission has the right to attend the Political and Security Committee, but does not enjoy the right of initiative it possesses in the first pillar.

A third development is the creation of specialised agencies to deal with specific regulatory and management tasks. While some have interpreted these initiatives as a step in the direction of more effective 'administrative integration' (Kreher, 1997), or a 'sensible outsourcing of specialised knowledge so the Commission can concentrate on its core tasks' (Christiansen, 2001b), they can also be seen as further evidence of the marginalisation of the Commission. That the Commission itself fears as much is evident from the White Paper on Governance. While acknowledging that the potential advantage of such institutions lies in 'their ability to draw on highly technical, sectoral know-how, the increased visibility they give for the sectors concerned (and sometimes the public) and the cost-savings that they offer to business' (European Commission, 2001a: 24), the Commission goes on to criticise their functioning and propound a highly restrictive view of where and how they should be deployed (Wincott, 2001). Indeed, Commission officials have in practice attempted to restrict the effective authority of agencies, as illustrated by its White Paper proposals for an independent European Food Authority (Majone, 2003).

This attitude is partly explicable in terms of a desire not to delegate real authority to a potential competitor. It also, however, reflects an understanding that agencies may in fact turn out to be not independent at all, but rather tools of the Member States. In his analysis of the creation of the European Environmental Agency (EEA), Majone (2003) is categorical in stating that 'comparing the preferences of the main political actors – Member States, EP, Commission – with the provisions of Council Regulation No 1210/90, one sees that the Member States clearly won the contest over institutional choice'. The Member States, moreover, succeeded in packing the influential management board of the organisation with their own representatives, thus further ensuring not only that the Commission's prerogatives in this crucial policy area were challenged but that their own were not.

The Member States and the Commission as an administration

The assertion of Member State power has not been restricted to policy or institutional developments, but has also been felt in respect of the Commission's internal organisation, functioning and resources. Although created as an independent body, the Commission is in practice dependent on national governments. The latter have used their various prerogatives – for example, as masters of the Treaty, members of the Conference of Member States, and co-partners with the EP in the budgetary authority – in ways that have impeded the ability of the Commission to carry out its responsibilities effectively.

First, the Member States have refused to take measures to streamline the College, even though, at least since the Spierenburg Report (Spierenburg, 1979), it has been generally accepted that the number of Commissioners makes genuine collegiality difficult, exacerbates problems of co-ordination, and introduces unnecessary complexity into the lines of accountability between the College and the services. The national governments' insistence on retaining the principle that the larger countries nominate two Commissioners and the small countries one has contributed to the difficulties of co-ordinating an already complex organisation, since a portfolio, including responsibility for one or more Directorates-General, has to be defined for each member of the Commission. Even the decisions taken at Nice – one Commissioner per Member State from 2005 and fewer Commissioners than the number of Member States once the Union has more than twenty-seven members – do not promise a satisfactory resolution.

A second problem is the insistence on the part of Member States is that they each continue to be represented at the highest levels of the Commission administration in A1 (Director General) and A2 (Director) posts. Although the Commission aims as part of the human resources element of the Kinnock reform package (Kassim, Ch 2 this volume) to make merit the guiding principle for appointments at all levels of the organisation, some governments have been unhappy at the demise of the 'geographical quota', where fewer of their nationals now occupy top positions. Few, if any, would tolerate a situation in which none of their nationals heads a Directorate-General. As Desmond Dinan observes:

> given its multinational, multicultural and multilingual character, and given also the nature of the EU system, the Commission will never conform to neat political and administrative models. For reasons of legitimacy, a rough balance of nationalities will always be important. For reasons of prestige and national advantage, Member States will always seek to influence staff policy and the implementation of EU legislation. For systemic reasons, the Commission can never become simply an executive body. Thus the Commission can be reformed, but there are limits to how much it can be transformed. (1999: 33)

A lack of resources is a third difficulty, and one that is also highlighted by the current reform process. The Member States have continued to delegate additional functions to the Commission and many of them, such as the administration of the PHARE and TACIS programmes to assist former Communist states in central and eastern Europe, have involved new types of responsibility. Others, such as the various education programmes, may have been far narrower in scope, but have also made severe demands on Commission manpower. However, the willingness of governments to entrust new tasks to the Commission has been unmatched by a commitment to increase the resources, particularly the human resources, necessary to carry them out. The recourse to the creation of technical assistances offices, *Bureaux d'Assistance Technique* – better known by their French acronym, BATs – with the attendant questions surrounding the status of their employees, accountability and delegation on the part of the Commission, developed as a response to a serious shortage of personnel. Whether the Council is prepared to grant the Commission the staff that the latter needs, following a detailed review of the tasks of the administration and the human resources available to it, is unclear.[11]

Finally, although there seems to be some evidence that *cabinets* have been less ready since 1999 to act as spokesperson for the national capital and for *chef* and special *chef* meetings to resemble mini-Councils (Peterson and Bomberg, 1999: 39) – the consequence of Prodi's decision to insist on the multinationality of the Commissioners' private offices and to locate the Commissioner and the *cabinet* in the same building as the Directorate-General for which they are responsible – the Member States have continued to use other means to ensure that their interests are articulated and protected within the Commission. Certainly, the inclination and ability of Member States to place, and use, their nationals in the Commission as sources of information and influence varies considerably (Kassim *et al.*, 2001), but there is less respect for the independence of the Commission. Even in countries where Commission independence has historically been regarded as sacred, such as the Netherlands, contact with the Dutch Commissioner is no longer regarded as taboo (Soetendorp and Andeweg, 2001). Not only do Member States encourage officials from their national administrations to sit the *concours* (thereby, attempting to ensure 'their people' are placed in that institution), but both the emphasis on sending short-term secondees, and the way in which national administrations are striving to maintain close contact with fellow nationals in Brussels attest to the ways in which Member State influence extends to inside that institution (Kassim and Peters, 2001; Menon, 2003). As Kassim and Wright have put it, the Union's bureaucratic system is 'shot through with national officials and influences' (Kassim and Wright, 1991: 835).

The Prodi Commission: tactical naivety and weakness at the top

Despite the calibre of the College, some notable achievements (for example, in administrative reform and enlargement), and the fact that it continues to play a key role across many policy areas and a crucial part in the workings of the European Union, the Commission has not been able to recover its former status. Though the scope for entrepreneurialism and dynamism that characterised the Delors Commission may have been narrowed due to the (near) realisation of the aims of the original EEC Treaty, opportunities still existed for the Prodi Commission to restore the institution's reputation through astute political action, an ability to sell the Community method to national governments and other constituencies, or a demonstration of its indispensability to the functioning of the Union. However, a lack of effective leadership at the top and a series of tactical errors on the part of the Commission President have prevented the achievement of such aspirations.

Problems 'manipulating the machine'
Despite his political experience and inspirational leadership of Italy's Olive Tree alliance in the 1990s, as well as the formal powers granted to the office by

the Treaty of Amsterdam, the Commission President has not yet demonstrated effective command over the organisation. The early decisiveness shown by Prodi in declaring the Commission to be a putative government, which led him to locate Commissioners and their *cabinets* in the same premises as the Directorates-General for which they are responsible – just as ministers in the Member States are based in their departments – has not been followed up. The effects of this bold gesture, which was intended to improve vertical co-ordination – a long-standing problem in the Commission that had worsened under Santer (interviews, European Commission, January, November, December 2002) – may well have been to render horizontal co-ordination – also a perennial problem – even more difficult by making contact between *cabinets* harder, since they no longer work under the same roof in the Breydel building.[12] More importantly, the departmentalisation of the College has not been counter-balanced by the creation of a powerful centre under the President, capable of providing firm leadership and a political steer to the work of the Commission. While the Secretariat-General of the Commission, which supports the work of the College and which is responsible to the President, has been strengthened as part of the reform process, its role is largely administrative and the Commission's fourth Secretary-General, appointed in 2000, prefers an apolitical approach to the more interventionist inclinations of some of his predecessors (interviews, European Commission, January, November, December 2002). The President's *cabinet*, meanwhile, which has an explicitly political function, has not been particularly effective (interviews, European Commission, January, November, December 2002). This is a serious problem, since it is the President's team that is responsible for providing lines of communication with colleagues and the outside world, and the President has attracted severe criticism for failures with respect to both (see, for example, Parker, 2002a: 15).

In addition, the Commission President has attracted criticism for his lax treatment of individual Commissioners, who have apparently contravened Commission protocol by intervening in domestic debates.[13] His less than assured handling of controversial issues, such as the reform of the Common Fisheries Policy, where there was suspicion that national interests lay behind the intervention of a Commissioner and the removal of the sitting Director General, has also been cited as an indication of weakness.

Tactical errors and misjudgements

More serious, however, have been the President's interventions in debates whether about policy or about the future of Europe, many of which appear ill-judged (see Peterson, Ch 1 this volume).[14] Prodi's call, for example, for the creation of a single foreign policy supremo in the form of a significantly strengthened Commissioner for external affairs to replace the current Council

(Solana) – Commission (Patten) dualism drew widespread criticism, including from the latter as Commissioner for external affairs. Prodi's suggestion that there should be senior and junior Commissioners in future Commissions, meanwhile, alienated the very Member States – i.e. the smaller ones, who look to the Commission to defend them against steam-rolling by the larger states – most likely to support a strong Commission (*Financial Times*, 17 June 2002). In addition, Prodi's observation that the EU's Stability and Growth Pact was 'stupid' may not have been inaccurate, but 'it upset colleagues and infuriated MEPs and leaders of smaller countries who felt he should be upholding the pact, rather than ridiculing it' (Parker, 2002a: 15). Finally, colleagues were incensed by the Commission President's secret project to draw up a draft EU constitution. The so-called 'Penelope' document was intended, as the Convention enters its final stages, to put the President's vision of deeper integration at the centre of the debate about the Union's future, but the clandestine nature of its preparation was regarded by other members of the Commission as an act of profound uncollegiality (Parker, 2002b).

Colleagues and natural supporters of the Commission have all been alienated by these actions.[15] Even those who share the same vision as the Commission President worry that damage has been done to their cause, either because they consider that the timing was wrong or that they believe a more subtle and strategic approach should have been devised, or that a collective position on these important issues should have been agreed first. In tactical terms, by declaring such ambitious objectives, the Commission President may have committed a serious error, by effectively 'playing the Commission out of the game' (interviews, European Commission, January, November, December 2002). At the very least, his outbursts have been grist to the mill of Eurosceptics anxious to persuade their governments of the need to reign in an over-ambitious Commission.

A further problem has been tone. The increasingly desperate nature of the Commission's attempts to lobby in favour of its own institutional position were clearly revealed in its White Paper on Governance, which comes across as a defensive document, used to fend off perceived threats to the Commission's position within the EU system (Wincott, 2001). The White Paper emphasises the need to re-assert the primacy of the Community method, criticises institutions and structures it perceives as a threat – notably agencies and comitology – and subjects both the Council of Ministers and the European Council to sharp criticism for fostering sectorisation. Yet as Wincott (2001) points out, such criticism is hardly fair in that, as we have seen above, the Commission is being somewhat blind to its own failings in this regard. While confronting an unfavourable environment, with Member States anxious to re-assert their primacy, the Commission has not helped itself. A lack of effective leadership has contributed significantly to the Commission's continued plight.

Conclusion: the 'future of Europe' and the future of the European Commission

The decline of the Commission, evident since the early 1990s, has continued since the Prodi Commission took office, and there seems little possibility that the situation will be reversed. As noted above, Member States have proved reluctant to reinforce the Commission by providing it with extra resources. The summits at Amsterdam and Nice, along with the current debate about the so-called 'Future of Europe', reveal the extent to which the question of the role and status of the Commission has been instrumentalised by the Member States. Rather than addressing fundamental questions concerning the effective functioning of the EU system as a whole and the Commission in particular, they have chosen instead to focus their attentions either on the Council, or on their relative weight within the Commission, through debating the number of commissioners each Member State has the right to appoint. Even the debate about the lack of democratic accountability of the institution may well hinder rather than help a quest for effectiveness (Majone, 2002; 2003; Menon and Weatherill, 2002) and seems to have more to do with a prevailing and continuing obsession with ensuring national control, rather than ensuring that the Commission can play a full and effective role. In addition, there is a curious disjuncture between Member State suspicions and the reality of the Commission's role and ambitions. Prodi's wilder statements notwithstanding, the Commission no longer has the ambitious, imperialist aspirations that arguably characterised it under Delors. The obsession with control that they reveal implies that the Member States have failed to take this on board.

The decline of the Commission has important implications not only for the institution itself, but also for the performance of the Union as a system and the future of European integration – points often overlooked in both political and academic debates.[16] The Member States' assertiveness, their determination to circumscribe the Commission's power and impose their control, may hinder the ability of the Commission to carry out tasks that are crucial to the effective functioning of the system as a whole and may ultimately prove counterproductive to their own interests. First, the reasons that led the Member States to delegate key functions to the Commission in the founding treaties are as relevant today as they were in the 1950s. If there are objectives that governments want to attain, which can only be achieved collectively, it is rational for them to create independent institutions that facilitate the achievement of these goals, for example by ensuring that all contracting parties comply with their obligations, circulating information, or filling out the details of an incomplete contract. For the Member States to perform these functions themselves would simply be too costly. Second, and relatedly, intergovernmental decision making has inherent limits. The experience of the CFSP and of JHA hitherto illustrates how cumbersome, slow and ineffective the intergovernmental method tends to be. Policy makers and observers stress both the crucial role played by the Commission as a 'policy entrepreneur' and its ability to broker agreements between Member States on issues where consensus, or even a qualified majority, appeared difficult to achieve. The experience, technical expertise and synoptic vision that the Commission can bring to the table, moreover, surpass the capacities of individual Member States. Third, despite its organisational weaknesses, the Commission has, as a consequence of its functions and strategic location, accumulated technical expertise and know-how across the full range of EU activities, as well as knowledge of policy and process in the fifteen Member States, which is unrivalled by any single national administration. It would be foolhardy indeed to squander this inheritance. Fourth, given the weaknesses of the Council which is already, with fifteen Member States, a large, unwieldy and complex organisation that suffers from problems of internal co-ordination, the Commission plays a crucial stabilising and co-ordinating role.

All of these functions will increase in importance once the Union enlarges. Tomorrow's Union of twenty-five will have more need than ever of an effective, independent, and adequately resourced Commission. In steadily increasing their own autonomy at the expense of the Commission, the Member States may well, therefore, have called into question the continued effectiveness of the Union itself.

Notes

Anand Menon would like to acknowledge the support provided by British Academy small Grant SG-31906 and Hussein Kassim to express his gratitude to the British Academy for a small research grant.

1 The new subparagraph of Article 219 stipulated that 'The Commission shall work under the political guidance of its President', while Declaration No. 32 attached to the Final Act provided that 'the President of the Commission must enjoy broad discretion in the allocation of tasks within the College, as well as in any reshuffling of those tasks during a Commission's term in office' (see Falkner and Nentwich, 2000). As one observer has noted: 'The President's newly introduced powers relative to those of the overall team thus remain rather limited' (Wessels, 2001: 211).

2 This chapter examines this relationship as it developed during the time of the Prodi Commission. Given the increasingly complex nature and ever-expanding scope of the Union, it is now more difficult than ever to generalise about its functioning. Different Treaty provisions, informal norms, decision-making processes, actors and objectives exist in different policy sectors. From its complete formal autonomy in matters relating to competition policy, to its virtual exclusion from other aspects of Union activity, the Commission's role in relation to the Member States varies greatly. Space permits only partial coverage.

3 The first report of the Committee of Independent Experts (1999a), the submission of which precipitated the Commission's resignation, exposed serious shortcoings in the organisation, and followed months of negative press coverage, and an unprecedented level of antagonism between the Commission and the Parliament.

4 Gerda Falkner (2002) argues convincingly that negotiations in social policy ran counter to the trend.

5 It could be argued, moreover, that integration *à la carte* has disadvantaged the Commis-

sion to the extent that it constitutes a departure from the original Community method, where the Commission plays a central role.

6 It may be recalled that the appointment of Santer was itself the reflection of a desire on the part of the Member States to avoid ambitious candidates.

7 Although the Nice Treaty continued a process of 'communitarianisation' of the third pillar begun at Amsterdam, it is important not to exaggerate the extent to which Member States have loosened their control over policy. Co-decision will be applied to a major part of visa, asylum and immigration policy, but application to most provisions will be deferred to a later date. In the case of asylum, co-decision will not be applied before the Council has adopted Community legislation defining common rules and principles, though some decisions relating to immigration will be adopted under co-decision from 1 May 2004. Co-decision will, however, apply to judicial co-operation in civil matters. The Commission's powers remain unchanged.

8 The Commission also wants to be allowed to fill in framework directives as part of its executive role.

9 This section draws extensively from the excellent discussion in Hodson and Maher (2001).

10 In a complete departure from established practice, moreover, the EU's satellite centre in Spain has been designated a Council agency.

11 Following the peer review exercise carried out under the chairmanship of the Commission President, a request was made to the budgetary authority for circa 400 posts.

12 In fact, *cabinets* have sought to compensate for the lack of day-to-day contact by instituting regular semi-formal gatherings.

13 See, editorial, *European Voice*, 2 May 2002.

14 Other examples include his invitation in January 2000 to the Libyan leader, Colonel Muammar Al-Qadhafi, to visit Brussels, and his speech at Oxford University in April 2002 where, in the words of the leader of European Liberals, 'he said the UK should, basically, forget its alliance with the US and concentrate more on the EU' (quoted in Banks, 2002).

15 There has also been criticism from inside the Commission that the President has failed to respect both the rules on senior appointments and those on the multinationality of *cabinets* that he championed as part of the reform process (*Guardian*, 3 August 2000: 15).

16 Some have argued that developments in the 1990s, beginning at Maastricht and confirmed at Amsterdam, mark the transition from one era of integration to another. Postwar integration, underpinned by a 'teleological ideal' and 'federalist vision of an expanding, undifferentiated, and uniform Europe', characterised by the application of a single 'Community method' to all areas of policy, has given way to more flexible and pragmatic solutions to 'new more sophisticated, more differentiated and, in many areas, more modest national demands' (Moravscik and Nicolaidis, 1998: 16–17). Others, by contrast, see evidence of an 'integration cascade' (Wessels, 2001), where new areas brought within the scope of the Union are at first subject to intergovernmental decision-making, but are progressively communitarianised. However, while the first perspective fails to address, still less answer, fundamental questions about the Commission and its role in integration, the second somewhat complacently assumes that the Member States, as masters of the Treaty, remain ultimately committed to the 'Community method' and the centrality of the Commission.

Susanne K. Schmidt

6

The European Commission's powers in shaping European policies

The European Commission plays a central role in shaping the course of European integration. In recent times this became evident both with the successes of the Delors Commissions in building the Single Market as well as the crisis of the Santer Commission in 1998–99. A weakened Commission, which is still feared, will hamper the development of the integration project. Interestingly, compared with the European Court of Justice (Burley and Mattli, 1993; Garrett, 1995; Mattli and Slaughter, 1995, 1998; Alter, 1998; Garrett, *et al.*, 1998), as the other major supranational institution of the European Union (EU), the role of the Commission has aroused much less debate in political science.[1]

The theoretical discussion of European integration is still dominated by the debate between intergovernmentalism and neofunctionalism or supranationalism more generally (Moravcsik, 1998; Stone Sweet and Brunell, 1998). Against this background, the role of the Commission is easily dismissed or emphasised, without a systematic assessment of its strengths and weaknesses (but see Pollack, 1997). In contrast, as regards the ECJ, even intergovernmentalists agree that national governments have little influence over its rulings (Moravcsik, 1995: 623). By establishing the direct effect and supremacy of European law, the ECJ has provided the integration process with legal momentum (Shapiro, 1992). On this basis judge-made law may substitute for agreements of the legislative bodies – the Council of Ministers and the European Parliament (Berlin, 1992: 21). The Court benefits from the established independence of the judiciary, and the fact that in interpreting the Treaty the governments would have to decide unanimously against the Court and amend the Treaty (Alter, 1998: 137).

As for the Commission, its influence has been best established as regards its agenda-setting powers. Under qualified majority voting, it is easier for the Council to accept Commission proposals than to alter them. For the latter a unanimous decision is required. This decision rule allows the Commission effectively to pick the winning coalition among the Member States (Garrett and Tsebelis, 1996). Moreover, the Commission can also revert to the 'softer' instruments that it possesses. Thus, it can initiate policy debates, and it can try to foster agreements among the Member States. But this influence is difficult to establish beyond doubt.

This chapter argues that the Commission has further means to influence decision-making in the Council. These instruments have so far been neglected in the literature. It will be demonstrated that the Commission may use strategically its competencies as a guardian of the Treaty and as an administrator of EU competition law to force the adoption of proposals in the Council *which would have been rejected were it not for this combination of different Commission competencies.* Thus, unlike the 'soft' instruments that it has, in using this alternative instrument the Commission exercises its influence in a robust way, similar to its formal agenda-setting powers.

This chapter establishes this influence with view to the relationship of the Commission with the national governments and the Council. Hence, although the European Parliament has gained in importance in recent years, it shall not be discussed here. This seems justified as it is generally questionable whether one can establish a systematic influence of the EP, given its various allegiances to different parties and Member States. Most of the examples used here relate to the Single Market programme. Nevertheless, more recent examples indicate the validity of the argument developed here.

The analysis proceeds as follows. First the argument is outlined; then the different Commission competences are presented, and several examples are given of how they were used. Finally, the conditions are discussed under which the Commission exerts this influence and other studies on the Commission's powers are related to these findings.

The role of the Commission in European integration

The Commission is the guardian of the Treaty and monitors the implementation of EU law by the Member States, by initiating infringement proceedings where appropriate. It has also important competences for the direct implementation of agricultural and competition policy. In addition to making proposals to the Council, it has the responsibility to work on policy initiatives that often result in EU legislation (Edwards and Spence, 1997).

It is hard to establish in which ways the Commission may use these different competences to influence the course of European integration (Moravcsik, 1995: 615; Pollack, 1997: 124–8). There is a danger in readily assuming a significant role of the Commission, simply because it became active in a certain matter, without paying enough attention to possible counter-arguments. This can be demonstrated with the example of the Single Market project. Sandholtz and Zysman (1989) show how the Commission initiated it with the help of powerful economic actors, while Moravcsik (1991) just as convincingly argues that the programme can only be explained by reference to the interests of the dominant Member States. It is hard to prove beyond doubt the relevance of the launch of policy debates and other 'soft' instruments used by the Commission. Was the Commission influential in promoting a decision, or rather the Council presidency?

The continuing debate between intergovernmentalists and supranationalists contributes to this state of affairs. It seems quite tempting to take an instance where the Commission was active as a possibility to refute Moravcsik, rather than to discuss the conditions and constraints of the Commission's actions in greater detail (Schmidt 1996). However, there is a third, institutionalist perspective on European integration, which comes to a more sophisticated assessment of the Commission (Majone, 1996b; Pollack, 1997). Drawing on Williamson (1985), the delegation of different competences to the Commission is explained by the resulting advantages for the Member States. Transaction cost savings result if governments renounce the rights for the preparation of policy proposals, the administration of specific policies (such as agriculture and competition) and the control of implementation. In addition, delegation strengthens the commitment *vis-à-vis* third parties and among national governments. By delegating powers to the Commission, as 'guardian of the Treaty', and to the ECJ, the implementation of agreed policies can be made credible. By using various control mechanisms over the Commission (e.g. comitology), governments ensure that delegated competencies cannot easily be used against their own wishes. In addition, the Commission is constrained by relying on the continued co-operation of the Member States for the preparation, adoption and implementation of policies.

In this perspective, the Commission indeed has the opportunity to play an autonomous role within the European polity. However, because of the rational-choice foundations of these works, an unexpected loss of control over the Commission is precluded. Thus, Pollack concludes by stating that the Commission's role should not be exaggerated in view of different control mechanisms in place (Pollack, 1997). Even if one assumes that the Member States can effectively check an unintended loss of control, the Commission can be influential by using its agenda-setting rights. In this case, it does not violate the intentions of the Member States but exploits existing differences in their interests for its own ends (Hammond, 1996: 143).

In the realm of Single Market legislation (the focus of this chapter), the Commission has the formal monopoly in proposing legislation. Without a proposal of the Commission, the Council and the European Parliament (EP) cannot act. Moreover, while the Council can adopt the proposal with a qualified majority, it can only alter it unanimously. Whenever the Council decides with qualified majority (i.e. in the majority of cases), the Commission may have a significant impact on the decision outcome. The Commission may choose from different existing coalitions that are supported by a qualified majority the one that is closest to its own preferences (Steunenberg, 1994; Schneider, 1995; Garrett and Tsebelis, 1996).

Unlike arguments about informal agenda-setting powers, the Commission's influence through formal agenda setting can thus be established beyond doubt. This chapter makes a similarly robust argument by showing how the Commission can use its different competences to render more likely the adoption of its proposals by the Council. Acting strategically, the Commission can influence the decisions of Member States by unilaterally changing their default condition, making non-decisions more costly for them. Thus, the Commission exploits the direct effect and supremacy of EU law, and benefits from the greater independence of the ECJ.

The default condition (Ostrom, 1986: 12f.), i.e. the case of non-decision-making, plays a central role in the well-known 'joint-decision trap' (Scharpf, 1988). In cases of unanimous decision rule and a stable status quo position, Scharpf argues, a single country that benefits from the status quo may block a solution preferred by the majority. Although the joint-decision trap has been widely used as a concept in the study of European integration, few analyses of European decision-making processes take note of the default condition (but see Pollack, 1995; Hanson, 1998: 70).

In short, the argument is the following: by threatening a changed default condition, the Commission can ensure the adoption of proposals that go beyond its agenda-setting means of choosing a certain coalition in the Council. Without this threat, which leads Member States to adopt a proposal as a *'lesser evil'*, the Commission could not be successful with its proposal. Unlike existing studies that relate the influence of the Commission to its 'soft' competences of arguing and forging coalitions, its impact can therefore be firmly established.

The powers of the Commission

How can the Commission employ a supranational legal framework in the course of Council negotiations? The Commission, first of all, acts as the *guardian of the Treaties*. Under article 226 of the Treaty it has the right, and in a certain sense also the responsibility, to take action whenever Member States do not meet their legal obligations. Where national regulations conflict with European law, the Commission can initiate an *infringement procedure*, which will eventually lead to a court ruling if the government concerned does not respond to the requests.[2] Additionally, private actors may complain to the Commission or start proceedings in domestic courts (Weiler, 1994; Alter, 1996).

Crucial is that recourse to the ECJ involves only in part the implementation of measures which were agreed in the Council. Moreover, and more important in this context, it refers to the *direct application* of Community law. Because of the direct effect and supremacy of many Treaty provisions, established national orders are not only 'Europeanised' by explicit Council decisions. Rather, national rules may become obsolete in the light of Treaty provisions, as the famous *Cassis de Dijon* case has shown (Alter and Meunier-Aitsahalia, 1994).

look at core reading
for s2 wl.

The relevance of a possible direct subordination of national regulations under EU law is strengthened through other competences of the Commission, namely the administrative powers it enjoys under *EU competition law* (McGowan, 2000). National governments have only limited formal opportunities to influence the way the Commission handles its powers under competition law. Articles 81 and 82 (ex 85 and 86) are directed at private actors, prohibiting cartels and the abuse of dominant positions. Governments participate in advisory committees. Articles 86–9 (ex 90–4) deal with the actions of Member States. Their right to grant special rights or state aid to enterprises is restricted. For the control of state aid the Commission simply submits two reports per annum to a committee composed of representatives of the Member States.

For article 86 (ex 90) and the control of the conferral of special rights, no participatory role of the Member States is foreseen, although the Commission is granted the extraordinary right to issue generally binding directives (or specific decisions) for the Member States. Informally, as several directives under this provision have shown, the Commission consults quite closely with the affected governments (Schmidt, 1998a). Similarly, in other areas of competition policy, governments have multiple means to put pressure on 'their' Commissioners and the Commission as a whole when controversial measures arise, so that they may successfully prevent decisions (Ross, 1995: 130–5).

Thus, EU law draws a distinction between different market freedoms, which prohibit the discrimination of cross-border market transactions, and competition rules, which safeguard the competitive order of markets. On the one hand, the Commission may assist in the implementation of the Treaty and its market freedoms (the free movement of goods, capital, services and labour as well as the freedom of establishment) through its powers of guardian of the Treaty. On the other hand, the Commission has considerable powers regarding the market structure of individual sectors. Accordingly, the Commission has the potential seriously to interfere with those parts of the national economies that are *not* predominantly *structured by market principles*. As with the market freedoms, the scope of EU competition law is hard to define. This differs from national competition law which normally exempts certain areas (e.g. the utilities) (Schmidt, 1998b: 66). Moreover, unlike national competition rules, European competition rules have the status of primary law (Scharpf, 1996: 151). Although EU competition law is aimed only at hindrances of the Single Market, the likelihood of such disturbances has been interpreted very broadly. Since a country's national restrictions almost always hamper a potential economic activity of other European nationals in addition to governing its own citizens, there may be in fact few inherently national cases (Scharpf, 1999).

Thus, while both sets of rules complement each other, referring either to trade or to competition, they may partly serve as substitutes. Whenever national monopolies prevail it may be possible to promote liberalisation either by applying competition law, or by allowing foreigners to offer their services in this domestically protected market. Table 6.1 summarises the different powers which the Commission may exercise.

Table 6.1   The powers of the Commission

Competence	Target	Procedure
Infringement procedure (art. 226, ex 169), relating, for example to insufficient market freedoms	State actors	Interaction between **Commission** and **Member** State on the allegations, reference to the **European Court of** Justice
Control of cartels (art. 81, ex 85)	Private actors	Commission decisions amounting to: **Prohibition of the action**, requiring alterations, and/or imposing fines.
Prohibition of abuse of market power (art. 82, ex 86)	Private actors	
Control of subsidies (art. 87–89, ex 92–94)	State actors	
Control of the granting of special rights (Art. 86, ex 90)	State actors	Decision or directive prohibiting the action or requiring alterations

Appeal to the European Court of Justice

Precisely which policy areas are particularly prone to Commission action can hardly be determined in advance because of the evolving interpretation of the Treaty and market freedoms (Behrens, 1992). Thus, it is impossible to foresee the extent to which judicial policy-making can substitute for Council-made secondary law. Most of the examples given are related to competition policy. But the argument is not restricted to this area. The Commission has used (and is using) its powers under competition law to restructure a whole range of regulated sectors. Moreover, the Commission finds an alternative venue for action in its powers to implement the internal market freedoms.

The relevance of these powers has been noted in several case studies. Thus, Bulmer (1994) refers to the Commission's use of supranational legal pressures when analysing the Council's adoption of the merger regulation; Cowhey (1990), Montagnon (1990) and Sandholtz (1998) discuss European telecommunications policy in this context and for O'Reilly (1997) these rights are important to understand the agreement to liberalise air transport. However, a systematic analysis is still missing.

Explicit threats – the 'lesser evil' strategy

By threatening the national governments with the use of its different competences, the Commission can ensure the adoption of its proposal in the Council as a 'lesser evil'. Only in this way can governments avoid a lingering worst case scenario. This is illustrated below first through the example of the liberalisation of road haulage (see figure 6.1).

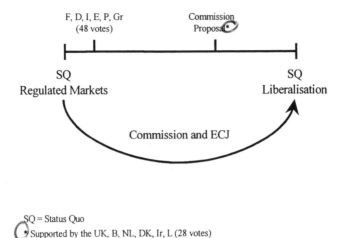

SQ = Status Quo

Supported by the UK, B, NL, DK, Ir, L (28 votes)

Figure 6.1   'Lesser evil': the liberalisation of road haulage

Despite the existence of a transport-specific chapter in the Treaty, the activity of the EC in this area remained limited in the 1960s and 1970s (Héritier *et al.*, 2001). Part of the problem was that, unlike the Benelux countries, the large Member States Germany, France and Italy regulated this sector with view to protecting the competitiveness of their railways. In the Council, the liberalisation of road haulage was directly linked to prior harmonisation. Some regulations emerged in this period dealing with a common tariff system and a contingent of licences that could be used for transport throughout the Community (Button, 1984: 42f., 77–9). Nevertheless, the traditional system of bilateral quotas remained strong. In addition, there were attempts to tackle various *harmonisation* issues, e.g. the different taxes on vehicles and fuel, social regulations concerning working times, and *technical* issues, e.g. the size and weight of vehicles. However, these efforts were not successful.

After several complaints to the Council about the stalling of transport policy, the European Parliament asked the ECJ to rule against the Council for failure to act. In 1985, the Court ruled that the Council of Ministers had violated the Treaty by failing to implement the free provision of services in the transport sector. For the Member States the ruling 'was an implicit threat that, if the Council did not redress the shortcomings in road transport quickly, the Court would directly apply the Treaty . . . which could have meant the instantaneous liberalisation of the road haulage market' (Young, 1994: 6). The Council was thus obliged to act. But, action remained difficult as Germany in particular maintained the link between liberalisation and harmonisation. In the subsequent negotiations, those actors interested in further liberalisation, namely the Netherlands and the Commission, repeatedly threatened to refer the matter to the Court again, if the Council failed to lift the restrictions quickly (*Süddeutsche Zeitung*, 22 December 1992).

In response to the ruling, the Council agreed to liberalise all transit transport from the beginning of 1993.[3] At the same time market access was harmonised (Basedow and Dolfen, 1998: Nr 169). It proved more difficult to implement the freedom to provide services within the Member States. This so-called *cabotage* was contentious as different competitive preconditions would become effective in domestic transport markets. German companies in particular felt disadvantaged by high taxes on vehicles and fuel. In view of the legal pressure, the Council agreed at the end of 1989 on a preliminary liberalisation of *cabotage*. In mid-1993, the understanding on the final liberalisation from mid-1998 onwards was achieved. This was part of a package deal that included a directive on minimum vehicle taxes and a directive on road pricing through a vignette (Gronemeyer, 1994: 271). How effective was the pressure of the Court that the Commission could refer to?

France, Germany, Italy, Spain, Portugal and Greece had originally opposed the liberalisation of road haulage (forty-eight votes), whereas only the UK, Belgium, the Netherlands, Denmark, Ireland and Luxembourg (twenty-eight votes) had supported it (Young, 1994: 15). Thus, without the legal pressure, liberalisation would have stalled, as the parallel agreement on harmonisation would have been difficult. But why was liberalisation through the Court a threat that made liberalisation through the Council to appear as a 'lesser evil' to the Member States? The 'lesser evil' strategy depends on the highly negative consequences of the Commission's threat for the Member States. Action through the Council prior to a mandated liberalisation by the Court, allowed the Member States – such as Germany – that were interested in a parallel harmonisation to achieve some of their goals. Because of the legal pressure, their negotiating position was weakened considerably, while those preferring liberalisation were strengthened. Nevertheless, the latter had an incentive to agree to (modest) harmonisation measures. If they had relied only on the Commission–ECJ tandem, they would have had to wait much longer, with the uncertainty of when the Court would finally rule, and the existing danger that the Court would – as in the inactivity verdict – again put further pressure on the Council for some liberalisation issues, rather than act by itself.

While the example of road haulage allows the clear presentation of the 'lesser evil' strategy, it is a case where the Commission is not particularly active. The European Parliament, rather than the Commission, called upon the Court. Only then did the Commission use the ruling of the Court to exert pressure on the Council. In other cases – e.g. the case of merger control described by Bulmer (1994) – the Commission used existing Court cases in a similar manner. But the Commission may also be more proactive as the second example, the liberalisation of electricity, will show (Schmidt, 1998b).

Despite the formal qualified majority rule, this case is one of *de facto* unanimity as France was firmly opposed to liberalisation. It is the largest electricity exporter and, therefore, it could not be outvoted (cf. Westlake, 1995: 111). It is therefore possible to focus on France and not necessary to reflect on the preferences of all Member States. As with to road haulage, negotiations in the Council on the Commission's proposal stalled. In light of the deadlock, the Commission brought cases of alleged infringement to the Court in 1994, arguing that the import and export monopolies of five Member States, including France, had to be abolished because of the market freedoms (Slot, 1994: 525). In view of this threat, France started co-operating in the Council. An agreement became possible in 1996, before the Court ruling set out the Treaty obligations of Member States. As the Court is unlikely to deviate excessively from a recent Council agreement (Everling, 1984: 323), governments could thereby keep the liberalisation process under their control.

In this case, the worst case scenario amounted to the negative consequences of an unplanned, i.e. Court-led liberalisation.[4] Because the Court would only rule on certain aspects of the existing electricity monopolies, uncertainty would result on the legal vulnerability of established orders. Given the long-term investments in the sector this was highly undesirable. In addition, it would be very difficult for the Council to overrule a verdict of the Court. Since the Court interprets the Treaty, which can be amended only unanimously, cases of precedent are very risky for the Member States. As long as one Member State benefits from the result of judicial politics, it can block the change and governments face a joint-decision trap in following up on the judgment. Thus, by being in a position to credibly threaten litigation, the Commission has the possibility *to alter the previously rejected option of a common European policy into a second-best solution that comes next to the non-defendable status quo.*

But why could Member States not prevent the Commission from acting this way, by putting pressure on their national Commissioner? Internally, the Commission decides by majority rule to pursue cases. Hence, government pressure on individual Commissioners could stop the Commission. Although governments may indeed sometimes be successful in this way, there are significant limits to such control, making 'lesser evil' a worthwhile strategy for the Commission. First, the Commission's overall credibility as a guardian of the Treaty and an administrator of competition law is at stake. Second, even total control of the Commission cannot fully prevent the 'evil' occurring. There are other actors, whose actions can partly substitute for those of the Commission. Private actors may directly turn to national or European courts to protect their rights. Acting purposefully or as a mere by-product of a court case, the significant costs of legal uncertainty and of highly binding judicial policy making of the ECJ may be brought about without much Commission input. This is what we have already seen with the examples of road haulage and merger control. The Commission, in turn, may exploit the ECJ action; without that control over it, it could not contain the situation any longer.

For the 'lesser evil' strategy, the Commission need not threaten with an uncertain legal situation or a direct liberalisation through the Court. 'Lesser evil' may also refer to direct financial losses. This is demonstrated by the example of the *liberalisation of air transport* (Argyris, 1989: 8–11; O'Reilly, 1997).

Following the *Nouvelles Frontières* ruling of the Court, affirming the applicability of European competition law on airlines, the Commission examined the bilateral agreements between airlines (CEC, 1986: para. 32). These hampered competition and infringed article 81 (ex 85) of the Treaty. Thirteen airlines were charged in 1986 and 1987 (CEC, 1987: paras. 36, 46) so that indirectly all national governments were concerned. Should the airlines not conform to the demands of the Commission, which were also detailed in proposals for two regulations submitted simultaneously to the Council, Commission decisions entailing high fines would come into force. In view of this threat, the Council reached an agreement on the Commission's proposals (the 'first package') in December 1987 (CEC, 1988, para. 46).[5]

The Commission may also impose opportunity costs in related areas. The liberalisation of alternative telecommunications networks (e.g. held by railway and electricity companies), for instance, was imposed by the Commission as the necessary price to pay for the authorisation of the co-operation of the French and German telecom operators, originally called *Atlas*. Otherwise the proposed merger would lead to excessive market dominance (Schmidt, 1998b: 170). The same reasoning was applied to the Netherlands and its Unisource involvement with the Swedish and Swiss operators. With Italy, a conflict about the licensing of the second mobile phone operator was used as a threat (Larouche, 2000: 56–9). Thus, pressure regarding various competition cases allowed the Commission to liberalise the use of alternative networks throughout the EU under article 86 para. 3 (ex 90 para. 3) from mid-1996 onwards.

In using its 'lesser evil' strategy, the Commission depends on the ECJ's parallel interpretation of the Treaty obligations. Before discussing the scope of the Commission's powers in the next section, it is useful to ask how far this strategy is still relevant today with an arguably weakened Commission[6] and a stronger emphasis on intergovernmental decision making. Certainly, the number of legislative proposals has declined, and with it the Commission's capacity to shape legislation. But it is not only interesting to understand how the Commission could act in the heydays of the Single market project. Today there are also cases that exemplify the pattern described here.

Thus, the current attempt to agree on an energy tax follows the same logic analysed in this chapter. As is well known, progress in tax policy is difficult because of the unanimity requirement. In view of the investigations in energy taxes launched by the Commission's DG Competition in several Member States, governments feel under pressure in the Council to agree on a directive (*Die Zeit*, 11 April 2001). Also relating to taxes, Internal Market Commissioner Bolkestein has opened infringement proceedings against Member States to harmonise the taxation of cross-border company pensions. So far, the discriminatory treatment makes it difficult for companies to offer EU-wide schemes and hampers the free movement of workers (European Commission, 2001b; *European Voice*, 21 February 2001). These cases against six Member States were taken further in February 2003 (European Commission, 2003b).

Another example comes from the area of corporate taxes. Here, all tax distortions of Member States were assembled in the so-called Primarolo report (2000), aiming at the self-commitment of Member States to reduce the resulting tax competition. On this basis, Competition Commissioner Monti has opened state aid proceedings against twenty of the sixty-six competition-distorting tax measures of the report in spring 2000 (Genschel, 2002: 230). Formal proceedings were opened for fifteen cases in July 2002. By February 2003, the Commission had taken negative state aid decisions on twelve of these cases, leading Competition Commissioner Monti to assert: 'Without our State aid proceedings, some Member States may well have not negotiated this year's tax package' (European Commission, 2003a).

These are all examples where the Commission uses the 'lesser evil' strategy to make progress in policy areas, namely taxes and private pensions, where integration has so far been hampered. But the strategy is also still used in more 'established' fields. Thus the Commission is trying to pry open railway networks by following up a complaint regarding an abuse of dominant position of the Italian railway (*Frankfurter Allgemeine Zeitung*, 9 and 10 July 2001). This may help in recent plans to speed up the liberalisation of railways (*Frankfurter Allgemeine Zeitung*, 1 January 2002).

In discussing the relevance of these Commission powers in the following section, the dependence of the Commission on the Court is analysed. In addition, existing analyses of the influence of the Commission on the EU policy process are related to the framework of analysis presented in this chapter.

The scope of the Commission's powers
By presenting its proposals as a 'lesser evil', the Commission can considerably influence decision making in the Council. But how relevant is this finding? In this sub-section, the preconditions of this strategy are first analysed, then other studies dealing with the Commission are discussed. On this basis, it will be considered whether the Commission may only further liberalisation or also re-regulation in this way.

The Commission can submit a proposal only as a 'lesser evil' if it manages to change the default condition of the Member States in such a way (or to present it as if it were changed) that the adoption of its proposal seems preferable. Since national governments can hardly alter the default condition which requires unanimity, a minority of governments, or even a single one, can determine the future policy just as the joint-decision trap predicts. Thus, the interest of some governments in the liberalisation of road haulage, air transport, telecommunications, and electricity made it impossible to prevent further pressure for liberalisation through a Treaty revision.

That the default condition can have this impact is mostly due to the Court. Hardly any attention has been given so far to the impact of the Court's independence on the Council's negotiations. Nationally shaped sectors can be subjected to EU law without explicit decisions of the Council. In addition, the

Court is very independent in its rulings. However, the Council can try to exert influence by passing secondary legislation, which the Court is likely to take into account. By agreeing in a timely manner the Council can ensure that an interpretation of the Court will not deviate too far from political consensus. This made it particularly attractive for the governments to find a compromise in the electricity case.

How far can historically defined systems be suddenly overtaken in this way? As the interpretation of the Treaty develops slowly (Behrens, 1992), EU legal requirements are often unclear. As a result, Member States may legitimately seek to postpone the adaptation process. Thus, in the infringement procedures in electricity, the French authorities argued that as no common policy had been agreed upon, it was legitimate to maintain the traditional national system of governance. However, if a Council agreement were generally a precondition for the application of the Treaty's rules, there would hardly be any scope for using the Treaty to put pressure on the Council. The Commission is therefore facing a difficult balancing act: changes that are too far-reaching cannot be requested, but incremental steps may be taken. In addition, neither the Commission nor the national governments can predict the Court's rulings as regards the scope of market freedoms.

Thus, in its ruling on the import and export monopolies for gas and electricity of 23 October 1997, the Court (ECJ, 1997a; 1997b; 1997c; 1997d) sided with the Member States against the Commission.[7] Although this does not mean that these monopolies are compatible with the Treaty, this ruling was a significant blow to the Commission. If the governments had foreseen such a cautious ruling of the ECJ, France would, most probably, have agreed only on a less liberal regime. In the last few years the ECJ has generally started to allow more scope for national policies, in particular in its case law relating to utilities (Scharpf, 1999: 166; Héritier, 2001).

How relevant are these findings for the process of European integration? The adoption of the merger regulation and the recent tax cases aside, the examples presented here relate mainly to the liberalisation of sectors. But can the Commission similarly influence re-regulation? On the one hand, re-regulation is promoted indirectly through liberalisation. It is rarely an option to simply liberalise highly regulated sectors. By promoting liberalisation the Commission is therefore in a good position to make proposals for re-regulation (Majone, 1992; Vogel, 1996). On the other hand, there are cases where the Commission can promote re-regulation in a direct manner. The default condition of decision making may favour a minority of governments wherever specific rights are already established in the Treaty. Due to the Treaty's emphasis on market freedoms and competition, most constraints on the Council favour liberalisation. The most liberal Member States, even if in a minority, are strengthened. In so far as positive rights can be drawn from the Treaty, the situation could, however, also be the other way around. Article 141 (ex 119) of the Treaty, in particular, mandating the equal pay for women and men, has been interpreted by the Court favourably for women (Fenwick and Hervey, 1995: 448; Pierson, 1996: 150f). Clearly, this case law could be used for a changed default condition favouring positive rights.

In addition, a similar pressure can be envisaged whenever the Treaty allows the exemption of high national regulations from the Single Market rules (Scharpf, 1998: 134; Genschel, 2000). In this case the threat relates to the danger of renewed market fragmentation. If some Member States are allowed to impose, for instance, higher environmental regulatory standards, this will re-fragment the Single Market. Governments that seek to avoid this danger have to agree on a directive. The governments that favour higher national standards are this time in an advantageous position in the Council. Under these institutional conditions, a 'race to the top' may emerge where higher standards are picked rather than risking new barriers to trade (the 'California effect' – see Vogel, 1995). In this context the recent caution of the ECJ with regard to the lifting of national restrictions is also important. How far the Commission may foster these legal constraints strategically, leading to higher standards, is a question for further research. Given that the Treaty of Amsterdam enhanced the means of Member States to regulate above EU rules (Pollack, 2000), this mechanism may play a more significant role in the future.

How far is it possible to conceptualise the results of other studies on the role of the Commission in a similar way? It is quite common to relate the influence of the Commission to the fact that, being a central actor, it is well positioned to exploit windows of opportunity (Kingdon, 1984) as well as fostering package deals. Windows of opportunity facilitate decisions by making them look more favourable than they did before. An example is the reform of the Common Agricultural Policy (MacSharry reform) that the Commission managed to achieve in the context of the Uruguay Round. While the reform had been blocked before, the Commission was successful when it pointed out that without concessions in agriculture the whole round could fail (Coleman and Tangermann, 1999: 399). The reform had become a 'lesser evil' in the light of the high cost of an unsuccessful round.

Regional policy provides another example. At the beginning of the 1980s the Commission failed to generate sufficient support for its Mediterranean pro-gramme. This situation changed in 1985, when Greece threatened to veto the accession of Spain and Portugal, if it did not receive financial means through this programme (Smyrl, 1998: 84). Again, this proposal became a 'lesser evil', given the importance of the Iberian enlargement.

The situation is similar when package deals are put together. The difference, of course, is that here positive incentives, rather than threats, are the key mech-anism. While a certain decision by itself is not acceptable, it becomes attractive if it is coupled with other decisions. With package deals and windows of oppor-tunity the Commission largely depends on *external* developments. On the contrary, I have shown how the Commission may use its *own* competences to alter the default condition of the Member States.

The Commission has a set of other means to influence the EU policy process that follow a different logic. Incrementalism is often emphasised ('Russian doll' strategy): by building on existing directives the Commission can gradually achieve concessions from the Member States, who feel obliged to take the next step by having agreed to the first (Ross, 1995; Héritier, 1997: 178). Another strategy is that of 'regulatory competition' by which the Commission prompts the Member States to suggest national regulatory patterns as solutions on the European level (Héritier et al., 1994). Although national governments like to maintain their national regimes, they prefer an EU policy that follows their national example to one where they incur adaptation costs. The Commission can then benefit from the fact that all Member States attempt to realise their 'second best' option and propose their national policy solutions at the European level.

With these strategies, the Commission exploits asymmetric information and benefits from the problem of collective action of the Member States. Member States would be careful not to agree on directives implying future obligations, if they were aware of them. Regulatory competition would fail if Member States could trust each other not to make proposals to the Commission. The precise mechanism which leads Member States to follow the Commission is less well established in those cases where the Commission is seen to increase its influence by means of coalitions with other actors. Examples include regional actors in regional policy (Marks et al., 1996; Tömmel, 1998), experts who participate in committees (Eichener, 1996; Héritier, 1997); as well as economic actors lobbying for certain integration goals (Green Cowles, 1995). That Member States agree in these cases to policies they initially objected to is due to a number of reasons: (1) they rely on expert knowledge or they are being pressurised by economic actors; (2) they suffer from information asymmetries and (wrongly) believe that the actors entrusted with the negotiations pursue the national interest; and (3) there is no set national government position, so that the actors in charge have some leeway.

Finally, it is necessary to discuss the relevance of the increasing importance of the *European Parliament* for the use of this strategy by the Commission. If the Commission can create and exploit its own favourable windows of opportunity by using its other competences, what impact is the European Parliament likely to have? In the literature, it is generally assumed that the EP is interested in furthering integration as much as the Commission is (Tsebelis, 1994: 137; Tsebelis and Kreppel, 1998: 44). Under this assumption, the extended rights of the EP under the co-operation procedure would not alter the instruments of the Commission. If one relaxes the simple assumption that the EP and the Commission pursue similar interests, it is questionable whether one can establish in general how the former will affect the latter's powers. Then its position will depend on national and party affiliation next to the institutional interests that influence its behaviour.[8]

Conclusion

This chapter has demonstrated that the Commission may use its powers as guardian of the Treaty and implementor of EU competition law to influence Council negotiations in a manner that goes well beyond its agenda-setting powers. By being able to *unilaterally* alter the status quo position of the Member States, the Commission's proposals appear to be a 'lesser evil'. Therefore, they are more likely to be approved by the Council.

The Commission may thus influence the Council's decision making beyond its agenda-setting powers. Despite their larger resources, national governments cannot prevent the Commission from acting in this manner, since they cannot change the default condition: either they lack the unanimous agreement required for Treaty amendments, or the Commission has recourse to external developments that cannot be altered.

So far, the relevance of the Commission's residual powers and of isolated court judgments has been often referred to in the literature. Nevertheless, this issue has not received the systematic attention it deserves. Moreover, it is cited frequently in support of a neofunctionalist explanation of European integration (Burley and Mattli, 1993; Leibfried and Pierson, 1995: 44), despite the weaknesses of neofunctionalism in dealing with institutions (Scharpf, 1988: 266). In contrast with the notion of 'spillover', this analysis makes an institutionalist argument focusing on the changing default condition of actors that may grasp the dynamics of integration more precisely.

But the options available to the Commission analysed throughout this chapter also have repercussions for institutionalist analyses. Although it is surprising – given Weiler's seminal analysis of the 'dual character of supranationality' that emphasised the connection between the Council's intergovernmentalism and the supranational legal context (Weiler, 1981) – institutionalist analyses often focus on the Council's decision making in isolation. But the Commission's possible manipulation of the default condition of the Member States is very significant for the operation of the Council. The likelihood of governments accepting a Commission proposal clearly depends on the value of existing alternatives, among which the default condition is particularly significant.

By combining agenda setting with its other competences, the Commission can push the Council into adopting proposals that would otherwise have been rejected. Further research is required to determine whether the Commission can use this strategy regularly to bring about – sometimes only very incremental – institutional change.

Notes

This chapter is the revised, partly shortened and partly extended, version of a previous article (Schmidt, 2000). I would like to thank all participants of the workshop in Oxford (May

2001) for comments, in particular Dionyssis G. Dimitrakopoulos, and Roman Claren for research assistance.

1 Several important works (Cini, 1996; Edwards and Spence, 1997; Nugent, 2001) on the Commission exist, but there has not been the same systematic interest in its powers.

2 The Commission is not the only actor who can seek to enforce European law. Similarly, national governments or private actors may intervene (art. 227 (ex 170), 230 (ex 173)), but traditionally this has been of little relevance.

3 Regulation 1841/88.

4 Eising (2002) interprets the case of electricity compromise as one of mutual learning in the Council, and dismisses the relevance of the Court proceedings. However, if this were the case, one would have expected France to implement the directive, which it did not without further pressure from the Commission.

5 Building on this first agreement, the second and third packages of liberalisation in air transport subsequently led to full competition by April 1997.

6 Smith (2000) argues that the Commission generally suffers from decreasing returns as workload increases and demands on its scarce resources intensify. It seems questionable whether this holds given that legislative output has declined.

7 Judgment of 23 October 1997, C-157/94, C-158/94, C-159/94 and C-160/94.

8 Hix (2002a) assumes that the EP is more interested in integration than the Member States. But his analysis shows that the EP partly pursues its own institutional interests to the detriment of further integration.

FRASER CAMERON AND DAVID SPENCE

7

The Commission–Council tandem in the foreign policy arena

Since the early 1990s there have been several institutional changes resulting from the growing realisation of the inextricable nature of the EU's 'external affairs' and the Common Foreign and Security Policy (CFSP). Yet, the fundamental problems remain (Hoffmann, 2000). As one observer appositely wrote after Amsterdam:

> Competition between the Commission and the Council for the ultimate control of European foreign policy is here to stay, and the Amsterdam Treaty does not definitely settle the issue, although it favours the Council. Even if the Treaty represents a concerted attempt to clip the Commission's external policy wings, the question remains: is the Commission or the Council most likely to produce something that looks like a European foreign ministry and a European diplomatic service? (Allen, 1998: 58)

The question was all the more pertinent in 2002 and 2003 during the Convention and the subsequent IGC, even if the management of the EU's external policy making did move on apace after Amsterdam. One of the main changes resulting from the Treaty of Amsterdam, coinciding with the start of the Prodi Commission, was the appointment of Javier Solana as the first High Representative for CFSP. Solana had a distinguished background as Spain's Foreign Minister and Secretary-General of NATO. At the same time, Chris Patten was appointed as Commissioner for External Affairs. He also had a distinguished background as a former British Cabinet Minister and last Governor of Hong Kong. Their respective appointments gave rise to much speculation about how they would work together and how the Council–Commission bureaucracies would cope with what seemed to be the inevitable turf disputes. Significantly, the appointment of Solana put paid to the previously mooted idea of a Commission Vice-President for external relations.[1]

Both Patten and Solana insist on their good relationship with each other but each sees flaws in the present system and both have produced proposals for change. The Commission advocates integration of the two positions under the authority of the President of the Commission. Solana, in contrast, has argued for increased powers and resources for the High Representative. At the Convention there were a myriad of proposals for reform of CFSP including very detailed measures relating to a merger of the two positions, which the IGC would find difficult to neglect.

This chapter sets the Solana–Patten relationship, and by inference the Council–Commission relationship, in the wider context of CFSP and overall external policy in the post-Santer era. It examines the undoubted 'Brusselisation'[2] of European foreign policy and assesses the EU's performance as an international actor, emphasising the Commission's practical role in this. It also discusses the various proposals aimed at raising the EU's profile and engendering a more coherent voice in international affairs.

CFSP in the 1990s: the institutional impact of Brusselisation

Although the EU has steadily increased its presence on the international stage, the CFSP did not have an easy first decade, partly because of structural problems and partly because of the major ongoing conflict in the Balkans. The pillar structure was much criticised while others doubted whether twelve, later fifteen, countries with different interests, capabilities, traditions and connections could ever establish a common policy in such a sensitive area as foreign affairs and security.[3] But few doubted the need for and desirability of CFSP, which was also a popular endeavour.[4] Despite all the problems, the role of the Commission has steadily increased through its control of the budget, its role in first-pillar decision making and instruments and its ability to provide continuity in an evershifting constellation of presidencies paralleled by institutional ambiguity.

As Yugoslavia disintegrated into civil war, some predicted that 'the hour of Europe' had arrived. However, as Chris Patten put it, 'It should have been the hour of Europe, but we blew it' (Patten, 2002). Far from the EU being regarded as the strong actor that could bang heads together and bring peace to the warring factions in Yugoslavia, it was regarded as weak and divided, both in the Balkans and in Washington. The whole Balkan experience, and Kosovo in particular, was a tough learning experience for the EU. But it did have two positive results. First, it demonstrated to Member States the futility of trying to pursue an independent, national policy in the Balkans. After a messy ten years' involvement together in the Balkans, the EU now has a common policy towards the region, encompassing foreign, trade and development policies wrapped up in the Stabilisation and Association Agreements (SAAs). The EU sanctions on Serbia helped to bring down Milosevic. A joint EU–NATO mission, involving Patten, Solana and Lord Robertson, helped defuse an incipient civil war in Macedonia while the EU helped broker a deal that allowed Montenegro to remain within Yugoslavia. Second, the Balkans experience led directly to proposals to establish a European Security and Defence Policy (ESDP), the most significant institutional development since the fall of the Santer Commission, and a vital step change in the CFSP.

As to the efficiency of the EU's external relations, there is also little doubt that the EU has been most effective in its immediate neighbourhood, where the Commission's role has been crucial. The top priority was assisting the candidate countries of central and eastern Europe in preparing for accession to the Union. This involved new contractual relationships as well as massive financial and technical assistance programmes. Further east, the EU offered partnership and association agreements with Russia, Ukraine and other former members of the Soviet Union. To the south, the EU established the Barcelona process, aimed at assisting the Mediterranean countries with economic development and providing for regular political dialogues. These agreements heralded the prospect of a 500 million-strong free trade zone stretching from Casablanca to Vladivostock, made concrete by decisions on enlargement at the Copenhagen European Council of December 2002. In sum, the EU has been a strong magnet for its neighbours and its ability to impose conditionality has ensured the spread of its norms, whether political or economic, throughout the continent. Significantly, in the development and negotiation of all these agreements and the enlargement process the Commission has been in the driving seat, providing the backbone for the negotiating teams as well as the financial and technical resources. There are few, however, who purport to see in the EU's clearly successful external relations evidence of the vitality of the CFSP itself. Indeed the EU's options seemed limited to speaking softly and carrying just one big carrot.

Further afield, the results have been mixed. In the Middle East, the EU has moved a long way in the past decade. It played an active role in the peace process, from the 1995 Madrid conference, bankrolling the Palestinian authority and promoting Solana's membership of the Mitchell Commission. The EU is also a leading member of the Quartet, a diplomatic arrangement with the US, the UN and Russia that meets on an *ad hoc* basis to discuss and co-ordinate policy towards the Middle East. But, EU policies towards other regions have developed at different speeds. In Asia, there has been a steady deepening of ties with Japan and China while, with Korea, the EU has strongly supported the sunshine policy of President Kim and sent a ministerial troika to North Korea in the summer of 2001 to try to maintain a dialogue with Pyongyang. In Latin America, the EU has become the main partner of Mercosur and the Andean Pact and has negotiated free trade agreements with Mexico and Chile. In Africa, the EU has concentrated on improving its development assistance, supporting regional economic integration and negotiating new agreements with South Africa. In all these areas, the Commission is the *de facto* operational arm of the EU's foreign policy through its management of the crucial first, and increasingly third, pillar policies and of the budget – including the CFSP budget.

In the purely political realm, the EU has not been able to build consensus in all areas. There have been isolated, yet important, disputes, for example over human rights in China or the fraught issue of how to deal with Iraq, which split the EU before and during the war against Iraq in 2003. But overall the trend has been towards greater EU cohesion in its external policies towards the rest of the world.[5] And if one places CFSP within the wider framework of the EU's overall external policies, the picture is positive. As Chris Patten put it (2001):

> there has been a real change of gear. At long last, European foreign policy is properly linked into the institutions, which manage the instruments needed for its accomplishment; external trade questions, including sanctions, external assistance, external aspects of Justice and Home Affairs including migration policy, terrorism and transnational crime.

So, the links now exist. But the problem is too many cooks in the kitchen and while 'surf and turf' dishes may be the fashion, turf disputes are not uncommon between them.

Assessment

Assessments vary when one looks at the CFSP from the perspective of the Commission, Council, Parliament, Member States, third countries or the general public. A Bosnian Muslim and a Kosovo Muslim may have very different views of the EU's role in the Balkans. Like other policy areas, the CFSP reflects the 'multiple realities' that make up the EU. But given the sensitive nature of foreign and security policy, there are additional tensions between the Member States (not just between large and small), between the institutions, and between the CFSP machinery and the growing influence of the NGO world. The CFSP is also a moving target. One week's failure to prevent the outbreak of conflict in Macedonia may lead to next week's success in arranging a cease-fire. And success in conflict prevention often passes unnoticed. Thus, a dominant issue for the Convention on the Future of Europe and a key agenda item for the following IGC was resolving the difficulty, if not impossibility, of isolating the CFSP from other external policies of the EU. As Patten has frequently stated, projecting stability may be achieved as much by enlargement, liberal trade policies and generous development assistance, contributing to improved living standards, than by any number of CFSP 'common strategies' or declarations. That the Commission is the initiator/manager in such policy areas should not be underestimated. And the EU's Treaty commitment to 'coherence' should likewise not be underplayed, including coherence in the distribution of institutional responsibilities, where both the presidency and the Commission have responsibilities anchored in the Treaty.

Patten, Solana and the Brussels CFSP machinery: bureaucratic warfare?

An early assessment of relations between Patten and Solana was that 'they are beset by structural problems that no amount of cordiality can eliminate' (*The*

Economist, 22 January 2000: 32). Today, cordiality remains a fact. Strangely, the urbane, British Conservative gets on well with the fiery Spanish socialist. They have made some joint trips, notably to the Balkans, and produced a few joint papers, such as that on *Wider Europe*, to the September 2002 Gymnich meeting, but arguably they could have done more together. For example, it would have been interesting to see whether they could have produced a joint paper to the Convention on reform of CFSP. Apparently such an effort was not even discussed. Although Solana and Patten do not frequently engage directly in turf battles, their rival bureaucracies often do engage in some bitter in-fighting.[6] Overall, however, there is more co-operation than hostility between the Council and Commission, despite the undeniable skirmishing. Each knows that there is a job to be done and professionals like to find solutions. Patten has summed up his role as follows:

> Javier Solana and I have different but complementary roles. We both develop external policies. Javier's role is to help the Council rally the Member States to our common policies and to represent those policies to the world. My role is to ensure that the EU can deliver on those policies, to come up with the necessary ideas and proposals, to implement them and to make sure that Europe's external action is consistent with its internal policies. (Patten, 2001)

'Even with the emergence of the CFSP High Representative, Member States look to the Commission to manage the nuts and bolts of that engagement, and to do much of the donkey work' (Patten, 2000b).

Solana, on the other hand, has stated (Solana, 2000a) that his task is to assist the presidency and the Member States to use the post of High Representative to create new momentum within the CFSP. We have to ensure that the EU provides a more coherent approach to the rest of the world. The Council has to guarantee that the Member States deliver on this (Solana, 2000b). In reality, though Solana may be regarded abroad as 'the EU's foreign policy chief', he is a chief with very few Indians and very little money. Patten, in contrast, has the money, the manpower and ownership of most of the instruments, which are first and third pillar policies. The High Representative is unable to order the use of specifically second pillar foreign policy instruments such as troop deployment or diplomatic demarches, while the External Relations Commissioner has considerable autonomous control of the first pillar instruments, which make up 90 per cent of the foreign policy toolbox at the EU's disposal. Patten has practical power. Solana has political profile. Even so, Patten himself has made no secret of his impatience with current arrangements. He accused Member States of making 'ringing political declarations', which they were 'reluctant to underwrite in money and staff', and lamented the 'unresolved tension' between intergovernmental activities and Community powers, so that the Commission gets left to 'wrestle with the contradictions and blamed for inadequate outcomes', its role 'that of the maid who is asked to prepare increasingly large and grand dinners in a poky kitchen with poor ingredients' (*The Economist*, online edition, 31 August 2000). There is a clear dilemma for the Commission.

As to the Council and its growing and changing secretariat, one of the most significant practical changes in CFSP after Amsterdam was the improvement of its operating machinery, formalised at Nice. While political oversight via the European Council and the General Affairs Council[7] remains unchanged, the motor running the CFSP has been greatly enhanced by the establishment of the Brussels-based Political and Security Committee (PSC) – known more frequently by its French acronym (COPS). The PSC's remit is to cover all aspects of CFSP including security and even defence issues. It meets at least twice a week and is the diplomatic hub around which the CFSP revolves. Comprising senior diplomats from the Member States, the Council Secretariat and the Commission, the PSC monitors international affairs, guides the work of the Military Committee and all CFSP working groups; prepares and oversees the implementation of CFSP decisions; leads political dialogues at official level and maintains links to NATO. The PSC also handles crisis situations and has engendered a series of its 'own' ESDP committees adding to the existing CFSP structures. The European Union Military Committee (EUMC) and the European Union Military Staff (EUMS) support the PSC. The EUMC is composed of the Chiefs of Defence represented by their military representatives and responsible for providing the PSC with military advice and recommendations. While the Commission has not so far participated in the meetings of the Military Committee, the Commission PSC representative (the director of the Commission's newly created CFSP directorate) has, on occasion, briefed it. The EUMS provides military expertise and support to ESDP, with a particular focus on the Petersberg tasks (peacekeeping, peace enforcement and support for humanitarian crisis situations, including evacuation etc.). Significantly, informal contacts between the Military Staff and the Commission's staff have grown apace since the outset. The Military Staff had to be aware of Community budgets and procedures, which were underpinning essential tasks such as de-mining, police operations, border guard and Customs training. As to the obvious need to evaluate civil–military issues in crisis management, a political–military committee and a civilian crisis management committee complete the picture. The PSC largely took over the work previously done by the Political Committee, which used to meet on a more leisurely monthly basis. Although it is nominally responsible to COREPER (as overall co-ordinator of the General Affairs Council), COREPER rarely intervenes in PSC business. There is thus a greater urgency about CFSP and an improved capacity to respond swiftly to crisis situations. But the long-term effects on the Commission's role and status remain difficult to determine.

Solana and the Council

The Amsterdam Treaty was deliberately vague on the responsibilities of the High Representative, stating that he 'shall assist the Council in matters coming within the scope of the CFSP, in particular through contributing to the formulation, preparation and implementation of policy decisions, and, when appropriate, acting on behalf of the Council at the request of the Presidency, through conducting political dialogue with third countries'. The High Representative is also supposed to 'assist the Presidency' in the external representation of the EU and in the implementation of decisions in CFSP matters. Given the vagueness of the provisions of the Treaty much depends on the personality of the office-holder. In appointing Solana to the post in October 1999, the Member States chose one of Europe's most distinguished statesmen. Solana's stature has clearly helped ensure that the EU's voice is heard regularly in Washington and other major capitals. Indeed, as rueful presidency officials have privately commented, visits to Europe by US Secretary-of-State Colin Powell often reverse the expected order of preference, so meetings between Powell and Solana have taken place privately before meetings with the Foreign Minister of the presidency. While the choice of a politician as opposed to a senior official for the HR post was by no means a foregone conclusion, such is the political role that Solana has carved out that it would now be unthinkable to replace him with a bureaucrat. Since Amsterdam, therefore, the Council's role has increased significantly as Javier Solana has become a growingly visible figure of European diplomacy.

Patten and the Commission

The first Commissioner for External Affairs was the former Dutch Foreign Minister, Hans van den Broek. Appointed in January 1993, van den Broek was to lead the Commission input into the fledgling CFSP. With his appointment, the Commission saw the creation of a new Directorate-General for External Political Relations, DG IA, under veteran EPC Commission expert Gunther Burghardt, in juxtaposition to DG I, External Economic Affairs,[8] under Sir Leon Brittan.

'Competition' is perhaps the obvious description of relations between the two Commissioners and their directorates-general; a competition made all the more entangled by the existence in the 1990s of other portfolios within the 'RELEX' family. The frequently public disputes between Commissioners van den Broek and Brittan were hardly conducive to efficient delivery of policy. And the seeming reticence of the Commission throughout the 1990s to use its hard-won right of initiative in CFSP, for fear of incurring Member State discomfort and opposition, compounded Commission weakness in CFSP. It is a moot point whether the diversity and in-built rivalry of the new structures explain the Commission's low profile in CFSP. After all, the EPC section of the Secretariat-General could have remained in the Secretariat-General and reported directly to the Commission President or been transferred to DGI, where there existed the benefit of a ready-made system of relations between headquarters and the delegations. This might have avoided the rivalry, which made so onerous the shift in management from purely trade and development matters to the weightier subject of foreign policy, with the concomitant evolution of administrative culture, which the Maastricht Treaty commanded.

The choice of the creation of DG IA and the bureaucratic rivalry seemingly caused by the need to find Commissioners and Directors-General adequate portfolios did much to keep the Commission from becoming the streamlined foreign service to which it might have aspired. The relations between Brussels and the delegations are a case in point. There was no recognisable career development and training path for staff at headquarters or in the field, and as new delegations opened to cope with the changing emphases in world politics, it was hard to ensure that staff abroad (including some 2,000 locally employed staff) were properly trained for the new functions they were to fulfil.[9] In sum, the overall need to co-ordinate was counterbalanced by the perception that Commissioners' independence and their DGs' autonomy must be preserved. This made management reform extremely difficult. Despite some improvements, this still remains the case. It leaves the Commission open to a takeover bid from the High Representative, a point to which we return below.

Patten takes charge

If the history of the 1990s is a sorry one, can that also be said of the Prodi Commission? The role of the Commission has certainly remained unchanged after the Amsterdam and Nice adjustments to the Treaty. So, the Commission remains 'fully associated' with the CFSP. But, most importantly, it implements the Community budget on which many CFSP policies and actions depend. Certainly, the re-organisation of the Prodi Commission, making Patten the chair of the five Commissioners dealing with external affairs, has led to a more coherent Commission approach to CFSP. Patten's determination to improve the delivery of EU assistance has also been appreciated by Member States – and recipients – though it is hard to find staff who sympathise with the split in responsibilities between policy making and project management. While logical in itself and clearly perceived as necessary following the tightening of budgetary supervision after the fall of the Santer Commission, it has added yet another layer of potential bureaucratic rivalry and infighting at a time when the Commission should arguably be girding its loins before the challenge of enforced transfer of many of its CFSP functions to the High Representative and the Council apparatus. Meanwhile, CFSP, where effectiveness of the policy itself is as hard to measure as the efficacy of the Commission's policy input, has become one of the key areas within the Commission, and much sought after by the same ambitious staff, who lament the rivalry they are forced to be part of.

Patten has tried to avoid open turf wars with Solana, preferring to wear his various hats of politician, manager and chief according to circumstances. Yet, in a letter to Member States' Foreign Ministers on 27 November 2000 about the new crisis management arrangements, he underlined the Commission's concerns. 'My problem with Javier's proposal is that as soon as something is designated a "crisis" he proposes it should at once become the object of a comprehensive joint action covering both Community and second pillar issues. Yet even in situations where possible military action creates an imperative for immediate decision-making, I would be unhappy about a Joint Action which strayed into the Community sphere'.

The concern is the submission of the Community method to the intergovernmentalism of the second pillar. Patten (2000b) himself argued that 'The – welcome – creation of the CFSP High Representative . . . has not helped . . . Indeed, it has given rise to some new institutional complications. It may also have increased the tendency for CFSP to usurp functions, which should be the responsibility of the Commission (e.g. the EC Monitoring Mission to the Balkans, which was dreamt up by CFSP and then left as an expensive baby on the Commission's doorstep'. Patten further argued that 'ambiguity about the limits of the Commission's role is particularly acute in the security field' and that the Commission 'should act as a 'reality check' on CFSP initiatives and 'beware of building parallel structures'. Others, and this has been emphasised consistently by some Member States in the Convention, are seemingly more concerned at the 'communitarisation' of the second and third pillars,[10] and have actually proposed parallel structures.[11]

What though of the Commission's internal organisation for CFSP? Though the Commission sensibly has not sought a role in the military dimension of ESDP, it has argued that it has an important role in non-military dimensions such as defence industrial co-operation, funding and training of police, customs officials and border guards, economic sanctions, de-mining operations, election monitoring, and restoring local administrations in societies emerging from conflicts. The Commission sees its contribution to CFSP/ESDP under the overall theme of conflict prevention, and its internal structures and procedures are being adapted to ensure that hitherto disparate policy areas form part of a coherent and co-co-ordinated whole.

To ensure this, a CFSP directorate was created after Amsterdam in what is now known as DG External Relations.[12] When EPC/CFSP stalwart Günther Burghardt left the general-directorship of DG External Relations to become Head of the Commission's delegation in Washington, his replacement, veteran agriculture Director-General Guy Legras, concentrated on creating a streamlined management framework for external relations, spearheaded by the creation of the 'Service Commun Relex', and the accompanying separation between policy making and project management, which passed to the new structure, as did around one hundred RELEX staff in early 2001. Unlike his predecessor Legras was not consumed with CFSP fervour. He saw his role as guardian of the *acquis communautaire* input into external policy making and did not intervene in the politics of the Commission's input to CFSP. This left a gap in the policy process, which many lamented. With the concentration on management taking prime focus for the Director-General, there was a case for boosting the role of his deputy. In effect, and on paper, this became the case. But the post of deputy Director-General in DG External Relations has never been part of the

Commission's line management and promotion structure. It is usually staffed by a senior national diplomat on secondment, and has often been left vacant for embarrassing periods while Member States sort out the implications. But the deputy Director-General is also the Commission's Political Director, a role that finds the incumbent abroad for the majority of the year in troikas of political directors and meetings worldwide. This has led to the *cabinet* of Patten intervening directly in the day-to-day work of the 'services' and establishing often-fruitful relations with staff at lower echelons. For example, like Pascal Lamy when he was Delors' *chef de cabinet*, Anthony Cary, *chef de cabinet* to Patten until his appointment as UK Ambassador to Sweden in the summer of 2003, developed a network of people with whom he felt confident of securing new ideas, quick drafts or help with policy briefs. This system may be more efficient than working through strict hierarchical procedures and it provides an ego boost to those involved. But it can also lead to frustration and resentment by those not in the inner circle.

Within the CFSP directorate falls the security unit, which is responsible for input to the POLMIL group, terrorism, arms control, small arms, non-proliferation, and the new 'crisis unit'. The other key policy unit comprises a team of some twenty officials covering conflict prevention, crisis management, CFSP in Africa and the newly introduced Commission contribution to the EU's rapid reaction capacity, the financial mechanism known as the Rapid Reaction Mechanism. Two further units deal with the business of sound financial management and legal implications (the CFSP Counsellor) and operations under the COREU or Cortesy network of inter-foreign ministry communication and the preparation of briefing for Council meetings (the European Correspondent).

In practical terms, the Commission's secure 'crisis room' is a focus for the Commission's co-operation (or input to?) the Council's 'Situation Centre' (SITCEN). The Commission has insisted on parity with Member States in reception of the information and documentation process in the SITCEN, while providing automatic transmission of information from its own heads of delegation to the Policy Unit.

Budgets

In the early years of CFSP, debates on policy were too often overshadowed by ideological arguments over whether an action was to be funded by Member States or the Community budget. The usual result was using the Community budget for CFSP actions, a vital feature on which the Commission failed to build adequately in the creation of its own role in CFSP. Such disputes remain a handicap to the efficient operation of CFSP, as does the woefully inadequate budget (circa 30 million euro in 2002), but they also explain the enduring co-existence of a CFSP mentality and a first-pillar mentality amongst Commission staff. The management of the Commission's input has been plagued with the vagaries and intricacies of the three-pillar system, which many would dearly have disappear after the next IGC.

An example of the confusion is the issue of whether the 'comitology' rules in the first pillar apply to CFSP. For example, the CFSP joint action on security co-operation with the Palestinian Authority saw the creation of an 'advisory committee' chaired by the presidency, a helpful and constructive innovation clearly aimed at enhanced coherence and efficiency. Yet, since the Commission is responsible for the management of the budget involved, it arguably should have chaired or, at least, co-chaired, the committee, as would be the case under the first pillar arrangements. The problem was that the committee might attempt to instruct the Commission by taking implementing decisions, which could undermine the Commission's role under the treaties. Of course, the term 'advisory committee' led to ambiguity. While there is no dispute about the Commission's role under the 'comitology' of the first pillar, art. 18.2 TEU confers responsibility for CFSP implementation to the Presidency, with the Commission fully associated (art. 18.4). But how would the Commission be associated and how would it perform its role in execution of the budget, including the right to modify or even reject projects, if its role were determined case by case by presidency decisions? Ambiguity remains despite the fact that the Commission's role in implementing civilian aspects of the CFSP has been partially defined in practice. The co-operation programme between the EU and the Russian Federation in the field of non-proliferation and disarmament (managed by the security unit in the CFSP directorate of the Commission) is a case in point.

Who speaks for Europe?

Despite being the largest financial donor in the Balkans, the OSCE logo on the ballot papers in elections in Bosnia and Kosovo underlined the EU's difficulty in getting its message across.[13] But it is not about the efficiency of the EU's public diplomacy, which is arguably improving (*European Voice*, 5–11 October 2000), not least because it was a major theme in the Solana–Patten joint report to the Lisbon European Council on the EU's failings in the former Yugoslavia. To describe the EU's external representation as confusing would be a huge understatement. If it were an individual, the CFSP would have long been enclosed in a psychiatric ward with doctors assessing how it could have survived so long with such a deep split personality. But its schizophrenia was programmed at birth and was only further complicated by the addition of the High Representative. In many parts of the world, including the US, Javier Solana is seen and increasingly described in the media as 'the EU's foreign policy chief', a shorthand term which irks some, especially the Foreign Minister holding the rotating presidency, but journalists cannot be expected to remember fifteen different telephone numbers and the press corps dealing with 'Europe' is to be found in Brussels, not in the country holding the presidency. Solana's telephone is more accessible and his media profile is higher than that of the rotating presidencies.

Who do the EU public and the outside world see as the focal point for representation of the EU? The appointment of the High Representative was supposed to give the answer. But, as one former Commission official has argued, the Treaty of Amsterdam was an 'exercise in collusive ambiguity' (Nuttall, 1997) and, indeed, outsiders might well be excused for thinking that there remains deliberate ambiguity if not obfuscation even after Nice. The answer to Kissinger's famous question is still not one telephone number and one person (*The Economist*, 5 August 1995). If you are an American foreign policy maker, there are several numbers to call, and they all need to be called frequently, which is precisely what the US Mission to the EU does. Amsterdam dropped the previous holder of the presidency from the troika but the EU side of the table at political dialogue meetings is still rather cumbersome with the presidency, the future presidency, the Council Secretariat (frequently with a speaking role since Amsterdam, though it is the Council Secretariat's external affairs directorate which provides the staff member and not Solana's personal team) and, not least, the Commission. It is often the case that there is more negotiating with the host country over seats for the EU delegation than over the substance of the agenda. Significantly, the only permanent members on the EU side of the table at Brussels-based troikas are the Commission (always called upon to comment on first and third pillar matters, where the diplomats representing the Presidency rarely have personal experience) and the Council Secretariat.

As to representation abroad, the embassies of EU Member States and the 128 Delegations of the European Commission are also encouraged (as well as enjoined by the Treaty) to co-operate locally and present a united front to their host country or international organisation, often in troika format. In practice, this co-operation varies considerably from country to country and is often dependent on local personalities. In addition, in many capitals there is no resident presidency representative, which somewhat complicates matters. The troika is basically a misnomer abroad, for the Council Secretariat is never present, except in the two cities where it keeps an office – New York and Geneva – for reasons of multilateral as opposed to bilateral diplomacy. Thus the Commission delegation is actually the only permanent part of the troika abroad. Presidency ambassadors with little personal experience of the Brussels machinery often tend to go it alone or invent procedures. More than one Member State ambassador has had to be formally reminded that the Commission is a permanent part of the troika. In important posts such as Washington and Moscow there is a further problem in that the larger Member States in particular often prefer to plough their own furrow rather than maintain EU solidarity. There is certainly considerable scope for Member States and Commission delegations to co-operate more effectively in third countries. Jointly the EU and the Member States run the largest diplomatic machinery in the world. With over 2,000 diplomatic missions and more than 20,000 diplomats, the EU has ten times more missions and three times more personnel at its disposal than the US. But as Solana has dryly remarked (2002), it is not obvious that the EU is ten times more effective than the US in foreign policy.

The EU's external representation is further complicated by the growing custom of appointing 'special representatives' to deal with particular problems. These envoys are appointed under the Joint Action procedure and their salaries and expenses are paid from Community funds (by the Commission). These special representatives have varied in their ability to ensure added value to the CFSP. They have certainly not been tasked with ensuring the vital inter-pillar coherence so sought after. Whether they are responsible to Solana, the Council or to their own Member State is a moot point. Significantly, there has been no serious attempt to structure their relationship with the local Commission head(s) of delegation, who often find themselves in an operational support role, without clear line management to cover the political implications. The basic question remains, and must soon be settled; which EU institution represents the EU (as opposed to the EC) abroad? EU institutions such as the European Parliament and other organisations, such as the Council Secretariat are not subjects of international law, and cannot therefore have their own representations abroad nor the diplomatic status that would be the concomitant. Commission staff are currently enjoined (but badly resourced) to provide assistance, facilitate contacts and provide a home' for visiting personnel from these key institutions. Should this all be changed? And what guarantee would there be of enhanced efficiency?

The future

There is no shortage of ideas to strengthen the CFSP and enhance the EU's role on the world stage, and no shortage of debate about the Commission's role and weight in the resulting arrangements. And the ideas are not new (*Financial Times*, 3 May 1995). A central theme of the European Convention concerned possible ways in which a more coherent CFSP could be developed. One of the most discussed proposals, advocated by many think tanks as well as the European Commission, concerns an amalgamation of the Solana and Patten functions (European Commission, 2002a). Some argue that the merger should take place within the Council; others advocate a merger within the Commission. The main argument for such a merger is that it would improve coherence and visibility. Some suggest that most Foreign Ministers would oppose any such merger, as it would inevitably shine the spotlight more on 'Mr CFSP', but they are equally, if not more, reticent to envisage a power shift to the Commission. Much will depend on whether the IGC accepts the proposal for an augmented European Council with its own president for a two-and-a-half- or five-year period. Clearly this supremo would overshadow Mr CFSP wherever he were located. Hence, perhaps, the growing backlash against the idea.

Commission views

In early December 2002, the Commission proposed significant institutional reforms, including in the CFSP area, in a major contribution to the Convention. The Commission proposed creating the post of *Secretary of the European Union*, as a Vice-President of the Commission with a special status. The EU Secretary would be appointed by common accord by the European Council and by the President designate of the Commission. He would report personally both to the European Council and to the President of the Commission, both of whom would be able to terminate his job. As a member of the Commission, he would also report to the European Parliament.

During an unspecified transitional period, the Secretary of the EU would exercise the Commission's right of initiative in CFSP 'according to the guidelines and mandates given to him by the Council, or of a group of Member States with a particular interest in a specific question and whose common interests might require action on the part of the Union'. At the end of the transitional period, the Council, acting on a proposal from the Commission, would rule (enhanced qualified majority) on the arrangements by which the Secretary of the Union would autonomously exercise the Commission's right of initiative in CFSP. Consequently, the Council would also have to rule on the extent of the Member States' right of initiative at the end of the transitional period. Perhaps recognising the radical nature of this proposal, the Commission added that even after the transitional period, a group of Member States could ask the Secretary of the Union to submit to the Council any proposal concerning the implementation of common objectives.

The College could debate CFSP but not block proposals by the Secretary of the Union after agreement had been obtained from the President of the Commission. It would be up to the President of the Commission and the Secretary of the Union to ensure consistency between CFSP and other areas of external action. The Secretary of the Union would also represent the Union *vis-à-vis* third parties with regard to foreign policy action and would be responsible for implementing common decisions. For this purpose, he would have access to 'a single administration resourced from the Council, the Commission and the Member States', placed under his authority, and benefiting from the administrative infrastructure of the Commission. The Commission's external delegations and the Council's liaison offices would become Union delegations managed administratively by the Commission and under the authority of the Secretary of the Union.

Other proposals

The two working groups at the Convention dealing with external affairs and defence had lengthy discussions but failed to reach unanimity on any major changes. While there was widespread agreement on the need to terminate the six-monthly rotating presidency in CFSP, there was less agreement on what to replace it with. At present, each presidency sets its own priorities, often in response to domestic concerns. The Swedes emphasise the Baltic region, the Belgians Africa, the Spanish Latin America and so on. It is useful that presidencies find the energy to organise meetings on these 'priority' issues, but there is an obvious problem of lack of continuity. Alternative solutions include an elected chair for two-and-a-half years or team presidencies. Yet another variation would allow the High Representative to chair the foreign affairs council. His post would no longer be combined with Secretary-General of the Council. The implications for meetings of subsidiary bodies, such as the PSC and the welter of CFSP and ESDP committees, have not been discussed. In the much simpler WEU setting, the Secretary-General chaired the meetings of ministers and often of ambassadors, with his support staff chairing meetings at lower levels. The same is true of NATO. But what role would remain for presidencies if such a system were adopted? And how would the roles of the two organisations be disentangled? More controversial proposals on the table include strengthening the provisions for enhanced co-operation, having regular meetings of defence ministers in a new Defence Council, abolishing the protection of national arms industries, and the establishment of a European diplomatic service with its own training facilities and personnel rotating between Brussels and upgraded EU delegations abroad.

For the foreseeable future, bilateral and EU foreign policy will clearly continue to co-exist. But there will be pressure to increase sharing of premises and other facilities as well as pressure to simplify the EU's external representation. There are thus far-reaching implications for the Commission's External Service, as Patten himself has foreseen, arguing, 'the revamping of our External Service is a major priority' (Patten, 2000b). This is acute not only in CFSP but in other international fora including the UN, G8, IMF and World Bank. Some changes are highly pressing. The question of financing has already been mentioned. Another problem area is the massive expansion in the number of political dialogue meetings. The Spanish 2002 presidency reckoned that the number of such meetings had doubled since their last presidency in 1995.

Conclusion

How to assess the Commission's present and future potential in the field of external affairs and CFSP? The EU has developed steadily as an international actor during the past decade. Much has been achieved but critics argue that much more could have been achieved with strengthened institutions. There is room for doubt. Foreign policy remains a sensitive area and Member States retain their *amour propre*. The UK initiatives in the Middle East in December 2002, for example, were not a formal part of CFSP. Foreign ministries are also reluctant to negotiate themselves into oblivion, not least because there remain unanswered questions about legitimacy. There also remain significant differences of foreign policy culture, experiences and expectations within the Member States, let alone the Commission.[14] At the end of the day, CFSP depends on the political will of its Member States and there are inevitable limitations in the conduct of foreign policy where national independence and identity rides high. In some important areas the EU finds itself hamstrung, but these areas are growing fewer as the Member States come to accept the advantages of working together. The national obsessions of some Member States may indeed have beneficial effects for the EU. The Union would never have paid so much attention to East Timor, for example, without the forceful prodding of Portugal over the years. And without the obvious national interest of France and the UK ESDP would probably not have reached the agenda.

The Commission has a clear interest in promoting a comprehensive vision of external relations and the CFSP, and in moving to a more proactive stance, where its ability and experience lend themselves to policy proposals. This means promoting a CFSP culture among Commission staff, and ensuring that training and career development encompass the resulting needs in terms of human resources and politico-administrative initiative. One could imagine the Commission delegations being far more proactive than hitherto in providing an early warning mechanism where potential conflicts affect EU interests and in co-ordinating a European response to political issues. The analysis of terrorist threats around the world is one obvious example, where continuity and permanent updating of information could arguably be better co-ordinated by the Commission than by rotating presidencies. While this might be desirable, the current standard of political reporting does not always match the Commission delegations' performance in the field of trade and aid. This should not be surprising, but it is certainly to be lamented. Importantly, political reporting by Commission delegations is automatically shared with the High Representative's policy unit. Further areas where Commission initiatives would be appropriate (and are increasingly forthcoming) fall into the areas of political dialogue and general policy frameworks such as the Transatlantic Agenda with the USA, joint declarations with Japan, Canada, India, and Russia etc.

It is unlikely, given the sensitivities of Member States, that significant changes to the Treaty's CFSP provisions will be achieved. Most Member States appear comfortable with present arrangements although there are several who recognise the importance of changes on the external representation front in light of enlargement. While CFSP reform figured largely on the agenda at the Convention and the subsequent IGC, changes are likely to be incremental in nature. The CFSP approaches puberty after a difficult childhood with little sign that its parents have overly high ambitions for its future. As Patten has recognised 'if the CFSP is to grow to maturity, it needs the nurture of both its parents, the Member States and the Community institutions. And – as any psychologist will tell you – the child is more likely to be happy and healthy if those parents love one another' (Patten, 2000a).

Notes

1 Declaration 32 of the Treaty of Amsterdam had noted 'the desirability of bringing external relations under the responsibility of a Vice-President'.
2 'Brusselisation' refers to the growing number of political and bureaucratic structures dealing ith CFSP in Brussels, both in the Council and Commission.
3 For a review of the introduction of the CFSP see Cameron (1999).
4 The European Commission's Eurobarometer polls have consistently shown high support for CFSP. See also Sinnott (1997).
5 The same can be said for EU support for the multilateral institutions.
6 The Prodi Commission, said Solana, had produced no meaningful initiative in its first nine months, apart from the ill-fated invitation to Libyan President Muammar Al-Qadhafi, which was subsequently withdrawn (*Der Spiegel*, 3 July 2000). Solana, seemingly comparing himself to Patten, stated to journalists that he had been no 'out-of-work politician' before becoming High Representative for CFSP, while Patten argued to a European Parliament Committee that CFSP had so far not produced much positive and needed 'flesh on the bones'.
7 There is now a General and External Relations Council at which different ministers may attend according to the agenda.
8 DG I covered commercial policy and relations with North America, China, Japan, the then Commonwealth of Independent States and non-EU Europe, including the crucial central and Eastern European countries.
9 It was not until December 2002 that a specific personnel development and training unit was established in DG RELEX.
10 French Foreign Minister Hubert Védrine criticised (*European Voice*, 6 July 2000) Patten's communication to the College (Patten, 2000) arguing that 'Patten wants to bring foreign policy under the control of the Commission, which was never agreed. He is trying to take on the roles of the Ministers'.
11 President Chirac proposed the creation of a 'light secretariat' to co-ordinate the work of a 'pioneer group' of countries joining together to promote greater integration (see *Financial Times*, 6 July 2000).
12 It is now housed on the 12th floor of the Commission's 'Charlemagne' building, and benefits from state-of-the-art security procedures and equipment, in preparation for the Commission's mooted role in conflict prevention and crisis management, especially since the implementation of the EU–NATO security agreement subsequent to the Copenhagen European Council.
13 The EU states contribute more than 60 per cent to the OSCE budget (the USA contributes around 10 per cent) and a majority of OSCE field missions are headed by EU Member State nationals.
14 For a description of foreign policy cultures and the role of national foreign ministries in EU affairs see Hocking and Spence (2002).

IRÈNE BELLIER

8

- After the sclusion/onned
- new statues/
- negotiations

The European Commission between the *acquis communautaire* and enlargement

The accession to the EU of ten new Member States in 2004 is perceived as a unique challenge, because of the number of the countries involved, their economic heterogeneity and cultural diversity. The enlargement will increase the territory of the EU by 34 per cent and the population by 105 million. The European Commission has prepared what is expected to be a massive change that may lead to the disintegration of the Union. Some highlight the EU's capacity to resolve all kinds of contradictions. As a former Director of the Forward Studies Unit put it: 'that is the secret of Europe . . . being able to share common objectives, particularly political objectives, and being attached to them in many diverse ways' (Vignon, 1997: 62).

The actual process of negotiation can be construed as the re-founding of the Union, in terms of (a) the institutions that must be adapted and (b) the content of the European project. It is against this background that this chapter considers the role of the European Commission in managing enlargement. Analysis focuses on the integration of the *acquis communautaire* in an attempt to highlight the diverse cultural representations of enlargement that emerge from the practices and discourses of the actors involved in the negotiations.[1] This chapter focuses on the strategic role of the European Commission, the metaphors associated with the adoption on the part of the applicant countries of the *acquis* and the way in which the **Commission acts as a mediator of sense.**

It is important to consider both the ways in which national and political cultures change when they are exposed to each other in the context of the negotiations that take place within an organisation, and the implications of that encounter for the EU's political dimension. The role of the Commission in these negotiations is very important for it provides a coherent view of the negotiating process and the reforms that applicant countries must undertake prior to their accession. This is by no means a straightforward process – not least because of the applicant countries' different levels of development. This is why the Commission has had to invent new instruments in its attempt to accelerate and direct the process within the framework defined by the European Council.

The Commission is responsible for steering the process of negotiation with third countries in general and with the applicant states in particular. 'Negotiation' is a broad term, which refers to several stages and issues, both material and immaterial ones ranging from the notion of *acquis communautaire* (EU legislation and ECJ rulings) to the values that contribute to the definition of a 'European model' of society.

The strategic role of the Commission

The political context

This process of enlargement was construed primarily in terms of temporality and to a lesser extent in terms of content and method. As a senior official of the Commission put it, 'the Member States took the political decision to enlarge the EU: we have to adjust the house' (interview, DG Enlargement, June 1999). To prepare the next step, the EU launched a process that may lead to the rebirth of the Community, in a phoenix-like manner.

The conclusions of the presidency at the Nice summit acknowledged the Commission's strategic role by endorsing the conclusions of the General Affairs Council in December 2000 concerning the strategy proposed by the Commission. The term 'strategy' is repeated five times in the page of the presidency conclusions that was devoted to enlargement (as compared to twenty-four times in the thirty-four pages of the whole document). This term implies a number of succeeding events, the use of deadlines as well as the preparation for the future.[2] The term 'strategy' incorporates a number of elements typically associated with war and other forms of action that require organisation, calculation and the orderly pursuit of a goal. In addition, it can have a reassuring influence: 'things are under control'. It is in this context that Commission officials have introduced the notion of 'own merits' as a rhetorical tool that allows the replacement of the notion of equality with the notion of equal opportunities. Furthermore, the use of deadlines highlights the efforts that must be made on the part of applicant countries to comply with EU requirements. The use of deadlines is also linked to the notion of 'speed' (of adaptation) that, in turn, highlights the political challenges that future members face.

Shifting positions

The accession of Eastern and Central European countries differs from previous enlargements. Despite differences in terms of economic development, in terms of temporality, previous applicants were like the member states in that they relied on a modern financial system and, more generally, shared the principles of capitalist economy. This enlargement differs because, as an official put it, 'the candidates come from the fridge, all their systems were paralysed'. Despite their significant experience in accession negotiations, many Commission officials interviewed for the purposes of this chapter, had to invent and employ new instruments.

Officials working on the PHARE programme used to work in collaboration with correspondents in other Directorates-General (DGs Agriculture, Internal Market, Environment etc.), and with a task force 'Enlargement' for the co-ordination of operations. The increasing number of activities put the Commission in a difficult situation on several occasions because of its limited staff.[3] Intra-organisational conflict gave the impression of sub-optimal preparation.

The Prodi Commission decided to re-group in DG for Enlargement (under the responsibility of one Commissioner) several services and programmes hitherto dispersed in three DGs.[4] Thirteen directorates have been constituted along geographic lines and their presentation in the directory reflects graphically the initial divide between first wave (Poland, Hungary, Czech Republic, Estonia, Slovenia and Cyprus) and second wave (Latvia, Lithuania, Slovakia, Bulgaria, Romania, Malta and Turkey) of candidate countries. Until 1997, it was common to consider the former countries closer to the EU standards and almost capable of sustaining integration when the others were still lagging behind. Although the official rhetoric changed in 1998 – with the new approach placing emphasis on each candidate's own merits, an implicit categorisation remained in place.[5]

Several units were created in the new DG to co-ordinate policy making, to manage resources and financial issues and specifically to deal with the flow of information and inter-institutional relations. Membership of the teams changed several times, and so did the lines of authority and *modi operandi*. The constant marginal changes reinforced a sense of incompleteness. Nevertheless, as a Commission official put it, 'Europe is going forward apparently with no ambition, but one can measure how it progressed since the beginning' (interview, DG Enlargement, June 2000).

The design of a strategy

The notion of a strategy suggests a planned and disciplined action for the successful attainment of the objectives. This is reflected in the vocabulary of the operations. 'Roadmaps', 'deadlines', 'objectives' and 'reports' are common words used in the texts as well as in the oral presentations of Commission officials. They consider themselves as 'the soldiers of the acquis' (interview, Enlargement Task Force, February 1999).

The officials of the Commission have had to invent new *modi operandi* and did so in a piecemeal manner typically legitimised on a *post hoc* basis. It started with the extension to the Eastern and Central European countries of the Generalised System of Preferences, a device invented for associating the less developed African, Pacific and Caribbean Countries with the European Union. After the adoption of the European Agreements and the definition in 1993 of the economic and political conditions (the 'Copenhagen criteria') for accession, the Madrid summit asked the Commission in 1995 to assess the candidates' applications and prepare a detailed analysis of the impact of enlargement on the EU. Agenda 2000 was designed in 1997 to address the challenge. The Commission started producing 'opinions' on each country with a prospective analysis of expected progress. In December 1997, the European Council meeting in Luxembourg launched a wider strategy. Its implementation begun in March 1998, for eight Eastern and Central European countries, Malta and Cyprus. This process culminated in the political agreement on the accession of these countries reached at Copenhagen in December 2002. The acceleration of the process took place while the EU was implementing the final phase of the EMU project and, more importantly, while the Commission was engaging in an ambitious process of internal administrative reform (see Kassim, ch 2 this volume) largely resulting from the downfall of Santer's Commission in 1999 (Georgakakis, 2001).

The Commission's comprehensive strategy paper of November 2000 contained both a 'strategy to go forward' and a 'communication strategy'. The second part of the main document was devoted to 'the pre-accession strategy' and was divided into six sections on the formulation of the partnerships for accession, PHARE-related financial provisions,[6] the 'Europe agreements' as a framework for the adoption of the *acquis communautaire* and the implementation of the priorities defined in the accession partnerships, new committees that would replace the meetings devoted to 'screening' (see pp. 142–3), the participation of the candidate countries to EU programmes, and a political forum for the discussion of issues of mutual and common interest: the European Conference. The remainder of the document outlined the progress made by the candidate countries. As regards economic criteria, country-specific references were made to inflation and unemployment rates, growth rates, foreign direct investment and trade, and detailed measures on public policies. However, the analysis of political criteria was not country-specific, perhaps because it referred to corruption, respect of minorities, etc. The document also elaborated on the notion of 'roadmap' which was meant to guide this process, help partners define a realistic agenda with regard to the individual chapters.[7]

Considered *in toto*, the document reflects the fact that the EU's strategy was both technical *and* highly political. Enlargement entails the expansion of the single market and the potential enhancement of the EU's strength. However, it also entails the adjustment of the EU's institutions and policies. As one Commission official has put it, it is the Commission's role – 'like the Church in the middle of a village' (interview, DG Enlargement, June 2000) – to keep discussions on track amid the submission and the withdrawal of various demands. The attitude of the Commission is best reflected in the politics of transposition of the *acquis communautaire*, an expression that is always used in French despite the fact that English is used in the negotiations, and whose meaning constitutes the focus of the actual negotiations.

The Commission as guardian of the *acquis communautaire*

The forthcoming enlargement has the ambition to sanction the transition of the applicant countries to a model of society thought to be more efficient and associated with success values.

The content of the acquis communautaire

The Commission starts with an assessment of the situation of the candidate country in terms of law, rules and institutions ('screening'). The analytical exercise proceeds by means of an exchange of views on legal documents over a period of time, through the making of two lists: the A-list includes tables on the EU legislation to be 'transposed' into national legislation, specifying dates, degree of implementation and the corresponding administrative structure; the B-list concerns soft law, the judgements of the European Court of Justice etc., which are essential but need not be transposed in the national legal orders. The objective is to promote the harmonisation of the applicant countries with EU law and prepare its implementation at street level.

The *acquis communautaire* is divided into thirty-one chapters, which are examined one by one by the applicant countries' experts and Commission officials. The process remains open until the end of the negotiations because EU law evolves constantly. As the Commission's strategy paper states 'On the basis of the progress made to date, the Commission considers that the time has come to outline a strategy to take the negotiations into a more substantial phase and point the way towards their conclusion' (European Commission, 2000: 28). The strategy is defined in five steps: first, the extant and candidate Member States are invited to negotiate on the substantive issues raised by the requirements for transitional measures; second, these requirements are analysed and put in one of three categories (defined by the Commission): acceptable, negotiable or unacceptable; third, a detailed roadmap provides a clear sequence of actions for tackling these issues; fourth, a proposal is made to facilitate the negotiations by 'setting aside' chapters with a limited number of remaining problems; finally, the time needed to complete the negotiations is defined.

The overall objective is to generate for the newcomers a clear view of the wider frame of which the rules are only a part and to help them find their ways in the European texts whose intelligibility is limited. Integrating the *acquis* is a *process* which relies on the adaptation of the candidate countries to the level of progress required by the Member States.[8]

The Commission follows up the questions related to 'the adoption, implementation and respect of the *acquis*', as a global enterprise which requires the mobilisation of governments and administrations, regional and local authorities, firms, and the professional organisations (sectoral and national). 'Screening' has a clear pedagogical dimension mediated by Commission officials: the representatives of the candidate countries come to realise the technical nature of the legal operations as well as the weight of the cultural differences. It led the

Commission to concentrate its efforts on capacity and institution building in Eastern and Central European states so as to allow them to deal with the European rules. These operations led to 'inventing' new tools, like twinning[9] formulated in 1999. The idea is that assistance should not be given only in terms of financial resources but transmitting administrative know-how too.

The technical nature of 'integrating the *acquis communautaire*' has not obscured the wider differences between the two systems. As far as Commission official are concerned, things are clear cut: 'They are far from our standards . . . we cannot say that they are underdeveloped as compared to other countries but they have to adjust on competition and way of life . . . an ocean separates us from them in terms of management culture' (interviews, DG Enlargement, May 1999).

Commission officials develop hegemonic discourses that on the one hand demonstrate a comprehension of the state of affairs in candidate countries while, on the other hand, they impose a common understanding of what the EU really is. The mental images they produce and project reveal significant *actual* differences. For instance, candidate countries are engaged in a two-fold process: state building and joining the EU. This is 'one of their problems' as a Commission official put it. 'Over a hundred years, Central and Eastern European countries never experienced territorial integrity, their notions of nation and national identities are radically different from ours' (interview, DG Enlargement, June 2000). Interestingly, some of the reasons expressed by the candidates for applying for EU membership seem to derive directly from Commission-projected discourse: 'on the EU stage things are predictable'; 'the notion of equal rights is enforced'; 'all the countries share the same rule of law and values of freedom' (interviews, representations of applicant countries, Brussels, June 2000). Although the adoption of EU rules is perceived – both by the Commission and the national representations of the candidate countries – as a very complex and tedious endeavour, these rules remain associated with a positive meaning and they are frequently evoked as the opposite of totalitarian ideology.

The diversity of national systems in Europe, is a political fact that generates a dynamic that the candidate countries use for their own purposes. Different national political cultures evolve on the European stage (Abélès and Bellier, 1996; Bellier and Wilson, 2000), cultural 'facts' are defined by practices and language interferes with the seemingly neutral and technical know-how of the Commission. Analyses made within Eastern and Central European states reveal that they are 'fishing' in the national markets to adopt the models and practices which could best apply to them. The impression that the EU is trying to impose a model certainly exists but the existence of such a model is largely questioned (Muntigl *et al.*, 2000).

It is the method that underpins the process of gradual, step-wise integration – not the political institutions or economic structures, or even the social model, that distinguishes the EU from other models. The Commission contributes to this method by constructing and defending what it calls the 'European interest'. In that context, the legal corpus of the *acquis communautaire* acquires a symbolic weight that reinforces the perception that the European Union differs from a free trade area.

The symbolic weight of the acquis communautaire

Integrating the *acquis* has become a tool in the hands of the Commission in its attempt to re-affirm the symbolic dimension of the Union. Many metaphors used by Commission officials reflect a classification that helps participants to think about the ways the European Union emerges as a wider space for political action. It relates to four spatial categories: 'a space under construction', 'a space for socialisation', 'a space of transition', 'a space of incorporation'. The terms used by administrative and political agents validate the idea that one does not observe a multilateral negotiation but a rite of transformation, through which the countries which had been historically separated from the Member States of the Union will be re-born in the common place.

Several interviewees have pointed out the fact that Eastern and Central European countries have been separated – or 'frozen out': 'in Poland they use the methods we had in Europe fifty years ago . . . the old mentality is always here'. Therefore, their newly found energy must be 'channelled'. As a Commission official put it, 'when they came out of the ice, they embraced extreme capitalism and now they realise the social consequences of deregulation'. With the fall of the Iron Curtain, divergence is progressively suppressed through discursive means used by Commission officials who attempt to maintain and promote coherence in the EU. These officials consider these countries as 'cousins' and this is a treatment within the linguistic register of 'brotherhood' that is not used for other countries. Membership requirements lead to the abolition of existing differences in the context of the EU 'family'. As an official put it, 'the day Poland will apply the whole of the *acquis*, family rules will apply to it, too'. The 'family' metaphor helps to consider that the negotiation for the transposition of the *acquis communautaire* will lead to an ontological change both within the applicant countries and in the Union.

For the Commission, enlarging the Union is not limited to a spatial dimension. Symbolically, it contributes to the mobilisation of these countries that were previously 'paralysed'. The implementation of EU programmes introduces hopes and fears, expectations and competition, rules and emotions. By the same token, the candidate countries which are in the process of forging a new destiny, they are required to absorb a set of far-reaching changes. As two representatives of Hungary and Poland put it 'the *acquis* is a heavy burden that has been imposed from outside and we have to translate it in our system; the large masses of Polish consider the *acquis* has a foreign body which has been tailor-made for the big members; Hungarian negotiators know the rules but on a personal ground some of them consider the process is too heavy (interviews, representations of applicant countries, Brussels, June 2000).

Absorbing the *acquis communautaire* entails the introduction of radical changes in several sectors in the applicant countries.[10] The end of the negotiations signifies the end of the transformation ritual. The applicant countries will be fully animated by the Union considered as a 'person'. By using many metaphors referring to vital parts of the Union such as heart, lung, blood and voice, Commission officials symbolise the construction of the Union and facilitate a process of identity building. Their transformation into full members will signify change of the EU as well and that is a crucial process whose technical aspect is in the hands of the Commission. A vast strategy of communication has been undertaken, which involves the Member States, the applicant countries, a multitude of organisations and partners, in which the Commission is a key stakeholder (Bellier, 1997a).

The Commission as mediator of sense

Transparent communication

The strategy of the Commission reflects demands stemming from the Member States, the candidate countries and, more generally, social groups. This strategy differs markedly from the strategy pursued by the previous Commission. Relying on new technologies, the Prodi Commission improved the EU's external communication policy (Bellier, 2000: 138–9) by publishing directories, official documents, as well as discourses and speeches of the Commissioners. Even reports regarding the candidate countries can be found on the relevant web site. The 'publicness' of these documents is controversial for the applicant countries: the objectivity of the reports, their national impact, their evaluative dimensions within the candidates cohort, are subject to debate. Their representatives frequently express thinly veiled anger and criticise the sources of documentation used by the Commission. The capacities are often criticised of experts upon which the Commission has relied for the preparation of reports which do not reflect the 'real country'. Writing reports and communicating them put under stress the evaluation system and the fact that the circulation of models, values and practices is a one-way process.

Commission officials highlight the divide between 'them' (applicant countries, not yet members of the 'family') and 'us' (part of the Union's family, Member States). They stress the key issue of the formation of a collective identity capable of constituting a group that is able to speak with one voice. That leads them to underline the pedagogical aspect of their work that, as they see it, will eventually render the EU more intelligible in the new countries. They admit that for most of the European citizens too, the EU is a kind of 'terra incognita'. As one interviewee put it, 'the discourse on Europe is monopolised by a small group of people who talk in an unintelligible fashion. In the candidate countries, this includes only a limited number of people such as civil servants, members of parliament and journalists' (PHARE Directorate, Brussels, June 2000). Making the EU intelligible is a central concern, but the whole system of explanation relies on the assumption that the *acquis communautaire* has a teleological dimension.

There are no common rules that can be avoided. Once the applicant country becomes a member, it joins the community of 'equals'.

The role of mediator performed by the officials of DG Enlargement, concerns two kinds of divided 'audiences'. The first such audience is the EU and the Commission. The second 'audience' is 'external' and extremely heterogeneous because it corresponds to the applicant countries. However, it is also limited to a manageable number of interlocutors, because diplomatic and official 'circles' mediate access. The officials of the Commission meet ministers, chief negotiators, local authorities and have no time to catch up with the reality on the ground. Indeed, desk officers are more exposed to that reality than their superiors who typically have a larger number of issues and countries to deal with (Bellier, 1999).

The cultural dimension of communication

Commission officials are active actors in situations that are characterised by the presence of multiple partners, changing configuration, loose and multiple identities attached to individuals, where the rules result from the politics of representation and the activities are defined by scarcity of time. They are frequently involved in situations they do not control even when they chair a meeting. English has become the main language of the process of enlargement, but French and German can also be used in Commission meetings, as can any of the official languages of the EU and those of the applicant countries. In the bureaucratic arena, the use of English creates a superficial impression that communication is flowing when meanings remain construed through other registers.

It is difficult for the Commission to deal with the cultural differences of the candidate countries in conjunction with those of the Member States despite the fact that most of its officials are used to it. As a female Director put it, 'here, in the Commission, we are used to inter-culturality, paying attention to the difficult comprehension of the other within the house . . . We use a mixture of languages, which is understood by ourselves only, and we do have different speaking attitudes and habits. Between us, it is not a problem but complexity of communication increases as contact with outsiders increases, first with the Member States' citizens, then with the citizens of the applicant countries'.

Metaphors and the enlargement strategy

No Commission official masters the incredible amount of information related to enlargement. Few actors have a clear idea of what it means beyond the immediate scope of the sector they deal with. The modalities are so complex and refer to such a limitless number of issues that enlargement seems to be assimilated only through key indicators and global metaphors. Qualitative data regarding social and cultural points are less frequently invoked than hard economic facts.

Most of the images take roots in the western repertoire of science and technology. For instance, 'New Europe' is frequently portrayed as a train. A former head of the Enlargement Task Force and various officials associated with the

PHARE programme often spoke in terms of the 'two rails' the Commission keep together: enlargement and the preparation of the candidate countries. 'My role is to avoid divergences . . . Colleagues from the opposite side concentrate on the other rail to support the development of the candidates (pre-accession partnership, PHARE programmes, etc.) to survey the evolution of the situation in other countries, their reform and institution-building. It is very difficult to balance these aspects and keep the rails together but it is also a necessity' (interview, Task Force, June 1999). Recently, the Commissioner Verheugen (2001) declared that 'The enlargement train has been given the green light and the way ahead is clear . . . It is going to be a high-speed train' (*Enlargement Weekly Newsletter*, 23 January 2001). The image of a dense object set in motion replaces, within the discursive register of enlargement, the discourse on 'Europe-building' where metaphors of architecture and civil engineering were dominant. The fact that a 'train' is composed of identifiable parts that can be differentiated (according to class or facilities) seems to reflect deep changes in the European project.

The image of the 'rails' replaces the foundations of the 'house' (Bellier, 1997a). Two objects are defined by the train and the rails metaphor, depending on the position of the speaker within the organisation. Sometimes the image refers to the corpus of rules whose transposition and implementation is a pre-requisite for accession to the Union. The material dimension thus becomes explicit. The image of a high-speed train reflects the more common sense of accelerating this process. It also refers to the technology required for the modernisation of the applicant countries as well as for guaranteeing the safety and security of both the 'train' (EU) and the passengers (countries). Sometimes the metaphor reflects the Union as a whole. 'Deepening' is associated with *qualitative* improvements in standards of living, methods and procedures, while 'widening' has a *quantitative* dimension typically associated with positive as well as negative meanings, such as the increased number of the Member States, the extension of the four freedoms (movement of goods, labour, services and capital).

The 'train' metaphor modernises the 'heroic times' defined by the 'Founding Fathers' (Schuman, Spinelli, Adenauer, Monnet, Spaak and others). The image also highlights two salient features of the 'New Europe'. First, it keeps moving towards a better destiny, a classical eschatological vision in European thought. Second, the Commission remains the locomotive, what Jean Monnet called '*l'avant garde de l'Europe en train de se faire*' (1976: 551).

The mediation of sense is one source of legitimacy for the Commission which has become the EU's 'intelligence centre'. Desk officers and policy specialists of DG Enlargement possess comprehensive evidence on individual countries. Specialisation by country or policy sector, responsible for the fragmentation of information, is partially compensated by the display of documents on the Commission web site.

Conclusion

For the first time in its history, the EU will integrate ten new Member States. This number, as well as the origin of the new members, represent a real challenge for the EU's capacity to progress. The New Europe will be more than four times bigger than the first European Community, and each country is bringing in the Union its official language, as well as its administrative and political culture. That creates a need to reform the EU's procedures and institutions in an attempt to improve its capacity to make and implement decisions.

The European Union had experienced a series of enlargement and the Commission monitored all negotiations with the newcomers, the United Kingdom, Ireland and Denmark in 1973, Greece in 1981, Portugal and Spain in 1986, Austria, Finland and Sweden in 1995. Negotiating with ten or twelve applicant countries was nothing new for the Commission's officials and, as 'brave soldiers', they followed up the political guidelines made by the extant Member States to include as soon as possible the Eastern and Central members of the European family. What the European negotiators gradually discovered, is reality in these countries. They also had to deal with two major changes of context: one stems from Europe's economic problems; the second corresponds to the progress of world governance and economic globalisation. As a consequence, the incorporation of the Central and Eastern European Countries induced the re-organisation of internal means and procedures. It was thought to affect the internal definition of the European identity, but it also led to a clearer redefinition of geo-strategic positions inherited from the end of the Cold War.

For the Santer and Prodi Commissions (which respectively commenced and concluded the negotiations), the cost of incorporating new members to the Union had to be thought, like in previous enlargements, in terms of budget costs and the re-allocation of funds that led to constant negotiations with the Member States which had to accept some of their sectors to benefit less from the Union. The operation of structural funds had to be carefully reviewed to take account of the newcomers' needs. The cost of the actual enlargement also had to be thought in political terms and a new equilibrium had to be found at the institutional level to allow the Union to survive the expansion in terms of decision making process. Economically, each of the newcomers might be a 'light-weight' but politically, and especially with the will of building a democratic Union, it has the weight of a sovereign State able to discuss its mode of association with others. We could observe, and the media reported on these facts, that the cohesive model initially thought by the founding fathers was no longer the sole representation of the political construct the negotiators of both sides had in mind.

The Community method proved its efficiency. In addition, the twin achievement of building Monetary Union while negotiating the enlargement was remarkable. But, the complexity of the game increased radically with the multiplication of partners, each one bringing in the Union its cultural and linguistic dimensions, as well as its political view of what a Union should be. In that respect, applicant countries are only partially reducible to the categories of 'small and big Member States' that are traditionally used for describing intra-EU discrepancies. Consequently, another set of negotiations had to take place in the European Convention to define a new constitution for the larger Union with the active involvement of representatives of Central and Eastern European countries. In this process, the central position of the European Commission which represents itself as 'the soul and the arm of the Union' became the subject of negotiation.

The European Commission has monitored the process at both the technical and the political levels which respectively entail the mobilisation of its officials for the implementation of the enlargement strategy and the promotion of institutional reform. While extant Member States highlight the efforts for change required on the part of the candidate countries, the latter have, unsurprisingly, focused on the EU's need to allow them to join at the earliest possible moment. The pivotal role of the European Commission is located at the intersection of these two logics. The Commission explains the *acquis communautaire*, defines programmes for building the candidates' capacity to implement EU law, co-ordinates its actions with those undertaken by other international organisations, and mobilises the energy of its officials who, *inter alia*, evaluate the progress made by the applicants and prepare their accession on the basis of 'merit'. The political dimension of enlargement combined with the technical nature of integrating the *acquis communautaire* have generated a series of tasks. Undertaken by the Commission, some of them reveal a new facet of this key organisation which was traditionally seen as the guardian of the Treaties and the source of legislative proposals. It is increasingly confronted with demands to explain the 'Community method' and make the process of integration intelligible to the newcomers as well as citizens of the Member States. It has had to develop new skills regarding information dissemination and communication policies. Until now, the EU did not suffer from the so-called 'democratic deficit' only. Indeed, it suffered from a 'communication deficit', an issue that was addressed by the Commission only recently. Cultural and linguistic diversity have further compounded this problem.

DG Enlargement produced the first comprehensive report on communication strategy for the purposes of the enlargement as late as March 2002. Informing the population remains the principal responsibility of the Member States and candidate countries' authorities, but the Commission's role entails interactions with the private and voluntary sectors in these countries. This is another change regarding the previous enlargements that were more or less all elite-driven. The political impact of joining the Union remains a major concern for the governments of the acceding states whose natural tendency is to consolidate their position in power, whereas the Commission seeks to improve their involvement in the wider process of integration. This endeavour is part of the effort to promote progress towards a 'European knowledge society', for which the Commission produced a white paper as early as 1995. In that respect enlargement entails an attempt to bring 'Brussels' – a term typically used to describe the Commission – closer to the diverse European societies.

Notes

1 This chapter is based on fieldwork conducted in 1999 and 2000 in DG Enlargement and the representations of Bulgaria, Hungary, Poland and the Czech Republic in Brussels as part of a larger study on the emergence of a European culture (Abélès *et al.*, 1993). In addition to interviews with officials, this chapter relies on content analysis of official documents and the discourse of the officials involved in the conduct of negotiations.

2 As a senior Commission official put it, 'we are already thinking about the post-enlargement stage' (interview, Enlargement Task Force, Brussels, February 1999).

3 Recruitment for posts funded by the EU budget is monitored by the Parliament and the large number of temporary posts is the controversial method which undermines the ability of the Commission to increase its staff.

4 These included the human and budget resources of the task force, PHARE (support for economic reconstruction) and other programmes such as ISPA (support for the development of transport and environment infrastructures), SAPARD (support for rural development and agriculture).

5 The categorisation (PECO in French, CEEC in English, the Baltic and the Balkans etc.) is politically interpreted in terms of collective and frequently opposing identities (the Northern and Latin countries, the Catholic and Protestant cultures, the Island and Continental 'attitudes', the small and big countries, etc.).

6 One third of this section was devoted to institution building and twinning.

7 In addition, the Commission has kept for itself the task of taking a position on three issues: the EU financial framework, the reform of the institutions and the success of the negotiations with the candidates who fulfil the criteria. Finally, the appendices present the conclusions of the 'regular reports' which are devoted to the situation of each country.

8 As stated by the European Council in Nice, 'the candidate countries are requested to continue and speed up the necessary reforms to prepare themselves for accession, particularly as regards strengthening their administrative capacity, so as to be able to join the Union as soon as possible' (European Council, 2000b: para. 9).

9 Twinning is an operation linking one or two Member States with one candidate country in an effort to promote changes in a particular sector of activity.

10 As a senior Commission official put it, 'We do have to foresee all the consequences for the family life' (interview, DG Enlargement, February 2000).

PART III

Conclusion

Dionyssis G. Dimitrakopoulos
and Argyris G. Passas

9

Governing without government?

The objective of this chapter is threefold. First, it brings together the main themes of this book and the key lessons highlighted in each contribution by identifying the patterns of change under Prodi. Second, it examines the Commission's proposals on its own future.[1] Finally, it assesses these proposals on the basis of the notion of 'parliamentarisation'. It does so in the light of (a) the views of the 'founding fathers' about the mission of the European Commission and (b) Giandomenico Majone's argument regarding the perils associated with the parliamentarisation of this organisation (Majone, 2002).

In lieu of a conclusion: patterns of change under Prodi

A number of major patterns of change under Prodi emerge from the preceding contributions. First, Peterson's analysis (Chapter 1) highlights a pattern of 'presidentialisation'.[2] Under Prodi, the post of President of the European Commission appears to have moved from being *primus inter pares* to being *primus solus*, albeit a contested one. In turn, this presidentialisaion is mirrored by the enhanced role of the Secretariat-General of the Commission which is highlighted by Kassim (Ch 2 this volume) as one of the main results of the internal reform process. The provisions of the Treaty regarding the appointment of the President of the Commission, the enhanced formal powers of the President and, to a lesser extent, Prodi's personal performance are the three factors that appear to account for the emergence of this pattern. Certainly, as Peterson's analysis demonstrates, Prodi's performance has been inconsistent. However, his activity in the area of institutional reform and, in particular, the way in which the Commission's proposals were prepared and presented has demonstrated at least awareness on his part of the need to lead from the front on big issues. In addition, one can also highlight his bold statements on the Stability and Growth Pact

(*Le Monde*, 18 October 2002). Indeed, although the conservative majority of the European Parliament challenged him to defend his comments, he put on a remarkable performance that eventually found widespread support amongst MEPs (*Le Monde*, 22 October 2002).

Second, Hussein Kassim's analysis demonstrates that individuals, methods and argument matter in the process of administrative reform. Indeed, as he argues, these are the key differences that distinguish this from previous attempts to reform the administration of the Commission. In particular, Kassim demonstrates that 'Kinnock matters' and underlines the Vice-President's entrepreneurial spirit as well as his emphasis on learning from past experience. Despite the inevitable problems generated by every reform effort, Kassim shows that 'the reform has been remarkably successful both in responding to the problems highlighted by the 1999 crisis and in implementing change, even if the extent to which it accomplishes its goals can only finally be judged in the long term' (Kassim, this volume, pp. 33–4).

Third, Cini's analysis reveals the importance of inclusive, as opposed to the elitist, leadership as well as Kinnock's attempt to create a common and consistent culture of impartial public service and a 'fresh organisational ethos' in the administration of the Commission. The difficulties in identifying and promoting an explicit and detailed conception of 'organisational culture' underlined by Cini's analysis may not be surprising. Indeed, as Dimier demonstrates in chapter 4 of this volume, the example of the reform of DG VIII between 1958 and 1975 shows that administrative reform is an expression of political conflict. Therefore, the lack of an explicit notion of organisational culture can be construed as a wise strategy that seeks to avoid the maximisation of opposition.

If the patterns of change in relation to the Commission as an organisation appear to be quite clear, the pattern of change with regard to its 'actorness' is patchy. If the relationship between the Council and the Commission is the core indication of the wider pattern of integration, Kassim and Menon give a range of examples from various policy areas which demonstrate that the status of the Commission in the wider institutional framework has been weakened (both directly and indirectly) throughout the 1990s as a result of a number of initiatives taken by the Member States, especially in the context of successive IGCs. As far as Prodi's tenure is concerned, Kassim and Menon highlight the Lisbon process (and the advent of the open method of co-ordination) whose implementation is 'orchestrated' by the European Council, as an example of the collective assertion of leadership on the part of the Member States. They also highlight the decision reached in Nice to extend the use of co-decision to seven new areas as further illustration of the pattern of 'continuing intergovernmentalisation'. More importantly, they underline Prodi's tactical errors and misjudgements with regard to the substance and the presentation of his proposals to the Convention and the defensive tone of the White Paper on Governance as evidence in support of their view that while operating in an unfavourable environment, 'the Commission has not helped itself' (Kassim and Menon, p. 101 this volume).

These arguments are in stark contrast with Schmidt's analysis which focuses on the institutionalised strategic use on the part of the Commission of what she calls 'the lesser evil strategy' for the liberalisation of previously protected markets. She highlights the examples of alternative telecommunication networks (since mid-1996) and, more recently, energy tax, the taxation of cross-border company pensions and corporate taxes where the Commission currently appears to be using the same strategy.

Cameron and Spence (Ch 7 this volume, p. 123) argue that 'the EU has been most effective in its immediate neighbourhood, where the Commission's role has been crucial' and highlight the examples of assistance to candidate countries of central and eastern Europe and the use of massive financial and technical assistance programmes. In addition, they underline (as does Bellier, ch 8 this volume) the major role of the Commission in the enlargement process. It has provided, they argue, 'the backbone for the negotiating teams as well as the financial and technical resources' (p. 123). As regards the key issue of the operation of the Patten–Solana tandem, Cameron and Spence argue that the reorganisation of the Prodi Commission 'has led to a more coherent Commission approach to CFSP' (p. 128) thereby highlighting the fact that the operation of the tandem is affected by the internal logic and operation of each of its components. Equally important were (a) Patten's successful effort to improve the delivery of EU assistance and (b) the emergence of CFSP as a much sought-after policy area for ambitious Commission staff. This picture is balanced by (a) the establishment of the post of High Representative for CFSP which has given rise to new institutional complications and (b) the need for better co-ordination on issues that concern the external representation of the Union.

The fact that changes under Prodi are more evident in the area of internal reform than in the Commission's 'actorness' is neither paradoxical nor unexpected. Any President has more control over the machinery of the Commission than they do over inter-institutional relations and wider political developments. For example, the President's and the Commissioners' powers of appointment allow them to appoint their 'own people' in key posts and push reforms forward. In addition, internal reform was by definition a much more pressing issue than policy development, even in the area of economic integration (the Commission's power base). Indeed, the reasons why and the way in which Jacques Santer's tenure was brought to an end has rendered reform the top priority for any successor, be they ambitious (like Prodi) or not.

Furthermore, it is the nature of the issue of 'actorness' that does not allow spectacular results to be produced over a short period of time. The area of CFSP provides a good example: the establishment of the post of High Representative for CFSP requires an adjustment on the part of the Commission, which controls powerful policy instruments, such as trade and a part of development aid, as much as it does on the part of the Council (as an organisation), individual

Member States and the first incumbent of the post. The creation of standard operating procedures and routines – in particular those that concern co-ordination and conflict resolution – *within* individual organisations is usually a time-consuming process. When more than one organisations are involved, this process inevitably takes longer and entails a degree of conflict. In this particular example, this process is more cumbersome for the Commission because established procedures tend to endure. Actors infuse rules with values that hinder subsequent change. The longer a rule or standard operating procedure exists, the more embedded it becomes in the values of actors (March, Schulz and Zhou, 2000: 72–3).

Ultimately, though, the influence of the European Commission will depend on (a) its relations with other elements of the Union's institutional framework and (b) its ability to either forge new alliances or revive old ones. This is precisely the objective of the Commission's proposals to the European Convention. The election of the next President of the European Commission by the European Parliament is a radical proposal that seeks to place the Commission-Parliament tandem at the heart of the Union's institutional framework. This is one variant of the 'parliamentarisation thesis' that is then contrasted with Majone's thesis (2002) on the perils inherent in this idea.

The proposals of the European Commission to the Convention: a platform for change?

The proposals of Romano Prodi's Commission to the Convention reflect the presidentialisation (Peterson, Ch 1 this volume) as well as the President's initial decision to keep no portfolio for himself. These proposals are important not only because of their content but also because the Commission used for the first time explicitly the terms 'governmental functions/tasks ' (European Commmission, 2002b: 7–8). This is certainly a risky strategy but also one that reflects Prodi's ambitions for the Commission.

Although scholars working in this area were aware that the Commission's two main powers – setting the legislative agenda and enforcing the rules – 'are the classic powers of a political executive' (Hix, 2002b) the Commission has consistently avoided the overt use of this term possibly because of its 'statist' and politically controversial connotations. The discussion that follows focuses on the proposals that concern the issues of composition, appointment and accountability, powers and operation of the European Commission which are then assessed on the basis of the notion of 'parliamentarisation' which we construe as a welcome trend towards the *explicit* politicisation of the Commission, the European Union and the process of integration as a whole.

Romano Prodi has consistently dismissed the argument that the College is currently too large. Indeed, immediately after his nomination he declared that he was trying to find a way to 'squeeze' the Commission's workload into nineteen portfolios (Prodi, 1999b: 1). In Prodi's opinion, the next College should comprise one national from each Member State, in line with the agreement reached by national governments in Nice (art. 4 of the Protocol on enlargement). Nevertheless, the President should – not unlike a national Prime Minister – have the right to structure the College (in line with the new provision of art. 217 adopted in Nice) around the 'core tasks' of the EU.

Arguably, external relations is one of the areas that would require the active involvement of a number of Commissioners. Indeed, one of the most ambitious proposals of the Commission was the creation of the post of Secretary of the Union[3] which would absorb the functions of (a) the High Representative for CFSP (who is also the Secretary-General of the Council) and (b) the Commissioner in charge of external relations (see Cameron and Spence, ch 7 this volume). The Secretary of the Union would also be a Vice-President of the Commission and would be appointed on the basis of a special procedure.[4] However, this is not the only radical proposal.

Prodi also proposed a new arrangement for the appointment of the President of the Commission which essentially swaps in this respect the roles currently held by the European Parliament and the European Council. According to this proposal the President of the Commission would be elected by the European Parliament and her appointment would require the approval of the European Council. The College as a whole would then need the approval of the European Parliament (European Commission, 2002b: 18). With regard to the Presidency of the Council,[5] Prodi proposed to maintain 'the six-monthly rotation for the Presidency of the European Council and the General Affairs Council' while for the other Council formations 'the Presidency could be exercised by a member of the Council elected by his peers for a period of one year' (European Commission, 2002b: 17).

As regards its legislative role, the Commission has proposed a rather radical simplification of the legislative process which would be combined with the re-assertion of the Commission's exclusive right of initiative that has been undermined throughout the 1990s (see Kassim and Menon, ch 5 this volume). The Commission's proposals also include (a) the generalised use of co-decision and QMV for the adoption of European laws and (b) the formalisation of the c urrent practice whereby the Commission has the right in the context of comitology to amend legal acts adopted by the legislator, for example in the light of technical progress.

Finally, the proposals of the Commission with regard to the executive f unction at the level of the EU are far-reaching. The Commission acknowledges that 'The exercise of the Union's governmental functions is something special' (European Commission, 2002b: 7) and seeks to draw comparisons between national and current EU-level arrangements. It makes essentially three bold proposals. First, the Commission's right of initiative 'must be made a general rule' (European Commission, 2002b: 8) with the exception of action that involves the use of military capabilities. This idea is closely linked to the proposed enhancement of the powers of the Commission in the co-ordination of economic policy. Under its proposals, the Commission must have the right to make proposals (as opposed to recommendations) with regard to the definition of the broad economic policy guidelines and the use of the warning system. These proposals could be amended but only by a unanimous decision of the Council. The second proposal entails the complete concentration to the Commission of the powers for the implementation of the rules laid down by the Council (art. 202 of the Treaty). This implies the elimination of the current exception that allows the Council to exercise these powers *directly* but obliges it, as a rule, to confer them to the Commission.[6] The third major proposal concerns the powers of the Secretary of the Union. After the end of a hitherto unspecified transitional period, the Secretary would autonomously exercise the Commission's right of initiative in terms of the CFSP. The Secretary would do so on the basis of arrangements decided upon (by enhanced majority) by the Council acting on a Commission proposal. In addition, the Secretary would represent the Union *vis-à-vis* third parties with regard to foreign policy issues and would also be responsible for implementing common decisions. This proposal is directly linked to the proposed extension of the arrangements that are currently used in the area of trade to the external aspects common policies[7] – including economic and financial issues (European Commission, 2002b: 12). The President of the Commission and the Secretary would ensure consistency between the two facets of the Union's foreign policy.

These proposals are ambitious and they constitute, to a large extent, another expression of Prodi's attempt to revitalise the European Commission and to place it back at the heart of the process of integration. More importantly, the first proposal (i.e. the election of the President of the Commission by the European Parliament) is an explicit attempt to implement Prodi's strategic decision to revive the Commission–EP tandem.[8] The next, and final, section of this chapter focuses on this crucial relationship and discusses the Commission's proposals to the Convention on the basis of the debate between the supporters of the 'parliamentarisation thesis' and its rival.

It does so for two reasons. First, this relationship has become, especially after the Single European Act and in particular in the 1990s, one of the defining characteristics of the Union because it has moved the EU closer than ever before to the model of a polity. Second, although the European Parliament has been a strategic ally of the Commission – especially under Jacques Delors – its activism was at the heart (along with other factors) of the downfall of Santer's Commission. This has had a major negative impact on the organisation that was previously seen as the 'motor' of integration (Barnier, 2000: 2). It is therefore submitted that if the European Commission is to be revived and if it is to regain its major role in integration, a more balanced relationship with the European Parliament has to be sought.

The 'parliamentarisation thesis' and its rival

The issue of democratic legitimacy of the High Authority, the Commission's forerunner, was a significant part of the founding fathers' thinking about the future development of the three Communities (see Monnet, 1976: 430, 446; Featherstone, 1994). Although the Schuman Declaration of 9 May 1950 did not contain a direct reference to a parliamentary body and highlighted clearly the independence of the High Authority, which was to be secured through the selection of 'independent personalities' (Schuman, 1950), this was not an indication of indifference *vis-à-vis* the explicit *politicisation* of that organisation. Rather, it probably reflected a strategy that was meant to promote the institutionalisation of the High Authority and the promotion of integration in the crucial initial stage of the 1950s, prior to the introduction of more explicitly political elements in the emerging institutional framework of the Communities (Monnet, 1976: 448).

The institutionalisation of the common framework and the significant progress made in the area of economic integration have highlighted the need for a more explicit politicisation of the largely elitist process of integration.[9] Competition for executive office is at the heart of accountable government in modern democracies. Since 1996 and the Treaty of Amsterdam, the issue has focused more specifically on the Commission–Parliament tandem. One cardinal argument that supports the 'parliamentarisation thesis' links closely the appointment and the operation of Commission with the European elections and, consequently, the European Parliament. Although many alternative scenarios[10] can be envisaged, the central component of this thesis is couched in the need to link *explicitly* and *directly* the election of Commissioners (or, as a first step, their President), on the one hand, and MEPs, on the other, in a manner that reflects the parliamentary model of 'domestic' government.

This arrangement would add clarity to an otherwise highly complex system. In simple terms, supporters of each political grouping or 'family' would more or less know the type of EU policies they are voting for *as well as* the political personnel who would put them into *effect*. In that sense, the choice of party could facilitate the emergence of the voters' preferred candidate for the presidency of the Commission or at least an EU-level policy programme which would then be put into effect if it were supported by an electoral majority reflected in the composition of the European Parliament.[11] This development would transform the European Commission. The European Commission would be expected explicitly to act along ideological lines. The adoption of this model would, it is argued (see Martin, 1990: 26) allow European elections to have 'immediate repercussions on the composition of the executive branch', similar to national elections. This is why this link could increase voter turnout in European elections.

Although there is no doubt that the formal powers of the European Parliament have increased remarkably, at least[12] since the Single European Act, voter turnout in European elections has decreased considerably.[13] Therefore, if the history of constant increases in the formal powers of the European Parliament has failed in the last two decades to lead to growing interest and involvement on the part of European citizens, linking directly the election of MEPs with that of the members of the European Commission may not change the situation. However, this is neither the only nor the most important criticism used against the 'parliamentarisation thesis' and, more specifically, its partisan variant.

Giandomenico Majone (1996a; 1996b; 2002) has consistently highlighted what he calls the 'perils of parliamentarisation'. He argues that in addition to the problem of *expertise* which traditionally supports the idea of delegation of significant powers to non-majoritarian institutions[14] whose officials have the required knowledge to deal with a regulatory problem, democracies face the problems of temporal *consistency* and *credibility* of their regulative policies. In light of the fact that politicians compete for votes, the consistency of regulative policies can be undermined by the electoral cycle because politicians are tempted either to introduce popular policy changes or, indeed, to avoid making necessary but unpopular changes. This, in turn, undermines the capacity of economic operators to plan their behaviour. The problem of credibility is more acute in international regulatory agreements. The credibility of these agreements relies on their enforcement by an independent third party that ensures that defection does not occur or, if it does, it is both detected and punished.

Thus, drawing on the experience of the US fourth branch of government (i.e. the regulatory commissions, agencies, boards etc. that combine functions of the three traditional branches in the area of regulation), Majone argues (2002: 385) that democracies need non-majoritarian institutions because they ensure 'consistency, fairness and expertise in regulatory policy-making'. As regards their legitimacy, these agencies are created, funded and limited by law. Thus, their independence does not mean that their decisions are made in a political vacuum. Finally, a process of judicialisation has added a court-like feature to the operation of these agencies and their use of discretion (Majone, 1996a: 12–13). In short, these agencies are both legitimate and capable of making and implementing regulative policies in a manner that can avoid the negative consequences of the electoral cycle. This is why they are particularly well suited to the problems of European regulation, which is plagued by heavy emphasis on law-making and weak enforcement (Majone, 2002: 386–7) and may have a suffocating effect on the Commission (Mény, 1999).

However, Majone has extended (2002) this logic to the European Commission by arguing that the Commission should become a part of a network of authorities that implement EU regulative policies but must keep for itself the role of the designer and co-ordinator of sectoral regulatory networks (Majone, 2002: 388). Clearly, in this scenario, there is no room for the more pronounced parliamentarisation of the European Commission.[15] The explicit parliamentarisation of the Commission through the establishment of the link between the election of MEPs and the President of the Commission (at least) is not compatible with the logic that permeates the agencies. In that scenario the President of the Commission would be expected to act in a manner that reflects the wishes of the parliamentary majority. Since both the Commission and the MEPs who would support it would be willing to be re-elected, they would be led precisely to the kind of electoral motivation that the fourth branch of government is meant to avoid.

This is why Majone explicitly calls for a return to basics on the part of the European Commission and identifies its contribution to the proper functioning and development of the *common market*[16] – by means of its powers to propose legislation, guard the Treaty and execute policy – as the Commission's 'core business' (2002: 390). This notion is, no doubt, supported – either explicitly or implicitly – by some national governments. To what extent, though, do these ideas differ from the aforementioned proposals of Romano Prodi's Commission to the Convention on the future of the EU?

Despite its merits, Majone's argument is unable, unlike Prodi's ideas, to capture the complex *political* reality in which the Commission must operate. The role of the Commission was and remains eminently political – not least because most Commissioners are career politicians (Hix, 2002b). Their daily tasks entail making – either explicitly or implicitly – choices amongst competing interests and values. Even if one assumes that the role of the Commission is merely that of a regulator, that role too has re-distributive effects. This is precisely why the Commission has to be politicised in an *explicit* manner. Indeed, in addition to being an 'arbiter' between state interests, the action of the Commission affects specific sections of society (and the electorate). Therefore, it is hard to see why the formal input of the electorate to the EU political process should not include a more pronounced role in the election of the President of the Commission.

The impact of the dual source of legitimacy of the EU is more evident in Prodi's proposal for the election of the next Commission President by the European Parliament. The aims of this proposal were twofold. On the one hand, it aimed to re-balance the roles of the Member States and the peoples in favour of the latter in regard to the election of the President of the Commission. On the other hand, in doing so this proposal sought to couch the Commission in the popular will as reflected by the majority of MEPs. Nevertheless, the requirement of a large majority (two-thirds of the votes cast) was wisely designed to avoid the perils of 'partisanisation' without obscuring the political element of this process.

Prodi's proposal was balanced in another sense too. It reflected both the original idea of the Commission as an 'independent' actor that would promote the 'general interest' as well as the more overtly political role that the Commission has assumed over time, especially under the inspired leadership of Walter Hallstein and Jacques Delors. The enhanced legitimacy of the President was meant, under Prodi's proposals, to be mirrored by his involvement in the appointment and the definition of the role of the Secretary of the Union who will play a prominent – though not exclusive – role in foreign policy. This is precisely the type of activity that cannot be captured by the emphasis on the mere regulatory part of the role of the Commission. The President of the Commission is a member of the European Council which is responsible for the definition of the general political guidelines of the Union (art. 4 of the Treaty). In addition, the Commission negotiates on behalf of the Union on the vast majority of trade issues, thereby contributing to the formulation as well as the implementation of the EU's foreign economic policy. Furthermore, it is a major actor in the area of development aid. These are eminently political tasks typically associated with executive, i.e. governmental, power.

Certainly, regulation *is* an essential part of the institutional role of the Commission[17] but it is neither the only, nor the most significant, one. This is why couching the selection of its key officeholders in the logic of the 'fourth branch of government' would be a mistake. Nevertheless, Prodi's proposal relies to a large extent on terminology that appeals to supporters of the fourth branch of government. The extensive use of the term 'general European interest' (European Commission, 2002b: *passim*) reflects Prodi's 'centrism' as well as an attempt to appease government *élites* that could be alienated by the idea of an overtly partisan European Commission President. This is why he chose to highlight the need for the Commission to remain an 'independent institution working for equal treatment between the Member States and embodying the principles of coherence, synthesis and concern for the general interest' as intended by the founding fathers of Europe (European Commission, 2002b: 4; see also Barnier, 2000: 8).

Prodi's proposal is certainly not perfect. Simon Hix (2002b) highlights two important weaknesses. First, the majority in the European Parliament does not reflect the opinion of voters on the EU because European elections are second-order electoral contests. Second, the fusion of legislative and executive majorities would turn the European Parliament into a rubber stamp for the Commission's policy programme. This is why Hix (2002b) advocates the direct election of the President of the Commission (see also Tabellini and Wyplosz, 2003). This proposal has its own weaknesses. For example, this election too could become a contest fought along *national* lines, probably expressed on the basis of the nationality of the candidates. However, both Hix's and Prodi's proposals share a key component: the explicit politicisation of the European Commission.

Certainly, Prodi's proposals can be analysed from three perspectives: (a) the perspective of the strategy that it reflects (i.e. the attempt to transform the Commission into a European government); (b) the perspective of the tactics employed where Prodi appears to have submitted a maximalist proposal without taking into account key elements of the current political conjuncture and the Commission's comparative advantage (e.g. in the area of implementation of EU rules and decisions) and (c) Prodi's capacity to mobilise the Commission as a collective body (see Peterson, ch 1 this volume).

This debate is ongoing and reflects the fact that the European Commission and the EU as a whole are at a significant point in their development. This book has sought to capture the difficult reality of Romano Prodi's Commission and to put it in its context. There is no doubt that the end of the intergovernmental conference will provide an opportunity for further research on this fascinating organisation.

Notes

1 That section of the chapter focuses on the proposals that the Commission adopted through its communications of May and December 2002 (European Commission 2002a; 2002b; Commission Européenne 2002).

2 A senior Commission official was quoted in *Le Monde* (3 June 2002) as having said that 'Prodi fait la politique, les autres travaillent sur leurs dossiers en faisant ce qu'ils veulent'.

3 There was consensus in the Convention on the creation of the post of the European Union Foreign Minister.

4 The Secretary would be nominated by common agreement of the European Council and the President designate of the Commission and would then be appointed subject to the approval of the European Parliament like the other members of the Commission.

5 The issue of the presidency exemplifies the question of 'political leadership' in the EU which was a major issue on the agenda of the Convention.

6 This arrangement was introduced by the Single European Act and was combined with the formalisation of comitology. With regard to the latter, the Commission has proposed the generalised use of advisory committees and, implicitly, the abolition of management and regulatory committees (European Commission, 2002b: 13). There was consensus amongst the members of the Convention – including representatives of national governments – on the need to 'simplify' comitology.

7 Defence and issues requiring military capacity would be excluded from this arrangement.

8 Another example of this strategy is the Commission's proposal of December 2002 regarding the reform of comitology in a sense that would be appealing to the European Parliament (interview with official of the European Commission's Legal Service, 13 May 2003).

9 The notion of politicisation implicitly refers to the question of legitimacy and its various forms. On this issue see Lord and Magnette (2002).

10 For example, they entail the selection of either the President or all Commissioners from amongst MEPs.

11 A general consensus emerged for the same reasons in the Convention on the election of the President of the Commission by the European Parliament on a European Council's proposal, the later deciding by QMV. This idea reflects the dual source of legitimacy of the EU.

12 Indeed, the European Parliament became a part of the Communities' budgetary authority in the early 1970s.

13 Turnout across the EU has dropped from 63 per cent in 1979 to 49.4 per cent in 1999 (UK Office of the European Parliament, 2003).

14 Majone (2002: 385) defines them as 'institutions that, by design, are not directly accountable to the voters or to their elected representatives'.

15 Majone (2002: 389) argues that Romano Prodi's decision to attempt to turn the Commission into a European government was 'probbly a strategic mistake'.

16 Majone's proposal also implies a very specific and limited (and – from the perspective of the EU as a whole – *limiting*) kind of future for the Commission.

17 This is why, in the light also of its increased workload, it must become both the designer and the co-ordinator of regulatory networks.

References

Abélès, M. and Bellier, I. (1996), 'La Commission Européenne: du compromis culturel à la culture politique du compromis', *Revue Française de Science Politique*, 46:3, 431–55.

_____, _____ and McDonald, M. (1993), *An Anthropological Approach to the European Commission*, unpublished report, December.

Ackerman, B. (1991), *We the People: Foundations*, Cambridge, MA, Harvard University Press.

Allaire, Y. and Firsirotu, M. E. (1984), 'Theories of Organizational Culture', *Organization Studies*, 5, 193–226.

Allen, D. (1998), 'Who Speaks for Europe? The Search for an Effective and Coherent External Policy', in J. Peterson and H. Sjursen (eds), *A Common Foreign Policy for Europe? Competing Visions of the CFSP*, London, Routledge.

Allison, G. T. (1971), *Essence of Decision: Explaining the Cuban Missile Crisis*, Boston, MA, Little, Brown.

Alter, K. J. (1996), 'The European Court's Political Power', *West European Politics*, 19:3, 459–87.

_____ (1998), 'Who are the "Masters of the Treaty"? European Governments and the European Court of Justice', *International Organization*, 52:1, 121–47.

_____ and Meunier-Aitsahalia, S. (1994), 'Judicial Politics in the European Community: European Integration and the Pathbreaking *Cassis de Dijon* Decision', *Comparative Political Studies*, 26:4, 535–61.

Aptel, C. (1995), *La Politique d'Aide Humanitaire de l'Union Européenne*, Working Paper 13, Bruges, Collège de Bruges.

Argyris, C. and Schön, D. A. (1978), *Organizational Learning*, Reading, MA, Addison Wesley.

Argyris, N. (1989), 'The EEC Rules of Competition and the Air Transport Sector', *Common Market Law Review*, 26:5, 3–32.

Babarinde, O. (1995), 'The Lomé Convention: An Ageing Dinosaur in the European Union's Policy Enterprise?', in C. Rhodes and S. Mazey (eds), *The State of the European Union, Vol 3: Building a European Polity?*, Harlow, Longman.

Bachrach, P. and Baratz, M. (1962), 'The Two Faces of Power', *American Political Science Review*, 56:4, 947–52.

_____ and _____ (1963), 'Decisions and Nondecisions: An Analytical Framework', *American Political Science Review*, 57:3, 632–42.

Banks, M. (2002), 'Jury Still Out on Prodi at Half-term', *European Voice*, 27 June–3 July, 3.

Barnier, M. (2000), *Pour l'Europe, deux temps et trois chemins*, note personnelle sur l'avenir de l'UE et la réforme des institutions, 8 May, www.europa.eu.int/comm/commissioners/barnier/speecig_fr.htm (accessed 3 March 2003).

Basedow, J. and Dolfen, M. (1998), 'Verkehrs- und Transportrecht', in M. A. Dauses (ed.), *Handbuch des EU-Wirtschaftsrechts*, München, Beck.

Behrens, P. (1992), 'Die Konvergenz der wirtschaftlichen Freiheiten im europäischen Gemeinschaftsrecht', *Europarecht*, 27, 2, 145–62.

Bellier, I. (1995), 'Une culture de la Commission Européenne? De la rencontre des cultures et du multilinguisme des fonctionnaires', in Y. Mény, P. Muller and J.-L. Quermonne (eds), *Politiques Publiques en Europe*, Paris, L'Harmattan.

_____ (1997a), 'The Commission as an Actor', in H. Wallace and A. Young (eds), *Participation and Policy Making in the European Union*, Oxford, Clarendon Press.

_____ (1997b), 'De la Communauté à l'Union Européenne', *Socio-Anthropologie* 2, 61–78.

_____ (1999), 'Le lieu du politique, l'usage du technocrate: hybridation à la Commission Européenne', in V. Dubois and D. Dulong (eds), *La Question Technocratique*, Strasbourg, PUS.

_____ (2000), 'A Europeanized Elite? An Anthropology of European Commission Officials', *Yearbook of European Studies*, 14, 135–56.

_____ and Wilson, T. (2000), 'Introduction', in I. Bellier and T. Wilson (eds), *An Anthropology of the European Union*, Oxford, Berg.

Berlin, D. (1992), 'Interactions between the Lawmaker and the Judiciary within the EC', *Legal Issues of European Integration*, 17, 17–48.

Bezes, P. (2002), *Gouverner l'administration: une sociologie des politiques de la réforme administrative en France (1962–1997)*, Doctorat de science politique, Institut d'Etudes Politiques, Paris.

Black, I. (2002), 'Kinnock and Patten Object to EU Foreign Policy Plan', *The Guardian*, www.guardian.co.uk/eu/story/0,7369,725077,html (accessed 31 May 2002).

Bossuyt, J., Laporte, G., Simon, A., Corre, G. and Lehtinen, T. (2000), *Assessing Trends in EC Development Policy*, Discussion Paper, Maastricht, European Centre for the Management of Development Policy.

Brown, A. (1995), *Organisational Culture*, London, Financial Times/Pitman.

Brunsson, N. and Olsen, J. (1993), *The Reforming Organisation*, London, Routledge.

Bulmer, S. (1994), 'Institutions and Policy Change in the European Communities: The Case of Merger Control', *Public Administration*, 72:3, 423–44.

Burley, A.-M. and Mattli, W. (1993), 'Europe Before the Court: A Political Theory of Legal Integration', *International Organization*, 47:1, 41–76.

Button, K. J. (1984), *Road Haulage Licensing and EC Transport Policy*, Aldershot, Ashgate.

Calori, R. (1995), Book Review of 'Cultural Perspectives on Organisations by M. Alvesson', *Organization Studies*, 15, 535–8.

Cameron, F. (1999), *The Foreign and Security Policy of the European Union: Past, Present and Future*, Sheffield, Sheffield Academic Press.

Castle, S. (2002), 'Prodi Team Warms up for the Second Half', *E!Sharp*, June, 10–4.

CEC (1986), *XVth Competition Report*, Brussels, Commission of the European Communities.

_____ (1987), *XVIth Competition Report*, Brussels, Commission of the European Communities.

_____ (1988), *XVIIth Competition Report*, Brussels, Commission of the European Communities.

Christiansen, T. (1996), 'A Maturing Bureaucracy: The Role of the Commission in the Policy Process', in J. Richardson (ed.) *European Union: Power and Policy-Making*, London, Routledge.

_____ (2001a), 'The European Commission: Administration in Turbulent Times', in J. Richardson (ed.) *European Union: Power and Policy-Making*, 2nd edn, London, Routledge.

_____ (2001b), 'Intra-institutional Politics and Inter-institutional Relations in the EU: Towards Coherent Governance?', *Journal of European Public Policy* 8:5, 747–69.

_____ (2002), 'The Role of Supranational Actors in EU Treaty Reform', *Journal of European Public Policy*, 9:1, 33–53.

Cini, M. (1996), *The European Commission: Leadership, Organisation and Culture in the EU Administration*, Manchester, Manchester University Press.

_____ (2000a), 'Administrative Culture in the European Commission: The Cases of Competition and Environment', in N. Nugent (ed.) *At the Heart of Europe: Studies of the European Commission*, 2nd edn., Basingstoke, Palgrave.

_____ (2000b), *Organizational Culture and Reform: the Case of the European Commission under Jacques Santer*, Working Paper RSC No. 2000/25, Florence, Robert Schuman Centre.

_____ (2002), 'Understanding European Union Institutions' in A. Wanleigh (ed.), *Understanding European Union Institutions*, London and New York, Routledge.

Cobb, R. and Elder, C. (1971), 'The Politics of Agenda-Building: An Alternative Perspective for Modern Democratic Theory', *Journal of Politics*, 33:4, 892–915.

Coleman, W. and Tangermann, T. (1999), 'The 1992 CAP Reform, the Uruguay Round and the Commission: Conceptualizing Linked Policy Games', *Journal of Common Market Studies*, 37:3, 385–405.

Commission des Communautés Européennes (1974), 'L'aide au développement, fresque de l'action communautaire', *Bulletin des Communautés Européennes*, 8.

_____ (1996), *Livre vert sur les relations entre l'Union Européenne et les pays ACP à l'aube du 21e siècle*, 20 novembre.

_____ (2000a), *Livre blanc: réforme de la Commission (partie 2, plan d'action)*, COM (2000) 200, http://europa.eu.int/comm/off/white/reform/indcx_fr.htm (accessed 12 February 2003).

_____ (2000b), *Communication sur la réforme de la gestion de l'aide extérieure*, 16 May, http://europa.eu.int/comm/external_relations/reform/intro/ (accessed 12 February 2003).

Commission of the European Communities (1997), *Agenda 2000 – Vol. I: For a Stronger and Wider Union*, COM (97)2000 final.

_____ (1999a), *For a European Political and Administrative Culture: Three Codes of Conduct*, March.

_____ (1999b), *Administrative Reform of the European Commission: Policy Issues*, 20 October, http://europa.eu.ing/comm/reform/administration/policy_issues_en.pdf (accessed 20 November 1999).

_____ (2000a), *Reforming the Commission*, Consultative Document, CG3 (2000) 1/17, 18 January.

_____ (2000b), *Reforming the Commission. A White Paper*, COM (2000) 200 final.

_____ (2003) *Commission Reform: 87 of 98 measures have been approved and implementation shows first benefits of Reform*, press release IP/03/133, 29 January, Brussels, European Commission.

Commission Européenne (2002), *Etude de faisabilité. Contribution à l'avant-projet de constitution de l'Union Européenne*, Brussels.

Commission/Inspectorate General (1999), *Designing Tomorrow's Commission. A Review of the Commission's Organisation and Operation*, Brussels, 7 July.

Committee of Independent Experts (1999a), *First Report on Allegations regarding Fraud, Mismanagement and Nepotism in the European Commission*, 15 March, www.europarl. eu.int/experts/report1_en.htm (accessed 12 February 2003).

_____ (1999b), *Second Report on the Reform of the Commission*, 10 September, www.europarl.eu.int/experts/default_en.htm (accessed 12 February 2003).

Coombes, D. (1970), *Politics and Bureaucracy in the European Community*, London, Allen & Unwin.

Council of Ministers (1988), Regulation (EEC) No 1841/88 of 21 June 1988 amending Regulation (EEC) No 3164/76 on the Community quota for the carriage of goods by road between Member States, *Official Journal of the European Communities*, L 163, 30 June.

Cowhey, P. F. (1990), 'Telecommunications', in G. Hufbauer (ed.), *Europe 1992: An American Perspective*, Washington, DC, The Brookings Institution.

Cox, T. (1994), *Cultural Diversity in Organizations: Theory, Research and Practice*, San Francisco, CA, Berrett-Koehler.

Cram, L. (1993), 'Calling the Tune Without Paying the Piper? Social Policy Regulation: The Role of the Commission in European Community Social Policy', *Politics and Policy*, 21:2, 135–46.

_____ (1994), 'The European Commission as a Multi-organization: Social Policy and IT Policy in the EU', *Journal of European Public Policy*, 1:2, 195–217.

_____ (1999), 'The Commission' in L. Cram, D. Dinan and N. Nugent (eds), *Developments in the European Union*, Basingstoke, Macmillan, 44–61.

_____ (2001), 'Whither the Commission? Reform, Renewal and the Issue-Attention Cycle', *Journal of European Public Policy*, 8:5, 770–86.

Crozier, M. (1963), *Le Phénomène Bureaucratique*, Paris, Seuil.

Cullen, P. and Yannopoulos, G. N. (1989), 'The Redistribution of Regulatory Powers Between Governments and International Organisations: The Case of European Airline Deregulation', *European Journal of Political Research*, 17:2, 155–68.

de Schoutheete, P. (2002), 'The European Council', in J. Peterson and M. Shackleton (eds), *The Institutions of the European Union*, Oxford, Oxford University Press.

DECODE report (1999), *Designing Tomorrow's Commission*, July 1999.

Dehaene, J.-L., von Weizsäcker, R. and Simon, D. (1999), *The Institutional Implications of Englargement: A Report to the European Commission*, 18 October, Brussels.

Den Boer, M. and Wallace, W. (2000), 'Justice and Home Affairs', in H. Wallace and W. Wallace (eds), *Policy-Making in the European Union*, 4th edn, Oxford, Oxford University Press.

Devuyst, Y. (1999), 'The Community-Method after Amsterdam', *Journal of Common Market Studies*, 37:1, 109–20.

_____ (2002), *The European Union at the Crossroads: An Introduction to the EU's Institutional Evolution* (Brussels: P.I.E. – Peter Lang).

Dimier, V. (2001a), 'Du bon usage de la tournée', *Pôle Sud*, 15:19–32.

_____ (2001b), 'Leadership et institutionalisation au sein de la Commission Européenne', *Sciences de la Société*, 53:183–99.

Dimitrakopoulos, D. G. (2001), 'Unintended Consequences: Institutional Autonomy and Executive Discretion in the European Union', *Journal of Public Policy*, 21:2, 107–31.

_____ (2003), 'Power, Norms, and Institutional Change in the European Union: The Protection of the Free Movement of Goods', *European Journal of Political Research*,

42:2, 163–84.

Dinan, D. (1999), *Ever Closer Union. An Introduction to European Integration*, 2nd edn, Basingstoke, Palgrave.

Doleys, T. J. (2000), 'Member states and the European Commission: Theoretical Insights from the New Economics of Organization', *Journal of European Public Policy*, 7:4, 532–53.

Dombey, D. (2002), 'Brussels Dreams of Becoming a Real Executive', *Financial Times*, 6 December.

Donnelly, M. and Ritchie, E. (1997), 'The College of Commissioners and their Cabinets', in G. Edwards and D. Spence (ed.), *The European Commission*, London, Cartermill.

Drake, H. (2000), *Jacques Delors: Perspectives on a European Leader*, London, Routledge.

Dryzek, J. (1996), 'The Informal Logic of Institutional Design', in R. Goodin (ed.), *Theory of Institutional Design*, Cambridge, Cambridge University Press.

Duhamel, O. (1999), 'Prodi, le printemps de la démocratie européenne', *Le Monde*, 29 March.

Dyer, W. G. (1986), *Cultural Change in Family Firms: Anticipating and Managing Business and Family Transitions*, San Francisco, CA, Jossey Bass.

ECJ (1997a), Judgment of 23 October 1997, Commission / The Netherlands, Case C–157/94, *European Court Reports*, I–5699.

_____ (1997b), Judgment of 23 October 1997, Commission / Italy, Case C–157/94, *European Court Reports*, I-5789.

_____ (1997c), Judgment of 23 October 1997, Commission / France, *European Court Reports*, I-5815.

_____ (1997d), Judgment of 23 October 1997, Commission / Spain, *European Court Reports*, I-5851.

Edwards, G. and Spence, D. (1994), *The European Commission*, Harlow, Longman.

Eichener, V. (1996), 'Die Rückwirkungen der europäischen Integration auf nationale Politikmuster', in M. Jachtenfuchs and B. Kohler-Koch (eds), *Europäische Integration*, Opladen, Leske und Budrich.

Eising, R. (2002), 'Policy Learning in Embedded Negotiations: Explaining EU Electricity Liberalization', *International Organization*, 56:1, 85–120.

Endo, K. (1999), *The Presidency of the European Commission under Jacques Delors: The Politics of Shared Leadership*, Basingstoke, Macmillan.

European Commission (2000), *Strategy Paper: Regular Reports from the Commission on Progress towards Accession*, 8 November, www.europa.eu.int/comm/enlargement.

_____ (2001a), *European Governance: A White Paper*, COM (2001) 428 final, 25 July, www.europa.eu.int/comm/governance/index_en.htm.

_____ (2001b), *The Elimination of Tax Obstacles to the Cross-Border Provision of Occupational Pensions*, COM (2001) 214 final, 19 April.

_____ (2002a), *Communication from the Commission: a Project for the European Union*, COM (2002) 247 final, 22 May, Brussels, European Commission.

_____ (2002b), *Peace, Freedom, Solidarity: Communication of the Commission on the Institutional Architecture*, COM (2002) 728 final, 4 December, Brussels, European Commission.

_____ (2003a), Final negative state aid decisions on special tax schemes in Belgium, the Netherlands and Ireland, Commission press release IP/03/242, 18 February, Brussels, European Commission.

_____ (2003b), Pension taxation: Commission tackles discrimination against foreign pension funds in six Member States, Commission press release IP/03/179, 5 February,

Brussels, European Commission.

_____ (2003c), *Reform of the Staff Regulations. Explanatory Fiches on the Package Agreed on 19th May*, Brussels, European Commission.

European Council (1999a), *Presidency Conclusions*, Cologne European Council, 3 and 4 June, http://ue.eu.int/en/info/eurocouncil/index.htm (accessed 14 February 2003).

_____ (1999b), *Presidency Conclusions*, Helsinki European Council, 10 and 11 December 1999, General Secretariat of the Council.

_____ (2000a), *Presidency Conclusions*, Lisbon European Council, 23 and 24 March 2000, Brussels, General Secretariat of the Council.

_____ (2000b), *Presidency Conclusions*, Nice European Council, 8 December 2000, Brussels, General Secretariat of the Council.

European Court of Auditors (1998), *Annual Report*, Office for Official Publications of the European Communities.

_____ (1998), *Annual Report*, Office for Official Publications of the European Communities.

European Parliament, Committee on Budgetary Control (1999), *Questions for the Hearing with Nominee Commissioner Neil Kinnock*, 30 August 1999–September 1999.

Everling, U. (1984), 'The Member States of the European Community before their Court of Justice', *European Law Review*, 5, 215–41.

Falkner, G. (2002), 'How Intergovernmental are Intergovernmental Conferences? An Example from the Maastricht Treaty Reform', *Journal of European Public Policy*, 9:1, 98–119.

_____ and Nentwich, M. (2000), 'The Amsterdam Treaty: The Blueprint for the Future Institutional Balance', in K. Neunreither and A. Wiener (eds), *European Integration After Amsterdam*, Oxford, Oxford University Press.

Featherstone, K. (1994), 'Jean Monnet and the "Democratic Deficit" in the European Union', *Journal of Common Market Studies*, 32:2, 149–70.

Fenwick, H. and Hervey, T. (1995), 'Sex Equality in the Single Market: New Directions for the European Court of Justice', *Common Market Law Review*, 32, 443–70.

Fischer, J. (2000), 'From Confederacy to Federation – Thoughts on the Finality of European Integration', in M. Leonard (ed.), *The Future Shape of Europe*, London, The Foreign Policy Centre and BSMG Worldwide.

Forster, A. and Wallace, W. (2000), 'Common Foreign and Security Policy', in H. Wallace and W. Wallace (eds), *Policy-Making in the European Union*, 4th edn, Oxford, Oxford University Press.

Franchino, F. (2000a), 'Control of the Commission's Executive Functions: Uncertainty, Conflict and Decision Rules', *European Union Politics*, 1:1, 63–92.

_____ (2000b), 'The Commission's Executive Discretion, Information and Comitology', *Journal of Theoretical Politics*, 12:2, 155–81.

Gagliardi, P. (1986), 'The Creation and Change of Organizational Cultures: A Conceptual Framework', *Organization Studies*, 7:2, 117–34.

Garrett, G. (1995) 'The Politics of Legal Integration in the European Union', *International Organization*, 49:1, 171–81.

_____ and Tsebelis, G. (1996), 'An Institutional Critique of Intergovernmentalism', *International Organization*, 50:2, 269–99.

Garrett, G., Kelemen, D. and Schulz, H. (1998), 'The European Court of Justice, National Governments, and Legal Integration in the European Union', *International Organization* 52:1, 149–76.

Garton Ash, T. (2001), 'The European Orchestra', *New York Review of Books*, 17 May.

Geertz, C. (1973), *The Interpretation of Cultures*, New York, Basic Books.

Genschel, P. (2000), 'Die Grenzen der Problemlösungsfähigkeit der EU', in E. Grande and M. Jachtenfuchs (eds), *Die Problemlösungsfähigkeit der EU*, Baden-Baden, Nomos.

――― (2002), *Steuerharmonisierung und Steuerwettbewerb in der Europäischen Union*, Frankfurt/Main, Campus.

Georgakakis, D. (2001), 'La Démission de la Commission Européenne: scandale et tournant institutionnel (octobre 1998–mars 1999)', *Cultures et Conflits*, 38–9: 39–71.

GRASPE (2001), *Cahiers du Groupe de Réflexion sur l'Avenir du Service Public Européen*, janvier 2001.

Green Cowles, M. (1995), 'Setting the Agenda for a New Europe: The ERT and EC 1992', *Journal of Common Market Studies*, 33:4, 501–26.

Gronemeyer, N. (1994), 'Die Entwicklung des EU-Kabotage-Rechts bis zur neuen Kabotage-Verordnung (EWG) Nr. 3118/93', *Transportrecht*, 17:7/8, 267–71.

Haas, E. ([1958] 1968), *The Uniting of Europe: Political, Social, and Economic Forces 1950–1957*, Stanford, CA., Stanford University Press.

Hammond, T. (1996), 'Formal Theory and the Institutions of Governance', *Governance*, 9:2, 107–85.

Hanson, B. T. (1998), 'What Happened to Fortress Europe? External Trade Policy Liberalization in the European Union', *International Organization*, 52:1, 55–85.

Hatch, M. J. (1997), *Organization Theory*, Oxford, Oxford University Press.

Hayes-Renshaw, F. and Wallace, H. (1997), *The Council of Ministers*, Basingstoke, Macmillan.

Héritier, A. (1997), 'Policy-Making by Subterfuge: Interest Accommodation, Innovation and Substitute Democratic Legitimation in Europe – Perspectives from Distinctive Policy Areas', *Journal of European Public Policy*, 4:2, 171–89.

――― (2001), 'Market Integration and Social Cohesion: The Politics of Public Services in European Regulation', *Journal of European Public Policy*, 8:5, 825–52.

Heritier, A., Kerwer, D., Knill, C., Lehmkuhl, D., Teutsch, M. and Douillet, A-C. (2001), *Differential Europe*, Lanham, MD, Rowman & Littlefield.

Héritier, A., Mingers, S., Knill, C. and Becka, M. (1994), *Die Veränderung von Staatlichkeit in Europa. Ein regulativer Wettbewerb: Deutschland, Großbritannien und Frankreich in der Europäischen Union*, Opladen, Leske & Budrich.

Hix, S. (2000), 'Executive Selection in the European Union: Does the Commission President Investiture Procedure Reduce the Democratic Deficit?', in K. Neunreither and A.Wiener (eds), *European Integration After Amsterdam*, Oxford, Oxford University Press.

――― (2002a), 'Constitutional Agenda-Setting Through Discretion in Rule Interpretation: Why the European Parliament Won at Amsterdam', *British Journal of Political Science*, 32:2, 259–80.

――― (2002b), 'The way to pick Europe's leader', *Financial Times*, 8 December.

Hocking, B. and Spence, D. (eds) (2002), *Foreign Ministries in the European Union: Integrating Diplomats*, Basingstoke: Palgrave.

Hodson, D. and Maher, I. (2001), 'The Open Method as a New Mode of Governance', *Journal of Common Market Studies*, 39:4, 719–46.

Hoffmann, S. (1966), 'Obstinate or Obsolete? The Fate of the Nation-State and the Case of Western Europe', *Daedalus*, 95:3, 862–915.

――― (1982), 'Reflections on the Nation-State in Western Europe Today', *Journal of Common Market Studies*, 21:1–2, 21–37.

_____ (2000), 'Towards a Common European Foreign and Security Policy?', *Journal of Common Market Studies*, 38:2, 189–98.

Hooghe, L. (2001), *The European Commission and the Integration of Europe*, Cambridge, Cambridge University Press.

Hope, V. and Henry, J. (1996), 'Corporate Culture Change – is it Relevant for Organisations of the 1990s', *Human Resource Management Journal*, 5:4, 61–73.

Hynes, N. (1999), 'Culture goes home', *Prospect*, March.

Jabko, N. (1999), 'In the Name of the Market: How the European Commission Paved the Way for Monetary Union', *Journal of European Public Policy*, 6:3, 475–95.

Jenkins, R. (1991), *A Life at the Centre*, London, Collins.

Joana, J. and Smith, A. (2002), *Les Commissaires Européens: technocrates, diplomates ou politiques?*, Paris, Presses de Sciences Po.

Joly, C. (1991), *Coopération au Développement: le Royaume Uni et la Politique Communautaire*, Paris, Economica.

Jones, E. (2002), *The Politics of Economic and Monetary Union*, Lanham, MD, Rowman and Littlefield.

Kassim, H. and Menon, A. (2003), 'The Principal–Agent Approach and the Study of the EU: Promise Unfulfilled?', *Journal of European Public Policy*, 10:1, 121–39.

Kassim, H., Menon, A., Peters, B. G. and Wright, V. (eds) (2001), *The National Co-ordination of European Policy: The European Level*, Oxford, Oxford University Press.

Kassim, H. and Peters, B. G. (2001), 'Conclusion: Co-ordinating National Action in Brussels – a Comparative Perspective', in H. Kassim, A. Menon, B. G. Peters, and V. Wright (eds), *The National Co-ordination of European Policy: The European Level*, Oxford, Oxford University Press.

Kassim, H. and Wright, V. (1991), 'The Role of National Administrations in the Decision-Making Processes of the European Community', *Rivista Trimestrale di Diritto Pubblico*, 31:3, 832–50.

Keohane, R. O. (1984), *After Hegemony: Co-operation and Discord in the World Political Economy*, Princeton, NJ, Princeton University Press.

Kingdon, John W. (1984), *Agendas, Alternatives, and Public Choices*, Boston, Little and Brown.

Kinnock, N. (1999a), The Roadmap for Renewal, Speech 99/133, 19 October, Brussels.

_____ (1999b), 'A Whistleblower's Charter for the European Commission', Speech, The Hague, 19 November.

_____ (2000), 'Publication of the Consultative Document on Reform', Press Conference, Speech 00/10, 19 January.

Kostakopoulou, D. (2000), 'The "Protective Union": Change and Continuity in Migration Law and Policy in Post-Amsterdam Europe', *Journal of Common Market Studies*, 38:3, 497–518.

Kreher, A. (1997), 'Agecies in the European Community: A Step Towards Administrative Integration in Europe', *Journal of European Public Policy*, 4:2, 225–45.

Laffan, B. (1997), *The Finances of the European Union*, Basingstoke, Macmillan.

Lambert, J. (1975), *The Times*, 20 July.

Larouche, P. (2000), *Competition Law and Regulation in European Telecommunications*, Oxford, Hart.

Leibfried, S. and Pierson, P. (1995), 'Semisovereign Welfare States: Social Policy in a Multitiered Europe', in S. Leibfried and P. Pierson (ed.), *European Social Policy: Between Fragmentation and Integration*, Washington DC, Brookings Institution.

Lemaignen, R. (1964), *L'Europe au Berceau*, Paris, Plon.

Levy, R. (2000), 'Managing the Managers: The Commission's Role in the Implementation of Spending Programmes', in N. Nugent (ed.), *At the Heart of Europe: Studies of the European Commission*, 2nd edn, Basingstoke, Palgrave.

_____ (2002), 'Modernising EU Programme Management', *Public Policy and Administration*, 17:1, 72–89.

Lewin, K. (1952), *Field Theory in Social Science*, London, Tavistock.

Lindberg, L. (1963), *The Political Dynamics of European Economic Integration*, Stanford, CA., Stanford University Press.

Linstead, S. and Grafton-Small, R. (1992), 'On Reading Organizational Culture', *Organization Studies*, 13:3, 331–55.

Lister, M. (1988), *The European Community and the Developing World*, Aldershot, Avebury.

Lord, C. and Magnette, P. (2002), *Notes Towards a General Theory of Legitimacy in the EU*, ESRC One Europe or Several Working Paper 39/02, www.one-europe.ac.uk/cgi-bin/esrc/world/db.cgi/publications.htm (accessed 27 May 2003).

Lowi, T. (1964), 'American Business, Public Policy, Case-Studies, and Political Theory', *World Politics* 16:4, 677–715.

_____ (1972), 'Four Systems of Policy, Politics and Choice', *Public Administration Review*, 32:4, 298–310.

Lundberg, C. C. (1985), 'On the Feasibility of Cultural Intervention in Organizations', in P. J. Frost, L. F. Moore, M. Reis Louis, C. Lundberg and J. Martin (eds), *Organizational Culture*, Newbury Park, CA, Sage.

Majone, G. (1992), 'Market Integration and Regulation: Europe after 1992', *Metroeconomica*, 43, 131–56.

_____ (1996a), *Temporal Consistency and Policy Credibility: Why Democracies Need Non-Majoritarian Institutions*, EUI Working Paper RSC No. 96/57, Florence, European University Institute.

_____ (1996b), 'The European Commission as Regulator', in G. Majone (ed.), *Regulating Europe*, London, Routledge.

_____ (2002), 'The European Commission: The Limits of Centralization and the Perils of Parliamentarization', *Governance* 15:3, 375–92.

_____ (2003), 'The Politics of Regulation and European Regulatory Institutions', in J. Hayward and A. Menon (eds), *Governing Europe*, Oxford, Oxford University Press.

Malek, T. and Hilkemeier, L. (2001), *The European Commission as a Learning Organization? Theoretical Considerations and Empirical Ideas*, paper presented at the ECPR Workshop Sessions, Grenoble, 6–11 April.

March, J. and Olsen, J. (1979), 'Attention and the Ambiguity of Self Interest', in J. G. March and J.P. Olsen (eds), *Ambiguity and Choice in Organizations*, 2nd edn, Oslo, Scandinavian University Press.

_____ and _____ (1983), 'Organizing Political Life: What Administrative Reorganization Tells Us about Government', *American Political Science Review*, 77:2, 281–96.

_____ and _____ (1989), *Rediscovering Institutions*, New York, The Free Press.

March, J., Schulz, M. and Zhou, X. (2000), *The Dynamics of Rules: Change in Written Organizational Codes*, Stanford, CA., Stanford University Press.

Marks, G., Hooghe, L. and Blank, K. (1996), 'European Integration from the 1980s: State-Centric v. Multi-Level Governance', *Journal of Common Market Studies*, 34:3, 341–78.

Martin, D. (1990), *European Union and the Democratic Deficit*, West Lothian, John Wheatley Centre.

Matlary, J. (1997), 'The Role of the Commission: A Theoretical Discussion', in N. Nugent (ed.), *At the Heart of the Union: Studies of the European Commission*, Basingstoke, Macmillan.

Mattli, W. and Slaughter, A.-M. (1995), 'Law and Politics in the European Union: A Reply to Garrett', *International Organization*, 49:1, 183–90.

_____ and _____ (1998), 'Revisiting the European Court of Justice', *International Organization*, 52:1, 177–209.

McDonald, M. (2000), 'Identities in the European Commission', in Nugent, N. (ed.) *At the Heart of Europe: Studies of the European Commission*, 2nd edn, Basingstoke, Palgrave.

McGowan, F. (2000), 'Competition Policy', in H. Wallace and W. Wallace (ed.), *Policy-Making in the European Union*, 4th edn, Oxford, Oxford University Press.

Meek, V. (1988), 'Organizational Culture: Origins and Weaknesses', *Organization Studies*, 9:4, 453–73.

Menon, A. (2002), 'A vote for inefficiency', *Financial Times*, 1 September.

_____ (2003), 'Member States and International Institutions: Institutionalizing Intergovernmentalism in the European Union', *Comparative European Politics*, 1:2, 171–201.

_____ and Weatherill, S. (2002), 'Legitimacy, Accountability and Delegation in the European Union', in A. Arnull and D. Wincott (eds), *Accountability and Legitimacy in the European Union*, Oxford, Oxford University Press.

Mény, Y. (1999), 'Europe: les pilotes et la machine', *Le Monde*, 4 September.

Metcalfe, L. (1992), 'After 1992: Can the Commission Manage Europe?', *Australian Journal of Public Administration*, 51:1, 117–30.

_____ (2000), 'Reforming the Commission: Will Organisational Efficiency Produce Effective Governance?', *Journal of Common Market Studies*, 38:5, 817–41.

Meunier, S. and Nicolaïdis, C. (1999), 'Who Speaks for Europe? The Delegation of Trade Authority in the EU', *Journal of Common Market Studies*, 37:3, 477–501.

Meyerson, D. and Martin, J. (1987), 'Cultural Change: An Integration of Three Different Views', *Journal of Management Studies*, 24: 6, pp. 623–47.

Mitrany, D. (1946), *A Working Peace System: An Argument for the Functional Development of International Organization*, 4th edn, NPC pamphlet No. 40, London, National Peace Council.

Monnet, J. (1976), *Mémoires*, Paris, Fayard.

Montagnon, P. (1990), 'Regulating the Utilities', in P. Montagnon (ed.), *European Competition Policy*, London, Pinter.

Moravcsik, A. (1991), 'Negotiating the Single European Act: National Interests and Conventional Statecraft in the European Community', *International Organization*, 45:1, 19–56.

_____ (1993), 'Preferences and Power in the European Community: A Liberal Intergovernmentalist Approach', *Journal of Common Market Studies*, 31:4, 473–524.

_____ (1995), 'Liberal Intergovernmentalism and Integration: A Rejoinder', *Journal of Common Market Studies*, 33:4, 611–28.

_____ (1998), *The Choice for Europe: Social Purpose and State Power from Messina to Maastricht*, Ithaca, NY, Cornell University Press.

_____ and Nicolaïdis, K. (1998), 'Keynote Article: Federal Ideals and Constitutional Realities in the Treaty of Amsterdam', *Journal of Common Market Studies*, 36: Annual Review, 13–38.

_____ and _____ (1999), 'Explaining the Treaty of Amsterdam: Interests, Influence, Institutions', *Journal of Common Market Studies*, 37:1, 59–85.

Muntigl, P., Weiss, G. and Wodak, R. (2000), *European Union Discourses on Unemployment*, Philadelphia: John Benjamins.

Ndoung, J. P. (1994), *L'Évolution du Fonds Européen de Développement prévu par les Conventions de Yaoundé et Lomé*, Bruxelles, Bruylant.

Norman, P. (1999), 'Leading From the Front', *Financial Times*, 16 September, 17.

North, D. C. (1990), *Institutions, Institutional Change and Economic Performance*, Cambridge, Cambridge University Press.

Nugent, N. (2001), *The European Commission*, Basingstoke, Palgrave.

_____ (2002), 'The Commission's Services', in J. Peterson and M. Shackleton (eds), *The Institutions of the European Union*, Oxford, Oxford University Press.

_____ and Saurugger, S. (2002), 'Organisational Structuring: The Case of the European Commission and its External Policy Responsibilities', *Journal of European Public Policy*, 9:3, 345–64.

Nuttall, S. (1997), 'The CFSP Provisions of the Amsterdam Treaty: An Exercise in Collusive Ambiguity', *CFSP Forum*, 3.

Olsen, J. P. (2002), 'Reforming European Institutions of Governance', *Journal of Common Market Studies*, 40:4, 581–602.

O'Reilly, D. (1997), *From State-Control to EC Competence Air Transport Liberalisation*, EUI Working Papers RSC No. 97/33.

Ostrom, E. (1986), 'An Agenda for the Study of Institutions', *Public Choice*, 48:1, 3–35.

Page, E. C. (1997), *People Who Run Europe*, Oxford, Clarendon Press.

_____ and Wouters, L. (1994), 'Bureaucratic Politics and Political Leadership in Brussels', *Public Administration* 72:3, 445–59.

Palier, B. and Bonoli, G. (1999), 'Phénomènes de path dependence et réformes des systèmes de protection sociale', *Revue Française de Science Politique*, 49: 199–220.

Parker, G. (2002a), 'The two Romano Prodis: The Tactless, Ineffectual Commission President and the Respected Italian Statesman', *Financial Times*, 23 December, 15.

_____ (2002b), 'Prodi loses colleagues' support after secret plan', *Financial Times*, 11 December, 4.

_____ and Bucle, T. (2003), 'Audit chief makes fierce attack on EU accounts', *Financial Times*; 13 March 2003, 12.

Patten, C. (2000a), *A European Foreign Policy: Ambition and Reality*, speech at the Institut Français des Relations Internationales, Paris, 15 June,www.europa.eu.int/comm/external_relations/news/patten/speech_00_219_en.htm (accessed 20 January 2003).

_____ (2000b), *External Relations: Demands, Constraints and Priorities*, Communication to the College, SEC (2000) 922, 26 May.

_____ (2001), *A Voice for Europe? The Future of the CFSP*, Brian Lenihan Memorial Lecture, Institute for European Studies, Dublin, 7 March, www.europa.eu.int/comm/external_relations/news/patten/speech01_111.htm, (accessed 20 January 2003).

_____ (2002), *Organised Crime in the Balkans*, speech at the UK Conference on Organised Crime, London, 25 November 2002, www.europa.eu.int/comm/external_relations/news/patten/sp251102.htm (accessed 20 January 2003).

Peters, T. J. and Waterman, R. H. (1982), *In Search of Excellence*, New York, Harper and Row.

Peterson, J. (1999), 'The Santer Era: the European Commission in Normative, Historical and Theoretical Perspective', *Journal of European Public Policy*, 6:1, 46–65.

_____ (2000), 'Romano Prodi: Another Delors?', *ECSA Review*, 13:1, 1–8.

_____ (2002), 'The College of Commissioners', in J. Peterson and M. Shackleton (eds), *The Institutions of the European Union*, Oxford, Oxford University Press.

_____ (2003), *The European Commission: Plateau? Permanent Decline?*, Oxford, St Antony's College European Interdependence Research Unit Discussion Paper 25.

_____ and Bomberg, E. (1999), *Decision-Making in the European Union*, Basingstoke, Macmillan.

_____ and _____ (2000), 'The European Union After the 1990s: Explaining Continuity and Change', in M. G. Cowles and M. Smith (eds), *The State of the European Union, Vol. 5: Risks, Reform, Resistance and Revival*, Oxford, Oxford University Press.

Peterson, J. and Jones, E. (1999), 'Decision Making in an Enlarging European Union', in J. Sperling (ed.), *Two Tiers or Two Speeds? The European Security Order and the Enlargement of the European Union and NATO*, Manchester, Manchester University Press.

Peterson, J. and Shackleton, M. (2002), 'The EU's Institutions: An Overview', in J. Peterson and M. Shackleton (ed.), *The Institutions of the European Union*, Oxford, Oxford University Press.

Pierson, P. (1996), 'The Path to European Integration: A Historical Institutionalist Perspective', *Comparative Political Studies*, 29:2, 123–63.

_____ (2000), 'Increasing Returns, Path Dependence, and the Study of Politics', *American Political Science Review*, 94:2, 251–67.

Pollack, M. A. (1995), 'Regional Actors in an Intergovernmental Play: The Making and Implementation of EC Structural Policy', in C. Rhodes and S. Mazey (eds), *The State of the European Union, Vol 3: Building a European Polity?*, Harlow, Longman.

_____ (1996), 'The New Institutionalism and EU Governance: The Promise and Limits of Institutional Analysis', *Governance*, 9:4, 429–58.

_____ (1997), 'Delegation, Agency and Agenda Setting in the European Community', *International Organization*, 51:1, 99–134.

_____ (2000), 'A Blairite Treaty: Neo-Liberalism and Regulated Capitalism in the Treaty of Amsterdam', in K. Neunreither and A. Wiener (eds), *European Integration after Amsterdam*, Oxford, Oxford University Press.

Primarolo report (2000), *Bericht der Gruppe 'Verhaltenskodex' (Unternehmensbesteuerung) an den Rat 'Wirtschaft und Finanzen'*, Tagung am 29. November 1999, Betr.: Verhaltenskodex (Unternehmensbesteuerung) EU Presse Mitteilung Nr. 4901/99 (29.2.2000), Brüssel, Europäische Kommission.

Prodi, R. (1999a), 'Discours devant le Parlement européen', Ms, 14 September.

_____ (1999b), Speech, Cologne European Council, 3 June, www.europa.eu.int/comm/commissioners/prodi/speeches/030699_en.htm (accessed 21 June 1999)

_____ (1999c), Statement on the European Parliament's compromise resolution on the Prodi Commission, 15 September, www.europa.eu.int/comm/commissioners/prodi/speeches/150999_en.htm (accessed 16 September 1999)

_____ (2000), Shaping the New Europe 2000–2005, speech to the European Parliament, 15 February, www.europa.eu.int/comm/off/work/2000–2005/index_en.htm (accessed 22 February 2003)

_____ (2002), The European Union's new institutional structure, speech to the European Parliament, 5 December, www.europa.eu.int/comm/commissioners/prodi/speeches/index_en.htm (accessed 22 February 2003)

Rosamond, B. (2000), *Theories of European Integration*, Basingstoke, Macmillan.

Ross, G. (1995), *Jacques Delors and European Integration*, Cambridge, Polity.

Sasse, C., Poullet, E., Coombes, D. and Duprez, G. (1977), *Decision Making in the European Community*, New York, Praeger.

Sandholtz, W. (1996), 'Membership Matters: Limits of the Functional Approach to European Institutions', *Journal of Common Market Studies*, 34:3, 403–29.

_____ (1998), 'The Emergence of a Supranational Telecommunications Regime', in W. Sandholtz and A. Stone Sweet (eds), *European Integration and Supranational Governance*, Oxford, Oxford University Press.

_____ and Zysman, J. (1989), '1992: Recasting the European Bargain', *World Politics*, 42:1, 95–128.

Scharpf, F. W. (1988), 'The Joint-Decision Trap: Lessons from German Federalism and European Integration', *Public Administration*, 66:3, 239–78.

_____ (1996), 'Democratic Policy in Europe', *European Law Journal*, 2:2, 136–55.

_____ (1998), 'Die Problemlösungsfähigkeit der Mehrebenenpolitik in Europa', *Politische Vierteljahresschrift*, 29, Sonderheft, 121–44.

_____ (1999), *Governing in Europe: Effective and Democratic?*, Oxford, Oxford University Press.

Schein, E. (1985), *Organisational Culture and Leadership*, San Franscisco, CA, Jossey-Bass.

Schmidt, S. K. (1996), 'Sterile Debates and Dubious Generalisations: European Integration Theory Tested by Telecommunications and Electricity', *Journal of Public Policy*, 16:3, 233–71.

_____ (1998a), 'Commission Activism: Subsuming Telecommunications and Electricity under European Competition Law', *Journal of European Public Policy*, 5:1, 169–84.

_____ (1998b), *Liberalisierung in Europa: Die Rolle der Europäischen Kommission*, Frankfurt, Campus.

_____ (2000), 'Only an Agenda Setter? The European Commission's Power over the Council of Ministers', *European Union Politics* 1:1, 37–61.

Schneider, G. (1995), 'The Limits of Self-Reform: Institution-Building in the European Union', *European Journal of International Relations*, 1:1, 59–86.

Schuman, R. (1950), *Déclaration du 9 mai 1950*, www.france.diplomatie.fr/archives/dossiers/schuman/pages/331a.html (accessed 17 December 2002).

Selznick, P. (1957), *Leadership in Administration: A Sociological Interpretation*, New York, Peterson.

Shapiro, M. (1992), 'The European Court of Justice', in A.M. Sbragia (ed.), *Europolitics: Institutions and Policymaking in the 'New' European Community*, Washington, DC, The Brookings Institution.

Shore, C. (2000), *Building Europe: The Cultural Politics of European Integration*, London, Routledge.

Simon, H. A. ([1947] 1997), *Administrative Behavior: A Study of Decision-Making Processes In Administrative Organizations*, 4th edn, New York, Free Press (Macmillan).

_____ (1976), 'From Substantive to Procedural Rationality', in S.J. Latsis (ed.), *Method and Appraisal in Economics*, Cambridge, Cambridge University Press.

Sinnott, R. (1997), *European Public Opinion and Security Policy*, Chaillot Paper 28, Brussels, WEU Institute for Security Studies.

Slot, P. J. (1994), 'Energy and Competition', *Common Market Law Review*, 31, 511–47.

Smircich, L. (1983), 'Concepts of Culture and Organizational Analysis', *Administrative Science Quarterly*, 28, 339–58.

Smith, A. (2003), 'Why European Commissions Matter', *Journal of Common Market Studies* 41:1, 137–56.

Smith, M. (1998), 'Autonomy by the Rules: The European Commission and the Development of State Aid Policy', *Journal of Common Market Studies*, 36:1, 55–78.

_____ (2000), 'The European Commission: Diminishing Returns to Entrepreneurship', in M. G. Cowles and M. Smith (eds), *The State of the European Union, Vol. 5: Risks, Reform, Resistance and Revival*, Oxford, Oxford University Press.

Smyrl, M. (1998), 'When (and How) Do the Commission's Preferences Matter?', *Journal of Common Market Studies*, 36:1, 79–99.

Soetendorp, B. and Andeweg, R. (2001), 'Dual Loyalties: The Dutch Permanent Representation to the European Union' in H. Kassim, A. Menon, B. G. Peters and V. Wright (eds) *The National Coordination of EU Policy: The European Level*, Oxford, Oxford University Press.

Solana, J. (2000a), The Development of a Common Foreign and Security Policy, keynote speech, Diplomatia, Rome, 26 June, http://ue.eu.int/en/summ.htm (accessed 20 January 2003).

_____ (2000b), 'Developments in CFSP Over the Past Year', *EPC-Journal Online*, 12 October 2000.

Spence, D. (1997), 'Staff and Personnel Policy in the Commission', in G. Edwards and D. Spence (eds), *The European Commission*, 2nd edn, London, Longman.

_____ (2000), 'Plus ça Change, Plus c'est la Même Chose? Attempting to Reform the European Commission', *Journal of European Public Policy*, 7:1, 1–25.

Spierenburg, D. (1979), Proposal for reform of the Commission of the European Communities and its services, report made at the request of the Commission by an independent review body under the chairmanship of Mr Dirk Spierenberg', Brussels, 24 September.

Spinant, D. (2002), 'Size matters . . .', *European Voice*, 14–20 November, 6.

Steunenberg, B. (1994), 'Decision Making Under Different Institutional Arrangements: Legislation by the European Community', *Journal of Institutional and Theoretical Economics*, 15:4, 642–69.

Stevens, A. (2000), 'La Chute de la Commission Santer', *Revue Française d'Administration Publique*, 95:369–79.

_____ and Stevens, H. (1996), The Non-Management of Europe, paper presented at the Eighth International Conference of the journal *Politiques et Management Publique*, Paris, 1996.

_____ and _____ (2001), *Brussels Bureaucrats? The Administration of the European Union*, Basingstoke: Palgrave.

Stone Sweet, A. and Brunell, T. L. (1998), 'Constructing a Supranational Constitution: Dispute Resolution and Governance in the European Community', *American Political Science Review*, 92:1, 63–81.

Straw, J. (2002), *Reforming Europe: New Era, New Questions*, London, Foreign and Commonwealth Office.

Strivens, R. and Weightman, E. (1989), 'The Air Transport Sector and the EEC Competition Rules in the Light of the Ahmed Saeed Case', *European Competition Law Review*, 10, 557–67.

Tabellini, G. and Wyplosz, C. (2003), 'Why a presidency is the best model for Europe', *Financial Times*, 25 February.

Tömmel, I. (1998), 'Transformation of Governance: The European Commission's Strategy for Creating a "Europe of the Regions" ', *Regional & Federal Studies*, 8:2, 52–80.

Tsebelis, G. (1994), 'The Power of the European Parliament as a Conditional Agenda Setter', *American Political Science Review*, 88:1, 128–42.

_____ and Kreppel, A. (1998), 'The History of Conditional Agenda-Setting in European Institutions', *European Journal of Political Research*, 33:1, 41–71.

Tsoukalis, L. (2000), 'Economic and Monetary Union', in H. Wallace and W. Wallace (eds), *Policy-Making in the European Union*, 4th edn, Oxford, Oxford University Press.

UK Office of the European Parliament (2003), *European Elections*, www.europarl.org. uk/guide/textonly/Gelecttx.htm#facts (accessed 10 February 2003).

Vignon, J. (1997), 'L'Europe face à la mondialisation', *Le Courrier*, 164:58–62.

Vogel, D. (1995), *Trading Up: Consumer and Environmental Regulation in a Global Economy*, Cambridge, MA, Harvard University Press.

Vogel, S. (1996), *Freer Markets, More Rules: Regulatory Reform in Advanced Industrial Countries*, Ithaca, NY, Cornell University Press.

Walker, M. and Traynor, I. (1999), 'Leaders unite to pick Prodi', *Guardian*, 25 March.

Wallace, H. (2000), 'The Institutional Setting', in H. Wallace and W. Wallace (eds), *Policy-Making in the European Union*, 4th edn, Oxford, Oxford University Press.

Weber, M. (1968), *Economy and Society: An Outline of Interpretive Sociology*, New York: Bedminster Press.

Weiler, J. H. H. (1981), 'The Community System: The Dual Character of Supranationalism', *Yearbook of European Law*, 1, 267–306.

_____ (1994), 'A Quiet Revolution. The European Court of Justice and Its Interlocutors', *Comparative Political Studies*, 26:4, 510–34.

_____ (1999), *The Constitution of Europe*, Cambridge, Cambridge University Press.

Wessels, W. (2001), 'Nice Results: The Millennium IGC in the EU's Evolution', *Journal of Common Market Studies*, 39:2, 197–219.

Westlake, M. (1995), *The Council of the European Union*, London, Cartermill.

Williamson, O. E. (1985), *The Economic Institutions of Capitalism*, New York, The Free Press.

Wincott, D. (2001), 'Looking Forward or Harking Back? The Commission and the Reform of Governance in the European Union', *Journal of Common Market Studies* 39:5, 897–911.

Wright, V. (1996), 'The National Co-ordination of European Policy-making: Negotiating the Quagmire', in J. Richardson (ed.), *European Union Power and Policy-Making*, London, Routledge.

Young, A. R. (1994), *Ideas, Interests and Institutions: The Politics of Liberalisation in the EC's Road Haulage Industry*, Brighton, Sussex European Institute.

INDEX